Improving Schools with Blended Learning

Improving Schools with Blended Learning is specifically designed to address the important issues needed to successfully modernise education within the context of technological change. It does this by first providing a clear roadmap for designing Blended Learning environments able to respond to the technological imperatives challenging schools at present, and then illustrating this roadmap via specific, original research that details the 'how to' aspects of a successful technology-based design process. School leaders, teachers, teacher education students and researchers will all find highly relevant information about how to manage for disruption in the new and informative approach to Blended Learning (BL) they will discover in this book.

This book arose from two different research projects the authors have been pursuing over the last 3–5 years, including school improvement research and Blended Learning research designed to investigate the role of technology in effective teaching and learning. By combining the insights gained from these two different research areas, this book is able to present a novel understanding of BL that is both insightful and clearly evidence-based.

Improving Schools with Blended Learning also provides several original contributions to specific knowledge in the areas of BL and school improvement that most educators will find highly useful, including the use of BL schemas, a clear and extended BL continuum, how to measure and evaluate the success of BL, how to scaffold teacher ICT knowledge and skills, and a specific process for contextualising applied BL in relation to the 'disruption' imperatives of the Knowledge Economy.

Tony Yeigh is an experienced research academic and Deputy Leader of the SCU TeachLab Research Group. He is an education professional, with a demonstrated history of successful research focused in the areas of Blended Learning, school improvement and school leadership.

David Lynch is Research Leader of TeachLab, a research entity focused on teacher education, and Professor of Education in the School of Education at Southern Cross University. He is the author of numerous books and articles on teaching and teaching improvement, specialising in whole-of-school teaching improvement.

Paul Fradale has been an educator for over 25 years; he's been involved in teacher training as a school leader, conference/seminar/workshop leader and a university lecturer. His doctoral dissertation and publications investigate shifting teacher practice within the context of Blended Learning.

Edward Lawless has had a 35-year career in education which has spanned four continents and multiple curricula in institutions around the world under face-to-face, blended and online conditions. He is passionate about reimagining education under flexible and sustainable Blended Learning conditions that can increase educational access and opportunity for all.

David Turner is Director of Professional Learning for the Queensland Association of State School Principals. He has enjoyed a successful career in educational leadership as principal in a variety of contexts and in university sector roles. He is interested in the leadership mindsets necessary for a rapidly changing world.

Royce Willis has a background in psychological science, currently working as a Research Officer and Casual Academic at Southern Cross University. Royce's research spans psychology, environmental psychology, sport psychology, psychophysiology, neurobiology and education. His education-specific research includes Blended Learning, school improvement, teacher identity, and teacher and student retention.

Improving Schools with Blended Learning

How to Make Technology Work in the Modern Classroom

Tony Yeigh, David Lynch, Paul Fradale, Edward Lawless, David Turner and Royce Willis

Routledge
Taylor & Francis Group

LONDON AND NEW YORK

First published 2021
by Routledge
2 Park Square, Milton Park, Abingdon, Oxon OX14 4RN

and by Routledge
52 Vanderbilt Avenue, New York, NY 10017

Routledge is an imprint of the Taylor & Francis Group, an informa business

British Library Cataloguing-in-Publication Data
A catalogue record for this book is available from the British Library

Library of Congress Cataloging-in-Publication Data
A catalog record has been requested for this book

ISBN: 978-0-367-40738-4 (hbk)
ISBN: 978-0-367-40740-7 (pbk)
ISBN: 978-0-367-80882-2 (ebk)

Typeset in Times New Roman
by River Editorial Ltd, Devon, UK

This book is dedicated to all teachers, school leaders and other school staff who work to improve teaching and learning in service of student outcomes and future possibilities. May your efforts never fail!

Contents

Figures

Tables

Preface

This is a book with a mission, to provide educators at all levels with the ability to undertake successful school improvement in a way that also responds to the disruptive influence of modern technology. The authors address this mission by integrating two corresponding and inter-dependent research-driven areas of education: school improvement and Blended Learning. School improvement is analysed in relation to the growing demands of the Knowledge Economy, which has intensified the need for schools to measure and report on the effectiveness of their teaching and learning outcomes. This has placed progressive pressure on schools and education systems in the form of a global 'improvement imperative' that requires ever growing transparency and accountability in terms of comparing and evaluating teachers, school leaders and student achievement in relation to state-based economies. In this respect a key contribution of the book is to articulate how Blended Learning can be implemented within the dynamics of this imperative as a necessary and effective improvement response that harnesses the power of technology to bring about positive change in the way we teach and learn in schools and classrooms, and which can have a positive effect on student achievement. From this perspective, Blended Leaning is 'unpacked' as a distinct pedagogy designed to support school improvement in ways that respond to the imperatives of the Knowledge Economy, while at the same time meeting the needs and purposes of the immediate school context. This understanding of Blended Learning is unique in the way it uses a context-driven design approach to provide practical solutions for the use of technology in support of school improvement in the twenty-first century. In this respect, the need for Blended Learning is also examined in relation to the impact of the current COVID-19 pandemic, which has necessitated an increase in online and blended skillsets on the part of both teachers and school leaders. Overall, the reader will experience a journey of discovery and practical application in this book that provides clear, systematic and concrete solutions to the challenges involved in undertaking school improvement within the context of twenty-first-century teaching and learning.

1 Education and schooling in the digital age

Relevant Australian Professional Standards for Teachers: 1.5; 1.6; 2.6; 3.2; 3.4; 3.6; 4.5; 6.2; 6.3; 6.4

Chapter synopsis

This chapter is about changes in society and their impacts on education, teaching and schooling. The chapter will first examine the transition of society from an industrial era, which spanned two centuries, to the fast-emerging and transforming knowledge era, which had its genesis circa 1996. The convergence of new technologies, including AI and robotics, and increasing processing power, is bringing rapid social change and disruption in the employment market, and corresponding disruption to education. This examination reveals a series of new socio-economic fundamentals focusing societies from the local to the global, embedding a greater reliance on and the use of technological innovations which together are redefining the concepts of work and home life. The 2000 era is witnessing exponential change that is challenging many long-held human maxims. These new fundamentals and the circumstance they are generating call into question what it means to be educated and, correspondingly, how such education should be undertaken.

Introduction

Welcome to an exciting period in human history. We are witnessing a seemingly endless array of technological innovations which over the past twenty years or so have accelerated to such a point that society is now fundamentally different to that when most teachers grew up and attended school themselves (Carl, 2009; Collins & Halverson, 2018; Fullan, 2016; Gross, 2019; Quong, 2016; Ross, 2010; Steele & Whitaker, 2019; TEMAG, 2014). Further, given their eighteenth-century hallmarks, schools still largely operate in ways that reveal a distinct contrast to the society they aim to serve (Carl, 2009; Fullan, 2016; Lynch, 2012; OECD, 2017a; Quong, 2016; Ross, 2010; Yeigh & Lynch, 2017). This is not to say that schools have not modernised. Nor that they have not invested in professionally developing their teachers. It is a comment on how the logic and staging of classroom teaching, despite pockets of change and innovation, remains largely unchanged (Berry, 2011; Burns & Gottschalk, 2019; Lynch, 2012; OECD, 2015; Tyack & Cuban, 1995; Vincent-Lancrin et al., 2019).

Let us elaborate on this assertion.

The organisation of schools and the arrangements inside the four walls of a classroom is such that schooling, with its 'one-size-fits-all' design heritage, is a contrast to a society built on individualism, choice, flexibility and exponential change. By this we mean schools and their teachers follow a state-mandated age-related curriculum – often the product of a ten-year review cycle – which inclines the teacher to 'cover content' irrespective of the individual needs of assigned students. National testing regimes, now prevalent in most countries, have the unintended consequence of reinforcing this mentality (Berry, 2011; Chenoweth, 2020; Lynch, 2012; OECD, 2017a; Vincent-Lancrin et al., 2019).

This is not to say that teachers do not endeavour to consider their student profiles when teaching. It is a comment on the limitations of such arrangements and how a curriculum mandate, coupled with lock-step progressions, dominates the 'what' and the 'how' of what teachers have to achieve and what they are accountable for in their classroom (Burns & Gottschalk, 2019; OECD, 2015). One might imagine that a teacher from a past generation could easily walk into any school and immediately recognise the organisational logic. This clear resemblance to history would not be so for many other professions which have been disrupted by technological innovation and change. Publishing, banking and healthcare immediately come to mind.

Thinking about how schools have remained largely the same over many generations of students, one could argue that teachers and schools have stagnated, resolved to continue doing what they have always done (Joram et al., 2020; Lynch, 2012; OECD, 2017a; Quong, 2016; Yeigh & Lynch, 2017). This is despite calls, over many years now, for fundamental change to occur in teaching and learning (Berry, 2011; Fullan, 2016; Hargreaves & Fullan, 2012; Hattie, 2009, 2012; Kaufman, 2015; Lynch, 2012; OECD, 2015, 2017a; Starkey, 2020).

This is not a criticism of teachers. Teachers care about their students. They want the best for them. It can be a challenging pursuit. Our point is that the histrionics and enculturating effects of traditional schooling coupled with a skills lag (Ertmer et al., 2012; Starkey, 2020; Yeigh & Lynch, 2017), a product of deficiencies in teacher education (Lynch, 2012; Yeigh & Lynch, 2017), are such that doing what has always been done often seems the most intuitive and easy path to follow. Besides, everyone has been to school and readily accepts the schooling logic as part of growing up. And therein lies the problem. This new world order is neither intuitive nor static.

The conundrum is that the people who work in schools today are still very much at the point of being able to capture amounts of value and productivity by doing what has always been done (Lynch, 2012). This could be attributed to the pressures for change being diluted by things such as producer capture, industrial agreements and the nature of the associated 'reward systems' or because, as a United States Teaching Commission Report (cited in Fullan, 2007, p. 275) once suggested, 'graduates are still being hired: if they (teacher education faculties) are failing they are doing so quietly'. But, and it is a big but, we live in a fast-changing world in which society and its economy now face daily challenges that invariably require ongoing innovations and change strategies if they are to thrive. As Yeigh and Lynch (2017), Fullan (2016), OECD (2015), Lynch (2012), Hattie (2011) and Christensen et al. (2011) all suggest, a disruptive model is needed to show a better way.

Welcome to the digital age of learning. We argue it offers the best of both worlds!

To fully appreciate the concept of digital learning one has first to understand how technology has fundamentally changed society and by direct association what it means for those who educate people for work and life in such a new society (Burns & Gottschalk, 2019). In the sections which follow, we provide an account of societal change, citing technological innovation and convergence as the key culprit. This outlining provides a foundation from which to appreciate the new fundamentals that schools and teachers must account for in their teaching and learning strategies today. Our central premise is that schooling, with its face-to-face classroom-centric focus, is not a bad thing. It is just that it is not sufficient on its own for a world where exponential technological innovation and disruption predominate our home and work life. Further, each learner has peculiarities which require of the teacher new capacities and capabilities for optimal outcomes. The traditional classroom alone just will no longer 'cut it', and because of this new, digital-based pedagogies such as **Blended Learning** have been introduced.

For the uninitiated, Blended Learning comes to mean using online learning technologies in the classroom or at home. But this is only half right. Blended Learning is the harnessing of all the good things about the physical classroom world with those of the online world to create a 'blend' in teaching and learning. Blended Learning comes to represent an opportunity for teachers to exploit the rapid technological developments that are occurring in information communication technologies while embracing the face-to-face classroom circumstance that is synonymous with growing up and attending school (Gepp & Kumar, 2020; Horn & Staker, 2017). At its heart, Blended Learning is an opportunity for teachers to meet the learning needs of all students, not just those who do school well and to propel teaching and learning into the digital age (Gepp & Kumar, 2020; Yeigh et al., 2020).

In short, it is our belief, given the profile of technological change that has occurred to date in society, that technology holds the power to transform teaching and learning in schools by enabling new capabilities and capacities that will benefit all learners in all circumstances (Fleurbaey et al., 2018; Starkey, 2020). We view Blended Learning as a fundamental first step in such a transformation (Gepp & Kumar, 2020; Yeigh et al., 2020).

A remarkable period in human history

The 2000 epoch is a truly remarkable period in human history (Fleurbaey et al., 2018). Technological innovations explode onto the market at a daily rate, only to be quickly replaced by a new, faster and better version (Schatzki, 2019). Take the mobile phone, for example. Its size has shrunk considerably over past decades such that its size has shrunk considerably over past decades making it compact enough to fit in one's pocket. When using a mobile phone, its gadgetry illustrates the phenomena of converged technologies. Although referred to as the 'mobile phone', its application far exceeds this rather erroneous name to include a video camera, digital camera, global positioning system, thermometer, calendar, compass, calculator, 'e-pad', web browser, diary, diagnostic tool, and the list goes on. The use of mobile phones, especially among young people, is so ubiquitous that to not figure its use in classrooms seems erroneous, and perhaps an example of schools refusing to move with the times.

Similarly, the motor vehicle, while still designed to take people from one place to another, has a central computer which governs the vehicle such that driving is now supported by all manner of creature comforts and technologically assisted mechanics. It appears only a matter of time before the 'driver' is made redundant and replaced by an auto-drive system. Diseases and ailments, once considered a death sentence, are now being efficiently dealt with by technologically advanced medicines and medical machinery. At the heart of such advancements is a cadre of highly educated individuals who are relying on schools to prepare equally highly educated people to join and eventually replace them.

These advancements represent a fundamental change in the structure of society, such that the way people live, socialise and work today has taken a radical departure from a relatively recent era in which the church, the school and the community were the mainstays of human knowledge, order and societal engagement (Schatzki, 2019; Tormos, 2019). Of importance to the message of this book, underpinning this fundamental change is a set of interwoven technological advancements (Victer, 2020), and thus we need to explore this phenomenon further.

The aforementioned advancements were created by human brainpower and networked ideas and stimulated by a consumer market driven by a seemingly insatiable desire for 'a better', more convenient, social and entertaining existence. In this new world, the consumer seeks a capacity to 'delegate' the drudgery of everyday life to a gadget, be connected and up-to-date 24/7 on topics and with people of interest for the most part, and have their next 'want' satisfied in a new and unique way, often with the expectation that it will be for free (Schatzki, 2019). While the consumer appears to be charting their own destiny, using technology to assist, the opposite is likely closer to the truth. Either way, we argue schools have a key role to play in all this, both from the standpoint of preparing people to operate in such a world – by this we mean from a consumer and producer perspective – and from the standpoint of critically analysing the potentials of innovations as an informed member of society.

So how did we get to this point in modern human existence?

Four industrial revolutions

This amazing world is the product of four **industrial revolution**s that have aggregated to define our modern-day society. The first occurred in the mid-1800s, when human labour capacities were increased by harnessing the power of steam and water into the production cycle, and the second in the late 1800s, when electricity replaced steam as a primary energy source. These two revolutions paved the way for the emergence of the mass production and consumption era that correspondingly transformed society from a largely rural agrarian society into an industrialised urban one (Schwab, 2016). This era also saw the birth of schooling as we know it today (Carl, 2009).

Adam Smith, in *The Wealth of Nations*, expressed the opinion that 'for a very small expense, the public can facilitate, can encourage, and can even impose upon almost the whole body of the people the necessity of acquiring those most essential parts of education' (Smith, 1801, p. 95). In effect, as industry expanded, mass schooling followed in its wake, mimicking it in logic, rationale and structure (Carl, 2009).

Once society had determined that educating the masses was a concept worth considering, discussions arose around what mass education should comprise. In the United States and Europe, for example, there was quick acceptance by the public to explicitly teach industrial, or 'vocational', skills to prepare the youth of society for participation in the emergent industrial economy; schooling had internalised the ethics and goals of the corporation (Grubb & Lazerson, 2009). These were centred around social order and hierarchies imposed by corporate practice and structure: compliance, conformity, knowing one's station, and accepting one's role in society (Carl, 2009; Grubb & Lazerson, 2009). Essentially, school was intended to socialise students into the roles they would play as adults in an industrial economy; this involved both socialisation and sorting students into categories for appropriate training for those roles (Labaree, 2005).

As these two early industrial periods continued, two schools of thought informed education: 'social Darwinism', as illustrated by the work of Herbert Spencer, and 'scientific management', as conceived by Frederick Taylor (Leyva, 2009). Spencer believed that the differences in humans could be viewed through the lens of evolution and at the time there was a strong measure of acceptance of this proposition among the upper, or ruling, classes (Leyva, 2009). It is worth noting that more than a century later, similar ideas were still being promoted, as evidenced by the bestselling but highly controversial 1994 publication of *The Bell Curve*, in which the authors contended that IQ is largely heritable and therefore able to explain the trends seen in American society (Herrnstein & Murray, 2010). This heritability of intelligence is strongly refuted by modern science, with environmental factors, including schooling, revealed to have much more of an impact (Dickens & Flynn, 2001; Nisbett, 2009).

Taylorism, as it came to be known, was the eponymous school of management thinking based on Fredrick Taylor's writings on 'scientific management', which sought to maximise efficiency, and focused on a foundational unit he labelled the 'task' (Stoller, 2015). This became highly influential and was soon applied to other fields, including education. Taylorism, in the context of schooling, sought to organise the day, quantify 'time on task', standardise practice and measurement of learning outcomes, all hallmarks of traditional schooling (Au, 2011). It is important to note that standardisation, operationalisation of routine and task simplification still feature heavily in debates about modern education and what should be considered 'best practice' (Ross, 2010). In education, Taylorism's legacy and impact can be seen in the traditional analogy of schools as factories: students are the raw material; curriculum learning is the product; training is via standardised tasks; students are sorted by ability; conformity is established by a bell-driven schedule; complex concepts and interdisciplinary contexts are simplified into discrete subjects and topics; content-driven pedagogy is esteemed over open-ended inquiry; teachers are deskilled with over-reliance on textbooks; and individuals are rewarded for individual performance in the form of test marks (Au, 2011; Ross, 2010).

The third industrial revolution occurred circa the Second World War when information technology and data processing spawned the development of the electronic computer. While electricity continues to power production, this third revolution started supercharging design, development and processing functions when labour became less 'hands-on' but more specialised because machines began to dominate production. This trajectory accelerated as machines became automated – 24/7, fast and efficient. By this time, schooling had become a central feature of many nations with legislation requiring students to complete secondary education. Certification of occupations became the norm, which in turn heightened the importance of success at school in order to enter a workforce which was increasingly specialised and codified.

The fourth industrial revolution, which started circa 1990 and continues today, is commonly known as the **digital revolution** and is referred to in the literature as the **Knowledge Economy**. In this era, machines are at the centre of many important decisions, while the human labour component of production is increasingly becoming obsolete. But while the labour side falls away, the human brain-power side nonetheless becomes critical for success, because knowledge and a capacity to use it in new and unique ways underpins this new order (Lansiti & Lakhani, 2020; Pitsis et al., 2020). Given this, traditional jobs, such as assembly line operators, printmakers, typists and bank tellers, have diminished in demand, while new jobs have arisen, such as relationship managers, coders, data analysers and all manner of e-designers.

This fourth revolution is different from the others because of two interrelated factors. First, the stand-alone computer has evolved into a series of powerful networked micro-processors, which have direct links to massive data stores and are installed in every conceivable device. These devices (think the mobile phone, your car, your medical device and even your fridge) have become consumer-centric, with a variety of software applications enabling users to customise, order, communicate, control and monitor at will. This circumstance is more commonly referred to as **connectivity** (Victer, 2020). Second is the increase in sensor capacities, used once again in all manner of devices and apparatus, that allow remote artificial intelligence to analyse massive real-time data sets at speed and in multi-dimensional settings. This capacity was previously only accessible to the human mind and at a much, much slower pace and scale (Friedman, 2016; Lansiti & Lakhani, 2020). The digital revolution is redefining what living means and what it now requires of people for home and work life.

For teachers and schooling systems alike, this new societal context is both an opportunity and a challenge. It's a challenge because it is a distinct contrast to the world in which most teachers have grown up and to the logic of what they have been prepared to do in classrooms (Lynch, 2012; Yeigh & Lynch, 2017). Further, exponential change magnifies this contrast for each new generation. It is an opportunity because technological advancements offer alternatives to the standard face-to-face 'chalk and talk' classroom learning paradigm and a potential to better meet the needs of *all* students.

To clarify our thoughts here, we are supportive of explicit instruction which research indicates to be a potent means for teaching and learning (Hattie, 2009). Our point about 'chalk and talk' is a comment on teachers using ongoing cycles of 'telling', 'note-taking' and 'assignments' and thus satisfying themselves that they have 'covered' the required content', a circumstance synonymous in high school settings. Parallel to this stagnation in teaching, technological advancements have exposed how the brain actually works and learns, which in turn generates a new set of considerations in the pedagogy of what occurs in classrooms (Guerriero, 2017; Guerriero & Révai, 2017; Joram et al., 2020). In the section which follows we briefly wade into the neurosciences to clarify such points.

Technological advancement: unpacking how people best learn

Technological advances have also spawned the neurosciences. This relatively recent field of science has unearthed how the brain works and how people learn and thus unpacks the anatomy of effective teaching (Kuhl et al., 2019). Brain-based research reveals the brain to be a series of neural connections which are strengthened as learning occurs, capturing and encoding unique information and skills that are experienced by the individual and which are weakened when infrequently used. Importantly, neural structures are influenced by both biology and environment (Goswami, 2008). The peculiarities of each learner, their genetic make-up and personal disposition, together with their experiences in life, including education, influences the structure and extent of connections in the brain and thus how each individual learner learns (Goswami, 2008; Kuhl et al., 2019). Parallel to this, evidence-based understanding of the brain enables the diagnosis of learning difficulties and provides a roadmap for how best to deal with such learning on an individual learner basis (Guerriero, 2017; Guerriero & Révai, 2017; Joram et al., 2020).

Importantly, this research is defining a new curriculum for teacher education. It is challenging long-held beliefs about how people learn, and correspondingly it questions many traditional classroom practices. Bringing the salient points of this research to bear on schools and teachers, findings can be understood through a series of principles of learning which teachers can use as a learning design framework:

1. Learning is incremental and experience-based
2. Learning is multi-sensory
3. Brain mechanisms of learning extract structure from input
4. Learning is social
5. Learning is mediated by emotions
6. Learning occurs throughout all stages of the human life span (Goswami, 2008, pp. 387–394).

So what do we take from this brief foray into the brain sciences? First, learners are not empty vessels waiting to be filled by teachers. Second, the process of learning can be codified and exemplified in principles which create a context for how lessons should be planned and delivered and what a school has to enable and support (Hattie, 2009; Lynch, 2012). The advent of neuroscientific research reinforces the individual nature of learning and highlights the complexities and logistics that schooling in the 2000s has to contend with if it is to be effective for all students. By this we mean schools as we know them today are designed for mass education: cohort learning not individualisation. This is a challenge of capacity and capability given traditional school design limitations. The logic of Blended Learning is to enable schools and teachers to build the required capacities and capabilities along lines attuned to a knowledge-based society (Horn & Staker, 2017; Yeigh et al., 2020).

Five considerations underpinning the preparation of young people

Having made these introductory comments about change and its impacts on schools and teachers, we need to restate our view that schools and the work of teachers are a necessary part of society because they prepare young people for future society. We are not arguing for schools to be phased out, nor teachers to be sidelined. Rather, we are arguing for a rethink, for a modernisation of schooling and teaching practice. In this respect our central argument has been that the system of schooling was conceived and developed to meet the needs of an earlier industrial revolution and, as society has changed fundamentally, it becomes incumbent on schools and teachers to change accordingly (Lynch, 2012). We contend that the powerful enculturating effect of mass schooling and its ingrained history on generations of people have rendered schools and the work of teachers blind to the need for a rethink and repositioning of what they do in classrooms (Lynch, 2012).

In light of this argument, the question then becomes change *what* and *how*? This question is answered explicitly in the culmination of chapters to follow. To elaborate on the *what* and *how*, we first need to outline the circumstances influencing our call for change and, in doing so, begin to scope the change considerations and thus front-end later chapters.

With these points in mind, our next section outlines a set of preconditions conceptualised by Nowotny et al. (2001) that reveal the anatomy of the Knowledge Economy. These preconditions take us back to the start of the fourth industrial revolution to identify the phenomena at play and to explain a new societal landscape. By direct association, this identifies what needs to be considered – designed for by education systems – to remain current and central if these systems are to adequately prepare young people for the future. These factors are: the growth of uncertainty; the growth of new forms of economic rationality; the transformation of time into the 'extended present'; flexible space; and increasing capacity for self-organisation. We turn first to the growth of uncertainty.

The growth of uncertainty

Earlier discussions have highlighted rapid developments of new technologies which have contributed to far-reaching societal changes. While technology solves problems and enables humankind to do tasks once unimaginable, it also unleashes uncertainty upon the populace. 'Uncertainty' can be understood as a state in which individuals find it impossible to attribute a reasonable definitive probability to the expected outcome of their choice. Instead, reality is perceived as a threatening series of possibilities inherent in economic life. Further, 'risk', once defined as an attempt to curtail uncertainty by assigning probabilities to expected outcomes, is now used to denote incalculability as an inherent feature of both knowledge production and social change (Nowotny et al., 2001). But herein lies the conundrum: a willingness to take risks remains a key element of human endeavour and decision making. To not take risks is to not progress society, and to not progress society is itself risky because society requires innovations and developments to satisfy human demands and to deal with intractable problems which negatively impact people, such as disease and poverty. Further, it has become increasingly difficult to determine who should take risks and for whom, to fathom the complexity of decisions made and to attribute blame (Nowotny et al., 2001).

Let us take medicine as an example. Thousands of babies are born each year with crippling diseases which are the product of defective genes passed from their parents. Science and technology offer an opportunity to banish such diseases by 'tampering' with these babies' genes. In effect, this is an opportunity to alter humanity, to play God as it were, and the possibilities – the risks – of what might also unfold creates a sense of uncertainty in the populace and thus debates rage. Governments intervene through laws to mitigate this uncomfortable uncertainty. This mitigation, in turn, creates a new set of uncertainties as the technology grows around it and the possibilities continue to create temptation . . . and the cycle continues.

A further example is the role science is playing in understanding the processes of the brain (OECD, 2017b). As we outlined earlier, researchers conclude that learning occurs through progressive construction of individual knowledge via neural connections, not simply through information transfer (i.e., the 'fill the empty vessel' logic). These findings are a contrast to traditional teacher education and thus have significant implications for schools and teachers because they question the relevance and effectiveness of what they currently do.

In simple terms, technology and science cannot provide society with 'truths', only with evidence for or against. Thus, far from being a source of secure knowledge and certainty, science and technology are sometimes viewed as being problematic and uncertain. We suggest that digital societies of the future will be characterised by a wide range of 'imponderabilia', unexpected reversals and other surprises. Digital societies will no doubt generate new kinds of moral questions, as well as questions of responsibility for our society's oft-cited political stagnation. Schools and teachers will be relied upon for the knowledge and skills to deal with such uncertainties; not just for transferring information about the issues, but preparing future citizens to critically analyse and question what has occurred and to be in a position to engineer a positive alternate response.

The growth of new forms of economic rationality

In a parallel evolution of science and society, a new type of economic rationality has emerged. This economic rationality acts as a principal filter in selecting, constraining and coping with an ever-increasing flow of new uncertainties resulting from developments that offer many and varied options. A major effect of this process is that industry and the research community relate to each other more dynamically. Consequently, the paths of basic research and future technological applications are converging, with 'end products' being assessed as profitable in the conventional sense and sidelined when returns are assessed as unlikely. That is, research now contends an economic rationality focused towards profitability, irrespective of the outcome and the sectors that may or may not benefit from it (Nowotny et al., 2001). In simple terms, if a product has no profit potential, it is not produced. Although logical from a commercial standpoint, this does create a dilemma for humankind when the product required might be for the common good. A case in point is the capital investment needed for a potential medical breakthrough to combat diseases afflicting those in shallow markets such as Africa.

The transformation of time into the 'extended present'

This parameter is characterised by expectations and anticipations, where actions, choices and decisions are made in relation to the 'here and now'. However, linking the present to the future (for the reasons detailed previously) becomes uncertain. While people have always had 'expectations and anticipations', the future is now experienced as an extended present in which decisions and actions can be made to shape the future. Thus, organisations are concerned with 'visioning' and the identification of trends and mega-trends (Nowotny et al., 2001). Data and one's capacity to collect and analyse it for profit outcomes has become king. In this regard Amazon and Google are examples of major corporations which have invested in and profited from what is termed 'big data' (Gunasekaran et al., 2018; Iqbal, 2016; Lansiti & Lakhani, 2020).

In relation to education, we note that recent state education publications in New South Wales (NSW), Australia, use data and extracted trends to define the future and, in turn, profess a new 'vision' for education and its schools, so demanding new roles and functions of its workforce (Department of Education, n.d.). The strategic plan that has subsequently emerged in NSW state education, for example, envisions the future as something the organisation can and will achieve. Various performance and accountability mechanisms are then implemented down the 'chain of command' as a process of ensuring the envisioned future is achieved. Continuing employment and promotion in this environment are subject to an employee's continued performance with respect to the performance and accountability mechanisms that have been set. The outcome for employees is increased 'administrivia' and a feeling of uncertainty within the organisation. While such processes are typical of education systems, the same is also not uncommon in other, non-educational modern organisations.

From a different perspective, the extension of time into the extended present also explains the 24/7/instant demand mentality that has emerged in consumption lifecycles. No longer are people prepared to wait. There is an expectation, which is a product of technological innovation engendering speed, for problems to be solved and services to be provided immediately. Correspondingly, users can do all manner of things on the Internet, at any time and with instant outcomes. Think paying bills and banking, browsing and ordering, getting an e-book or movie on demand, setting up service provisions, all without the need for human intervention. The only impediment at present to 'immediacy' is the speed at which physical deliveries can be made. But technology is already at play as drones are tested with the potential to shorten delivery times from days to minutes.

This flexible supply and consumption mentality is seductive to busy and connected people. It is no less so for young people who are equally engaged in the digital world. This mentality, however, has not yet met the school gate, and we therefore ask what a flexible schooling regime might look like? This is a tough one, as it confronts a central premise of schooling – which is conformity and standardisation. Could one imagine a tide of demand that might catch schools unaware and force the hand of teachers as the Monday to Friday, 9am to 3pm, age-related grouping becomes untenable for parents and restless 'connected' youngsters? Could Google, Amazon or Microsoft step in with a new device that makes schools redundant (Starkey, 2020)?

Flexible space

Associated with the shift of time into an extended present, 'space' itself is able to be modified by information and communication technologies so that distance is reduced or even eliminated (Nowotny et al., 2001). Advancements in online learning, virtual reality and augmented reality have made it possible to manipulate time and space according to the whims and imagination of users. The possibilities of flexible space provisions for education appear endless and transformational for the analogue classroom (Starkey, 2020).

Let us expand the concept further.

The processes that have compressed time and distance through advances in information communication technologies and travel, often referred to as 'globalisation' and 'connectivity', have led to the intertwining of the world's economic and cultural systems. Corporations and individuals alike now have instant access and impact on all sectors of the Internet-connected world, at least if they live in the West. When distance becomes compressed and bridged in this way, 'flexible' knowledge becomes 'first-hand', accessible and up-to-date to all those who are 'connected' in the digital age. This has direct implications for schools. In contrast, schools trade on the transfer of knowledge from teacher to student using sequential age-related grade levels and a propensity for cycles of 'tell–write–assess' because it is intuitive, efficient and traditional, the path of least resistance.

Imagine if the potentials of flexible learning could be meshed with the objectives of traditional classroom plans. You could imagine students attending school for the benefits of socialisation, direct human instruction and physical demonstrations and practice. Not to mention the care provisions that busy working parents require. But also imagine its union with technological innovation through an assembly of online learning with virtual and augmented reality. Students could be taken to all parts of the world in a moment, or into the the structure of a single cell to see its marvels unfolding (Starkey, 2020). Factor into this the customisations that can be made to meet the profile of users and you have begun to engineer the school of the future. This blend in learning in effect harnesses the best of the traditional school with that of technologies, creating a truly transformative learning experience for every learner. On a strategic plane, Blended Learning also maps a transition pathway for teachers and schools. A pathway which, to date, has remained locked in the complexities and logistics of prevailing education change management theory and a mindset that takes its cues from an outdated past.

An increasing capacity for self-organisation

According to Nowotny et al. (2001), the self-organising properties of contemporary society are the capacity to define its boundaries and thus constitute everything beyond itself as 'context'. Consequently, the more complex the system becomes, the more powerful is its potential for interacting with the environment. A move in Western education systems to devolve various 'central office' responsibilities to schools through programs such as 'school self-management' (Lynch, 2012) is one such example. Another example is the capacity for the home entrepreneur to develop a 'shop' online in a matter of minutes, without the encumbrance of traditional physical space and the drudgery of home–shop travel. This capacity for self-organising is an aspect of the digital age that enables the school and its teachers to design, customise and deliver teaching and learning in the scope, size, time and circumstance of their choosing. In effect, this phenomenon encourages the school to constitute itself as a flexible and highly client-centred institution.

What does this all mean for schools and teachers?

We have outlined to this point a series of arguments and insights to highlight a misalignment that exists between schooling today and the societal context it now seeks to prepare young people for. Table 1.1 captures our discussions to compare the attributes of modern-day society (the fourth industrial revolution – 1990 onwards) with that of the previous societal era (the first, second and third industrial revolution era – 1800 to 1990).

The table chiefly highlights the first through third industrial revolution eras as having a continuing societal maxim built on physical labour, specialisations, standardisations, routines and efficiency. Importantly, these eras together span nearly 200 years: a contrast to the fourth industrial era which is just thirty years old. The means to production was limited to those who had extensive capital and the system of things relied on conformity and rigid sets of control. This logic built a sense of certainty in the community in that jobs were for life and often handed down from father to son.

At the core of this book is an assumption that the fourth industrial era represents a radical transformation from the previous three. In this industrial era the maxim of society has changed rapidly, to place a premium on human brainpower, customisations, individualisation, flexibility and a capacity to self-organise for effects. Production is now limited only by the imagination of the designer, which then permeates to the end-user. Creativity and innovation dominate the workplace with multiskilling, collaboration and personal agency the order of the day. The self-organisation capacity of this era allows many people to work from home and correspondingly operate their own 'corporation' from their home office using virtual spaces.

Table 1.1 represents a blueprint for the school of the 2000s and a corresponding set of considerations for organising its teaching and learning functions. This table indicates a starkly different societal circumstance that is in contrast to the organisational logic of the traditional school that had its genesis in the 1800s. This fourth industrial revolution society is known as the Knowledge Economy. This is the term we adopt to capture the world in which young people are growing up and toward which schools and teachers are preparing them.

Table 1.1 Comparing schooling in industrial eras: characteristics and outcomes

Time period	Theoretical profile	Societal profile	Desired schooling outcomes	School organisation attributes
First, second and third industrial revolution – 1800 to 1990	Certainty Inflexible workspaces/ conditions Time as regimentation mechanism Reliance on significant capital and physicality for work and production. Standardised product outputs	Movements from agrarian, rural lifestyles to urban, mechanised factories and mass production Individual work specialisations Emphasis on physical production with standardisation Low – medium levels of education required for work Skills and jobs for life Physical workplaces	Compliance Conformity Accepting roles Completing routine or simple tasks Efficiency Competition Problem minimisation	Sorting students Daily schedule Distinct subjects Memorisation, recall of content/ skills Ability tracking Individual rewards
Fourth industrial revolution – 1990 +	Self-organising capacities Uncertainty Flexible spaces Time transformed into the extended present New economic rationalities	Movement from labour centric factories to home-based and flexible digital work environments Networked work specialisations Emphasis on digital design and innovations that lead to improved physical and digital production outputs High levels of education required for work Multi-skilled/ capacity to transform skill capacity Virtual workplaces	Creativity Collaboration Flexibility Agency Innovation Problem solving	Open-ended inquiry Teamwork Interdisciplinary study Student ownership of learning 24/7, flexible arrangements Customisation and individualisation

Chapter summary

As previously stated in this chapter, one can only marvel at the scope and speed of technological innovation that has created today's modern society with all manner of gadgetry, insight and opportunity; a circumstance that has emerged through four interlinked industrial revolutions. Each revolution accelerated possibilities through technological innovation and convergence.

Societies of the 1800s were enlightened enough to realise the need for a systematic education, that society was changing for the better and that its people needed to be better positioned for what was unfolding. They imagined and conceived a system of things to capture and care for the thousands of young people who found themselves growing up in urban settings and who required a stratified set of skills for a stratified system of work.

This system became universally known around the globe as *schooling*. Certainty through job security was the order of the day, and young people moved orderly from school to a job over a period of nearly 200 years, even if certainty came with laborious employment, restriction to their hometown and a relatively early death. In periods of doubt about their lot in life during this early period of schooling, religion provided guidance and comfort through a message of certainty of a better afterlife. Schools were a fit to the order of the day and were accepted as a part of one's growing up and then participating in a stable and familiar society, fulfilling traditional life outcomes.

In the more recent thirty or so years, technological innovation and convergence have transformed every aspect of society and life. No longer is there a job for life – even qualifications have finite life-spans. Exponential change, fuelled by human brainpower and consumer demand, hunts out and disrupts long-held traditions and practices to offer a faster, more efficient and effective means of doing things. While modern society offers abundant opportunities and potentials and has emancipated the masses through new insights and labour-saving gadgetry, it is dependent upon human brainpower for effect. To be transported through time from 1800 to 2020 would render even the most enlightened person of the time confused and bewildered; society has changed so profoundly and fundamentally.

The problem being responded to by this book is that despite this profile of profound and fundamental change, the organisation and positioning of schools remain relatively unchanged in the modern era. In this respect, new societal maxims illustrated through human capacities for creativity, collaboration, flexibility, agency, innovation and problem-solving have failed to dominate the logic of curriculum design and delivery, instead giving way to state-mandated curriculums which place a premium on narrow national testing outcomes. This circumstance has the effect of rendering schools largely misaligned to the modern workplace and society, and thus jeopardise the life chances of many.

Moving schools from the analogue world of the past to the digital age of the present is a substantial undertaking, an undertaking that will require significant repositioning of both resources and mindsets. In writing this book, we present the reader with both a challenge to change but importantly a way forward toward making this change. As we signalled in an earlier section, Blended Learning, which couples classroom practice with the digital world and its possibilities, comes to represent the bridge for change and a potent means through which teachers are able to transform their classrooms by building personal capabilities and harnessing new capacities to deal with the profile of individuals who currently occupy seats at the tables of their future. We will investigate Blended Learing in more detail beginning with Chapter 3, but first we examine more specifically how knowledge operates at the heart of the Knowledge Economy, and how this requires a profound level of education reform, in Chapter 2.

Glossary

Blended Learning   A distinct, technology-driven pedagogy designed to harness the power of technological disruption in positive ways that can assist modern teaching and learning to address the imperatives of the Knowledge Economy.

Connectivity   A state in which all manner of devices and equipment are linked together through technological means to create a network of semless coordinated and compatiable activity.

Digital revolution An era in modern times where technology has increased to such a point that machines make decision and all manner of activities are managed or enacted through the use of digital means.

Industrial revolution A revolution in industry, driven by technological innovation, which commenced during the eighteenth century disrupting and redefining home and work life.

Knowledge Economy An economic circumstance where production and consumption is based on an inter-play of intellectual capital and technological advancement.

References

Au, W. (2011). Teaching under the new Taylorism: High-stakes testing and the standardisation of the 21st century curriculum. *Journal of Curriculum Studies, 43*(1), 25–45.

Berry, B. (Ed.). (2011). *Teaching 2030: What we must do for our students and our public schools: Now and in the future*. Teachers College Press.

Burns, T., & Gottschalk, F. (2019). *Educating 21st century children: Emotional well-being in the digital age*. Educational Research and Innovation.

Carl, J. (2009). Industrialization and public education: Social cohesion and social stratification. In R. Cowen & A. M. Kazamias (Eds.), *International handbook of comparative education* (pp. 503–518). Springer International Handbooks of Education, vol. 22. Springer. https://doi.org/10.1007/978-1-4020-6403-6_32

Chenoweth, K. (2020). *Schools that succeed: How educators marshal the power of systems for improvement*. Harvard Education Press.

Christensen, C. M., Horn, M. B., & Johnson, C. W. (2011). *Disrupting class: How disruptive innovation will change the way the world learns*. McGraw-Hill.

Collins, A., & Halverson, R. (2018). *Rethinking education in the age of technology: The digital revolution and schooling in America*. Teachers College Press.

Department of Education. (n.d.). Strategic Plan 2018 to 2022. https://education.nsw.gov.au/about-us/strategies-and-reports/strategic-plan

Dickens, W. T., & Flynn, J. R. (2001). Heritability estimates versus large environmental effects: The IQ paradox resolved. *Psychological Review, 108*(2), 346.

Ertmer, P. A., Ottenbreit-Leftwich, A. T., Sadik, O., Sendurur, E., & Sendurur, P. (2012). Teacher beliefs and technology integration practices: A critical relationship. *Computers & Education, 59*(2), 423–435.

Fleurbaey, M., Bouin, O., Salles-Djelic, M. L., & Nowotny, H. (2018). *A manifesto for social progress: Ideas for a better society*. Cambridge University Press.

Friedman, T. L. (2016). *Thank you for being late: An optimist's guide to thriving in the age of Accelerations*. Penguin.

Fullan, M. (2007). *The new meaning of educational changes*. Teachers College Press.

Fullan, M. (2016). *The new meaning of educational change* (5th ed.). Routledge.

Gepp, A., & Kumar, K. (2020). How to improve teaching using blended learning. In L. Makewa (Ed.), *Theoretical and practical approaches to innovation in higher education* (pp. 80–90). IGI Global.

Goswami, U. (2008). Principles of learning, implications for teaching: A cognitive neuroscience perspective. *Journal of Philosophy of Education, 42*(3–4), 381–399.

Gross, S. J. (2019). *Applying turbulence theory to educational leadership in challenging times: A case-based approach*. Routledge.

Guerriero, S. (Ed.). (2017). *Pedagogical knowledge and the changing nature of the teaching profession*. Educational Research and Innovation. OECD Publishing.

Guerriero, S., & Révai, N. (2017). Knowledge-based teaching and the evolution of a profession. In S. Guerriero (Ed.), *Pedagogical knowledge and the changing nature of the teaching profession* (pp. 253–269). OECD Publishing.

Gunasekaran, A., Yusuf, Y. Y., Adeleye, E. O., & Papadopoulos, T. (2018). Agile manufacturing practices: The role of big data and business analytics with multiple case studies. *International Journal of Production Research, 56*(1–2), 385–397.

Hargreaves, A., & Fullan, M. (2012). *Professional capital: Transforming teaching in every school.* Teachers College Press.

Hattie, J. (2011). Challenge of focusing education reform. *The Australian*, June 7. Retrieved July 7, 2011, from www.theaustralian.com.au/business/news/rethinking-education-the-challenge-of-focusing-reform/story-fn8ex0p1-1226069556190

Hattie, J. (2012). *Visible learning for teachers: Maximising impact on learning.* Routledge.

Hattie, J. A. C. (2009). *Visible learning: A synthesis of over 800 meta-analyses relating to achievement.* Routledge.

Herrnstein, R. J., & Murray, C. (2010). *The bell curve: Intelligence and class structure in American life.* Simon and Schuster.

Horn, M. B., & Staker, H. (2017). *The blended workbook: Learning to design the schools of our future.* Jossey-Bass.

Iqbal, U. (2016). Google business secrets. *The Journal of Internet Banking and Commerce, 21*(2). www.icommercecentral.com/open-access/google-business-secrets.php?aid=75285

Joram, E., Gabriele, A. J., & Walton, K. (2020). What influences teachers' 'buy-in' of research? Teachers' beliefs about the applicability of educational research to their practice. *Teaching and Teacher Education, 88*, 1–12.

Kaufman, K. (2015). Information communication technology: Challenges and some prospects from preservice education to the classroom. *Mid-Atlantic Education Review, 2*(1), 1–11.

Kuhl, P. K., Lim, S. S., Guerriero, S., & van Damme, D. (2019). Neuroscience and education: How early brain development affects school. In P. K. Kuhl, S. S. Lim, & S. Guerriero (Eds.), *Developing minds in the digital age* (pp. 25–36). OECD Publishing.

Labaree, D. F. (2005). Progressivism, schools and schools of education: An American romance. *Paedagogica Historica, 41*(1–2), 275–288.

Lansiti, M., & Lakhani, K. (2020). *Competing in the age of AI: Strategy and leadership when algorithms and networks run the world.* Harvard Business Review Press.

Grubb, W. N., & Lazerson, M. (2009). The education gospel and vocationalism in an international perspective: The promises and the limits of formal schooling. In R. Maclean & D. Wilson (Eds.), *International handbook of education for the changing world of work.* Springer. https://doi.org/10.1007/978-1-4020-5281-1_121

Leyva, R. (2009). No Child Left Behind: A neoliberal repackaging of social darwinism. *Journal for Critical Education Policy Studies, 7*(1), 365–381.

Lynch, D. (2012). *Preparing teachers in times of change: Teaching school. standards, new content and evidence.* Primrose Hall.

Nisbett, R. E. (2009). *Intelligence and how to get it: Why schools and cultures count.* WW Norton & Company.

Nowotny, H., Scott, P., & Gibbons, M. (2001). *Rethinking science: Knowledge and the public in an age of uncertainty.* Polity.

OECD. (2015). *Schooling redesigned: Towards innovative learning systems.* OECD Publishing.

OECD. (2017a). *Schools at the crossroads of innovation in cities and regions.* Educational Research and Innovation. OECD Publishing.

OECD. (2017b), Neurotechnology and society: Strengthening responsible innovation in brain science. *OECD Science, Technology and Industry Policy Papers*, No. 46, OECD Publishing. https://doi.org/10.1787/f31e10ab-en

Pitsis, T. S., Beckman, S. L., Steinert, M., Oviedo, L., & Maisch, B. (2020). Designing the future: Strategy, design, and the 4th industrial revolution—An introduction to the special issue. *California Management Review, 62*(2), 5–11.

Quong, T. (2016). Facts don't change behaviour, stories do. *Australian Educational Leader, 38*(3), 70.

Ross, E. W. (2010). Exploring Taylorism and its continued influence on work and schooling. In *Social studies and diversity education: What we do and why we do it* (pp. 33–37).

Schatzki, T. R. (2019). *Social change in a material world: How activity and material processes dynamize practices*. Routledge.

Schwab, K. (2016). The fourth industrial revolution: What it means, how to respond. *World Economic Forum*. www.weforum.org/agenda/2016/01/the-fourth-industrial-revolution-what-it-means-and-how-to-respond/

Smith, A. (1801). *An inquiry into the nature and causes of the wealth of nations*. J. Decker.

Starkey, L. (2020). A review of research exploring teacher preparation for the digital age. *Cambridge Journal of Education, 50*(1), 37–56.

Steele, D., & Whitaker, T. (2019). *Essential truths for principals*. Routledge.

Stoller, A. (2015). Taylorism and the logic of learning outcomes. *Journal of Curriculum Studies, 47*(3), 317–333.

Teacher Education Ministerial Advisory Group [TEMAG]. (2014). *Action now: Classroom ready teachers*. Teacher Education Ministerial Advisory Group, Australian Government.

Tormos, R. (2019). *The rhythm of modernisation: How values change over time*. Brill.

Tyack, D. B., & Cuban, L. (1995). *Tinkering toward utopia*. Harvard University Press.

Victer, R. S. (2020). Connectivity knowledge and the degree of structural formalisation: A contribution to a contingency theory of organisational capability. *Journal of Organization Design, 9*(1), 1–22.

Vincent-Lancrin, S., Urgel, J., Kar, S., & Jacotini, G. (2019). *Measuring innovation in education 2019: What has changed in the classroom?* Educational Research and Innovation. OECD Publishing.

Yeigh, T., & Lynch, D. (2017). Reforming initial teacher education: A call for innovation. *Australian Journal of Teacher Education, 42*(12), 112–127.

Yeigh, T., Lynch, D., Turner, D., Fradale, P., Willis, R., Sell, K., & Lawless, E. (2020). Using blended learning to support whole-of-school improvement: The need for contextualisation. *Education and Information Technologies, 25*, 3329–3355. https://doi.org/10.1007/s10639-020-10114-6

2 The case for education reform

Relevant Australian Professional Standards for Teachers: 1.5; 1.6; 2.6; 3.2; 3.4; 3.6; 4.5; 6.2; 6.3; 6.4

Chapter synopsis

Over the course of the past twenty years, governments across the globe, together with their respective education systems, have grappled with changes in society that are unprecedented in modern human history. Chapter 1 outlined this circumstance as a transitioning of society from an industrial paradigm to one built on knowledge through the Knowledge Economy. In Chapter 2 we examine how knowledge operates at the heart of the new economy and explore the capacity to use knowledge in new and interconnected ways that require education reform. This reinforces the need for modern, technology-driven societies to have high performing education systems, and to this end, Chapter 2 also investigates the extent to which schools and teachers have witnessed a corresponding push for increased national **standardised testing regimes**, ongoing updates occurring in school **curriculum**s and calls from various quarters of society and the economy for study area mandates. To understand how this changing focus for government education policy positions education reform, Chapter 2 will use examples of reform that have taken place in Australia over the past five decades, noting this is a societal circumstance which also typifies education activity in most developed countries. From this perspective the main focus for Chapter 2 will be to identify the pressure points for changing education policy position, as well as the associated societal elements which intervene to make such policies a success or otherwise. The chapter concludes by providing analysis of such a circumstance in order to propose a series of key and corresponding educational reforms considered necessary to progress the quality of education within a knowledge economy framework.

Introduction

In Chapter 1, circumstances leading to the emergence of the Knowledge Economy were outlined, and the impacts on schooling briefly discussed. In summary, the emergence of the 2000 era Knowledge Economy has become a significant factor in societal change that is being driven by the exponential growth in computing power and increasing connectivity between digital devices. Feeding such change is human brainpower, which Schiemann (2012, 2014) refers to as **Talent**. Our central argument is that by direct association, schools and the work of their teachers – the school's 'Talent' – are implicated in what is now required for such a new world.

Further to the changes that technological innovation has brought to the world, recent examples of unpredictable events like pandemics and natural disasters related to climate change add to the complexity and unpredictability of the world, and the environment future generations will need to work within. *The Big Lockdown of 2020* (i.e., COVID-19) brought to light the shortfalls of a society that took for granted the uncertainty of a complex world, not to mention the level of technology use in schools, as well as technology access issues, when schools were forced to close and use online learning exclusively for an extended period of time (Li & Lalani, 2020; Taylor, 2020). Taken together, the 2000 era is in fundamental contrast to the traditional schooling logic embedded in the 1800s and the trajectory that modern society is now following. The case for a reform of schooling is intensifying.

This chapter provides an argument for the reform of schools to meet the profile of a Knowledge Economy. This call for reform is now critical as schools play a central role in preparing young people for the future, a future that is not static like the work circumstance of the 1900s. With this goal in mind, the chapter begins with an examination of what we term the 'rhetoric of reform'. This examination provides an insight into the challenges that schools and system leaders face in reforming schools, a challenge that is an unintended consequence of governments seeking to intervene in education outcomes. Correspondingly, a later section argues that a 'false dichotomy' has emerged in the school reform debate, primarily because old mindsets are trying to solve new problems. Further to this, we argue the need for a new curriculum. These arguments are juxtaposed with an examination of the concept of capability and how this twenty-first-century workplace logic redefines 'the what' and 'how' of what schools should focus their instruction upon. We turn first to the 'rhetoric of reform', where our goal is to shine a light on why schools fail to engage in the level of reform necessary and to introduce a reform logic that is built upon 'new mindsets' focused on building school-wide capability, rather than preoccupying itself with 'outmoded' operating logics and imposed compliance regimes.

The rhetoric of reform

Education reform has been a preoccupation with governments of all political persuasions across the globe, particularly in Western societies over past decades, largely because of the economic benefits that an educated population generates. The improvement driver of choice for governments has been to ultimately tie funding to schools with performance benchmarks through the use of national testing regimes. This is illustrated in Australia by the National Assessment Program – Literacy and Numeracy (NAPLAN)[1] and through various testing regimes in the USA (Kaestle, n.d.). The scope of such tests has been chiefly literacy and numeracy achievement at junctions in the student progression through schooling, which has had the effect of narrowing the focus of teacher work in classrooms. The punitive nature of public testing reports inadvertently forces the teacher to essentially 'teach to the test' and place less emphasis on curriculum elements that fall outside the scope of such tests (Apple, 2001; Vrasidas, 2015). The problem with this approach to school improvement is that it is primarily an industrial-age mindset. It is not about meeting the profile of a fast-evolving societal context but endeavouring to use 'compliance and uniformity' as a performance proxy that has created competition between schools and birthed national leagues tables. On another front, standardised testing has become an excuse for governments to shift funding commitments, blaming schools and teachers for poor results. In summary, after four decades of standardised testing in the United States, with Australia's NAPLAN or with international comparisons using the Programme for International Student Assessment (PISA) ranking exemplars, and the resulting culture of 'performativity', no substantial improvements have been delivered. This drive for improvement has also limited the focus of teachers, school leaders and education system leaders. This might have been a defensible position pre-1990, but the type of skills required of graduating students today is in fundamental contrast to the past and now an aberration. Our point here, is that it has become apparent that standardised testing is encouraging the wrong direction when school reform is a desired outcome.

In Australia, educational policy, while somewhat forward-thinking in rhetoric, has been patchy at best in implementation terms. For example, the *Melbourne Declaration on Educational Goals for Young Australians* (MCEETYA, 2009) articulated two goals: that Australian schooling promoted 'equity and excellence', and that all young Australians become 'successful learners, confident and creative individuals and active and informed citizens' (Ministerial Council on Education, Employment, Training and Youth Affairs [MCEETYA], 2009). The report's commitment to action for 'strengthening accountability and transparency' states that 'schools need reliable, rich data on the performance of their students because they have the primary accountability for improving student outcomes' (2009, p. 16). Despite this rhetoric in 'the declaration', the focus on accountability and improvement has only heralded the start of a period of standardised test comparisons, including the 2010 launch of the 'MySchool' website in Australia,[2] which is now used by parents to choose the school for their children and the suburb in which they should reside. This has enabled parents to decide where their children should enter the schooling system, and perhaps this is a good thing, but the narrowness of such testing is deceptive, and the point we make is that the concern should be with the scope of the actual 'education' with which their children exit the system!

Another response by governments to reform schools is exampled in a document entitled *A Shared Challenge: Improving Literacy, Numeracy and Science Learning in Queensland Primary Schools* (Masters, 2009). This commissioned report was to address the state of Queensland's poor schooling performance in comparison to other Australian states. Again, the recommendations were based on 'best practice research' but the system reverted to type and responded to it by implementing yet another layer of accountability that included 'school reviews' (School Improvement Unit, 2017).

The same year as the Master's (2009) report, further Australasian research became a significant focus for educators. John Hattie's (2012) study of the impact on learning on a wide range of factors pointed educators to approaches that had the largest effect size. Hattie's suggested 'hinge point', the minimum average effect size of 0.4, was what teachers should aim for in their charges and through annual systematic priorities became the new performance benchmark in the classroom. Correspondingly, schools set out to cherry-pick those teaching strategies that had the largest effect size without consideration to teaching context and content and pedagogic design principles (DeWitt, 2018). Once again, the rhetoric of what is said to work becomes the focus rather than the application of a comprehensive pedagogic strategy (Coe, 2002).

As in the United States, which has over four decades of standardised data demonstrating little improvement (Hanushek, 2016), the gains in Australia are less than encouraging (Harrington, 2013; Thomson et al., 2019). It could be argued that a focus on accountability, transparency and performance within school systems has resulted in little 'improvement'. Industrial-age thinking on improving the 'production line' appears not to have provided an appropriate return on investment. Australia's declining performance in PISA comparisons is another concerning data set (Thomson et al., 2019).

A focus on effective instruction, as a result of policy and system intervention and the research of Masters (2009) and Hattie (2012), has further increased the rhetorical value of 'direct instruction' and 'explicit instruction' strategies over skill sets also deemed important in the digital economy. We are not saying the research is wrong, nor that is it of little value; quite the opposite, as we believe it is. Our argument is how education systems use such knowledge to enact policy positions, which then distract schools from responding appropriately. We will return to this point.

We have argued that while twenty-first-century skills or 'transversal skills' (UNESCO, 2015) appear in national curricula, higher value has been placed on such things as reading levels and test scores, a 'systematic curriculum', accountability and transparency, and such skills get little attention. We agree the fundamentals of education, such as reading competency, are critical to school and later life success, but to create a circumstance where the rewards for schools and teachers are solely connected to them is wrong and unfortunately reduces teacher agency in the teaching and learning process. We're not taking teachers off the hook, as it were, here. They must be highly educated themselves and have demonstrated capacities to teach effectively. Our point is that in the affirmative, the teacher is constrained by external circumstances which only seek to strengthen the rhetoric of education policy positions which are wrong-footed for the current era.

Put simply, we argue that the results of this lack of focus on the skill sets needed for a Knowledge Economy (the fourth industrial revolution era) and beyond is fundamentally creating a negative impact on the employability of school graduates (McGunagle & Zizka, 2020; Wolff & Booth, 2017).

In addition, the promise of technology in schooling has not yet been realised. What needs to be understood is that it is not only about the technological device. Technology is rapidly changing the world, but it has not yet changed schooling because the focus has largely been on the hardware through the introduction of computer labs, the purchase of class sets of iPads, the installation of interactive whiteboards across a school and 'one-to-one' programs. For the types of disruption seen in other sectors of the economy to occur in education, school leaders and teachers will need to consider not just the hardware, or a narrow set of measures intended to improve an outdated system, but will be required to entirely reimagine their work. Schooling has been somewhat protected to this point because it has not attracted the level of capital investment that other sectors of the economy have due to its almost universal 'not for profit' status. That is until the COVID-19 pandemic of 2020 forced an immediate response by educators and a shift in approach through technology as the need for 'remote learning' was hastily thrust upon them.

Further to this is the idea that the innovation required in realising the potential of these technologies to improve learning and prepare students for the Knowledge Economy cannot be achieved using the traditional industrial-age schooling mindsets. What this resulted in is the replacement of old technologies with new ones. For example, the whiteboard being replaced with an electronic whiteboard, the feint-ruled pad being replaced by a computer used as a word processor. Significant resourcing, investment in hardware, subsequent technical support, professional learning and the like has not really brought measurable improvement, or indeed student satisfaction or engagement (Kelley et al., 2020; Willis et al., 2019; Yeigh et al., 2020). Our argument here is that the same creative thinking and innovation that has produced the technological advances across society is now required by school leaders and teachers.

An example of how an industrial age mindset and a narrow focus on improvement has held back innovation in the learning space, including the effective implementation of Blended Learning, is the establishment of a dichotomy between explicit instructional strategies and the more divergent strategies that might contribute to the types of skills student will need to succeed in the fourth industrial revolution. For the successful implementation of a whole school Blended Learning approach, we argue this is a false dichotomy. We now explain our logic.

A false dichotomy

As previously discussed, research has demonstrated that most high-yielding teaching strategies include explicit, teacher-directed instruction, and this has predisposed teachers and school leaders to overvalue these pedagogical practices. Or, more correctly, to undervalue the active learning pedagogies, including problem-based learning and inquiry. What we argue here is that the dichotomy created is problematic for the skills necessary in the fourth industrial revolution.

This 'false dichotomy', as presented in Figure 2.1, has been the result of a system of education that has attempted to improve schools using an industrial-age mindset and an overreliance on processes concerned with 'test score' improvement. Like achieving faster production lines in the factory, this approach has failed to recognise how technological advances would bring more significant disruption. As an example, achieving a 10 per cent more efficient production line in a factory producing motor vehicles was never going to 'compete' with the efficiency robotics would achieve. We therefore hold the position that while explicit instruction is essential in a high-performing system, it is insufficient for the results needed in the fourth industrial revolution. It is, in effect, a 'false dichotomy' in a now irrelevant pedagogical debate.

We propose this as a false dichotomy because schools need the strategies that appear at both ends of this continuum if they are to prepare students for an unknown future. The convergent thinking of teaching strategies that focus on specific foundational skills, and the divergent thinking of teaching that builds the skills necessary for the network society, are both necessary. This is also the potential of harnessing the best of 'face-to-face' teaching with the best technology has to offer, as realised in Blended Learning. The contention in this book is that Blended Learning offers the considered planning of required pedagogy that ensures the foundational skills in literacy and numeracy that have been the focus of education systems in recent times, and the transversal skills considered essential for the fourth industrial revolution through the mindful application of technology.

We also argue that more focused consideration of transversal skills is another element necessary in preparing students for the fourth industrial revolution. While this book is not chiefly concerned with issues of curriculum, we will briefly discuss this in the next section to further illuminate the potential of Blended Learning in a Knowledge Economy circumstance.

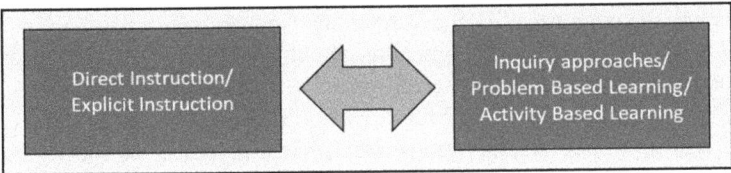

Figure 2.1 False dichotomy.

A new curriculum

As we outlined in Chapter 1, the industrial age curriculum was designed for transferring knowledge and as a sorting process to direct individuals to appropriate areas of employment. It is based on what 'content knowledge' was deemed to be important and not how to think, solve problems, ask questions, be creative, synthesise ideas or apply critical thinking. The sorting process provided large numbers of school leavers – often early leavers 'exited' because they 'didn't make the grade' – to fill the labour-intensive needs of farming, mining and factory production lines. At the other end of schooling, mastering the curriculum and achieving higher grades enabled a far smaller number of students to pursue higher callings, such as the leadership of government, the church or army and to become 'captains of industry' (Berry, 2011; Lynch, 2012). This sorting is evident in how schools still function today: 'grade' level grouping of students, performance presented as A–E grading, test scores being valued most, university entrance scores and the establishment of a hierarchy of disciplines. This hierarchy has given a higher educational value to subjects like physics, chemistry, mathematics and English, valuing them more highly than 'the arts' (Robinson, 2017).

This hierarchy is another dichotomy established in education that can be described as 'false'. In the complexity of the fourth industrial revolution, solutions to problems facing humanity are increasingly emerging from transdisciplinary thinking and creative processes, not necessarily from narrow fields within a single discipline. These are the skills identified as twenty-first-century skills (see Rios et al., 2020), the soft skills (see Howes & Taylor, 2020), and transversal skills (see Pastor, 2020), and they can appear in existing national or systemic curriculum mandated by government, including the Australian Curriculum.[3] It is not uncommon to read the rhetoric about these skills in various curriculum documents and education policy position papers but, in the main, current schooling practices do not focus on these skills, they focus on what can be understood as an industrial definition of academic performance. By this, we mean basic skills, recall of knowledge and the articulation of long-established perspectives (Duncan et al., 2016; Lynch, 2012). While important as 'the basics' are, a personal capacity to transition some into actions embodying the dynamic circumstances of a fourth industrial revolution, where innovation, creativity and change abound, is largely missing in current curriculum considerations.

A new curriculum is not a prerequisite to implementing Blended Learning. In fact, we come to see the emergence of a new curriculum as an additional outcome of implementing Blended Learning. Meaning, the logic and potentials of Blended Learning, as Chapters 3, 6 and 7 outline, invariably encourage the teacher and the school to rethink its curriculum as technology opens up potentials and capacities for teaching and learning. Our key point here, however, is that a whole rewrite of the school curriculum, or a refocusing of the skills to be developed within an existing curriculum, and delivered through Blended Learning, offers teachers an opportunity to greatly enhance the learning of students, better preparing them for a changing world, and to increase their respective agencies in the education process. Understanding the false dichotomies presented here, in terms of pedagogy and curriculum, is a first step in unleashing the potential of Blended Learning (Figure 2.2).

Having now made introductory comments about the rhetoric of reform and the need for a new curriculum, we briefly pause to capture our key messages thus far.

For many years, calls for the reform of schools from various sectors (government, business and industry, and education consumers) has dominated the media and debates in published literature. Governments have tended to respond with instruments such as standardised testing and a back to basics curriculum, which, while newsworthy and

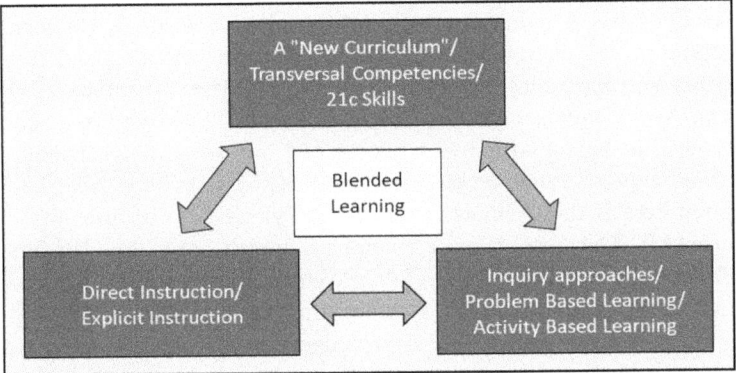

Figure 2.2 A new curriculum.

resonating with the general public, tend to focus the attention of teachers away from engineering a curriculum for the future to one that is best placed in the past. This is not to say that basic skills are not important. They most certainly are. But it's a point about how calls for school reform fall far short of what's required. In summary, a repeating rhetoric of reform coupled with various false dichotomies have muddied the waters on what now needs to occur in our schools and the work of our teachers.

So how do schools and their teachers transition to a new paradigm in schooling? How does one escape the clutches of reform rhetoric and false dichotomies and increase the agencies of schools and their teachers in a modern-day schooling circumstance?

To answer this question, we introduce the concept of **Talent Management**. Talent Management unpacks the required fourth industrial revolution mindset and positions the school's teaching 'Talent' for Knowledge Economy work and the changing world unfolding before them.

The management of Talent in schools

In Chapter 1, we outlined how the emergence of the Knowledge Economy has redefined society such that the consumer now demands choice, flexibility, and real-time service provisions. By direct association, this new workplace is preoccupied with problem-solving, innovation and creativity, trading manual labour requirements for mechanisation, automation and robotics. Service provision has gone from 'face-to-face' and 'within-time constraints' to digital and 24/7.

This transformation of the workplace has correspondingly moved the manager's focus from ***Labour* Management** to *Talent* Management, in effect placing a premium on what can be termed 'knowledge work', where managers reposition themselves as 'the leaders' and concern themselves with unleashing the Talent before them, working to position and support the collective Talent for novel work, focused on interpreting and evolving the school curriculum for the fast-evolving landscape that is the 2000s (North & Gueldenberg, 2011). The Talent in schools, of course, is the teacher.

The term Talent Management thus comes to mean a transformation of the workplace whereby the manager's focus moves from labour oversight and supervision to *talent enablement*, placing a premium on the potentials that 'knowledge work' offers for fourth industrial revolution-based industries such as the school (North & Gueldenberg, 2011). Blended Learning in this circumstance is a mechanism for enabling and supporting such required changes and repositioning schools for the 2000 era. In effect, Talent Management represents a new mindset for how teachers are positioned within a school, the type of work they need to be supported to work on and the focus of what they do with students. We further explore Talent Management in Chapter 5.

Our key point here is that schools are no longer viewed as factories that just sort and certify performance. They are custom enterprises which view their student charges as tomorrow's Talent and apply a parallel Talent Management mindset to prepare, position, enable, engage and support tomorrow's future citizens. Continuing this logic, we argue that teachers are thus a key part of the Knowledge Economy in that they expose, exploit and harness knowledge and its potentials so as to prepare young people for future work and life. They are in effect the main 'service provider' in a school and thus come to represent the school's chief resource. A resource that we term 'Talent'. To understand this circumstance and to connect it to a call for school reform we draw on John Stephenson's (1999) concept of capability and William Schiemann's (2012) theory of Talent Management.

A workplace that is constantly consumed with inventing the new and transforming the old is dependent upon 'brainpower'. This type of worker is highly skilled, continually learning and is motivated to create, invent and innovate. Stephenson (1999) defines this as the capability factor: 'an all-round human quality, an integration of knowledge, skills, personal qualities and understanding used appropriately and effectively – not just in familiar and highly focused specialist contexts but in response to new and changing circumstances' (1999; emphasis added).

The broad nature of capability makes it impossible to draw up the kind of lists of traits, characteristics, 'desirabilities' and essentials that are common with 'competencies'. 'Competence' is often defined with an emphasis upon personal traits, characteristics or skills that may be directly linked to effective (or outstanding) job performance. Competence has its hallmarks in the first and second industrial revolution, where workers were preoccupied with ensuring products complied with long-held and established norms. Capability is thus the looking forward to the fulfilment of potential where competence looks back to the demonstration of actuality. Figure 2.3 locates the concepts of competence and capability where Y comes to represent the traditional workplace mindset – what we termed in Chapter 1 as the *Taylorist-based industrial era mindset* – and Z the *new workplace mindset* concerned with constant change and Talent. We now explain this logic.

The Taylor-based industrial era mindset of the 1800s affirms the emergent world as 'the same' as it always was, but with more 'problems' to grapple with. This mindset is illustrated by position Y. In this position, workers are dealing with familiar problems for which they have learned familiar solutions. Keeping production at an established level and quality is the priority. Relating this to schools and the work of teachers, position Y is a classroom circumstance that is content-focused, uses a homogenised set of curriculums, teacher-centric activities, and with technology as an afterthought. One can see how standardised testing would flourish and fit nicely in such a circumstance.

In the contrasting mindset, the world, because of new technologies, the structure of a new kind of labour market, the universalism of popular culture, the need for self-assertion, and patently different life prospects existing for young people, is seen as radically different. Correspondingly, it follows that workplace activities need to be radically

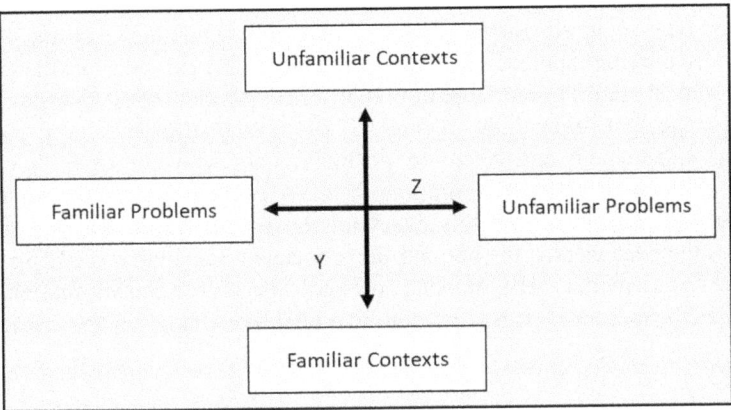

Figure 2.3 A way of looking at the world of actions (adapted by the authors from Stephenson, 1999, p. 2).

different. This mindset is represented by position Z in Figure 2.3, where incumbents have less familiarity with the context. In position Z there are no solutions available 'to buy', as problems must be formulated before they can be solved. Professional activity is, therefore, characterised by courage, planned risk-taking, imagination, intuition and creativity (Stephenson, 1999). According to Stephenson (1999), it is an ability to operate in both position Y and Z that very often distinguishes experts or what can be termed 'expertise'. We propose that to set and rely upon a standardised test as a key indicator of success in such a circumstance is a futile attempt to capture performance that is illogical in a fast-changing and evolving world.

Locating this within classrooms and the work of teachers, we refer back to Chapter 1, where we defined this as a schooling context comprising organising elements such as open-ended inquiry, teamwork, interdisciplinary study, student ownership of learning 24/7, flexible arrangements, customisation and individualisation. Blended Learning in this context is the central mechanism through which such knowledge and skills are able to be transitioned for effect into the traditional classroom circumstance. We now elaborate this assertion.

Blended Learning as a mechanism for school reform

For the uninitiated, Blended Learning comes to mean using online learning technologies in the classroom or at home. But this is only half right. Blended Learning is the harnessing of all the good things about the physical classroom world with those of the online world to create an explicit, sophisticated, deliberate 'blend' in teaching and learning. Blended Learning comes to represent an opportunity for teachers to exploit the rapid technological developments that are occurring in information communication technologies while embracing the face-to-face classroom circumstance that is synonymous with growing up and attending school (Gepp & Kumar, 2019; Horn & Staker, 2015). At its heart, Blended Learning is an opportunity for teachers to meet the learning needs of all students, not just those who do school well, and to propel teaching and learning into the digital age (Gepp & Kumar, 2019; Yeigh et al., 2020).

We now return to the Talent Management logic. To this point, we have outlined how government policy positions have created an environment which is an ill fit to the Knowledge

Economy and the work and home life it sets up and enables. This economy is a fundamentally different type of world to the previous industrial revolution eras and thus requires a fundamentally different approach to how people are 'managed' and 'positioned' within it. Talent Management comes to represent how such a new positioning is conceptualised.

Talent Management essentially comprises the systematic attraction, identification, development, engagement and retention of individuals who are of high worth to the organisation (Schiemann, 2012), or in simple terms engaging the appropriate workforce for the job ahead. So, what does this mean for the school leader who seeks to position their Talent – their teachers – for optimal performance? Schiemann (2012) presents what he terms the 'ACE model'. His model comes to represent a transformational model of leadership that focuses on how leaders optimise effective change in their Talent via three dimensions:

- Alignment: the degree to which leaders align staff to the vision, mission and goals of a change program.
- Capabilities: the degree to which leaders ensure that staff have access to the relevant resources, skill sets, and professional learning required to enact the change program.
- Engagement: the degree to which leaders can inspire and motivate staff to engage in the change program.

This model is transformational in that it 'emphasises leaders' developing a compelling vision, providing individualised support, and intellectual stimulation to staff, and engaging them in the achievement of shared goals' (Sun & Leithwood, 2015, p. 500). Importantly, this model can provide a framework to contextualise research in educational leadership through the lens of alignment, capabilities and engagement, which can be linked to prior research in the area of leadership impact as follows:

- Leithwood (2013) found *aligning* teachers by 'direction setting practices' and *building their capabilities* by 'developing people, redesigning the organisation and managing the instructional program' (p. 636) were useful strategies employed by successful leaders.
- Specific to transformational leadership, Moir et al. (2014) found that teachers preferred transformational leaders who developed *engagement* through high levels of interpersonal skills such as trust and *aligned* their staff by placing a premium on student achievement.
- Behaviours which impacted most on student learning were those resulting in what Marzano et al. (2005) referred to as 'second-order change' (p. 113). These included *aligning* through ideals and beliefs, *capability building* by intellectual stimulation, and *engaging staff* by way of affirmation.
- The principal's role is to ensure teachers are *aligned* and *engaged* by bureaucratic structures that promote teacher autonomy through 'open and innovative-stimulating (vision-building, intellectual stimulation) actions' (Buske, 2018, p. 274).
- Notably in the research of Robinson et al. (2009), the dimension with the most substantial effect, 'promoting and participating in teacher learning and development', involves school leaders participating *in* and *with* teacher learning and development, which is considered an essential aspect of Schiemann's (2014) conceptualisation of *organisational readiness*. This notion sits at the heart of the ACE model and proposes that school leaders who are able to transform and direct alignment, capabilities and

engagement in support of the change agenda surrounding a school improvement initiative are better able to enact positive improvement outcomes.

At a conceptual level, the ACE model can be viewed as a representation of the theory of planned behaviour (TPB), which suggests an explicit relationship exists between attitudes, intentions and behavioural engagement (Ajzen, 1991; Lamorte, 2018). We also note that Dinham (2016) reported similar findings concerning the impact of this relationship on the role of school leaders in the United Kingdom and Australia.

In this respect, our application of the ACE model is echoed by Macklin and Zbar (2017), who argue that school improvement, and therefore student learning outcomes, stands or falls on school leadership and what it does. Our central argument is that positioning teachers for Blended Learning comes to represent a systemic process of aligning, engaging and building the capability of teachers. Blended Learning as a pedagogy also has the organising potential to increase the capacity of the teacher to cater for the diversity of the modern classroom and the inherent need to customise learning for each individual student. We explore the premise of Talent Management and school leadership in Chapter 5.

Chapter summary

What this chapter has outlined is that fundamental changes in society and technological advances have changed the definition of what a successful school should produce, yet the persistence of legacy pedagogies anchored firmly in the industrial era in which they were designed, and the failure of such pedagogies to meet current needs, have been compounded by a well-intentioned yet deeply flawed emphasis on standardised testing. This has given rise to several rhetorical flaws such as a false dichotomy between the inclusion of both convergent and divergent skill sets, and accountability regimes instead of Talent Management regimes. We concluded this chapter with an introduction to the ACE model for gauging school readiness for change, a construct that will be explored at an operational level in later chapters. In Chapter 3 we will introduce Blended Learning more formally, as well as connect it to some of the key ideas about technological disruption and school reform as presented in Chapters 1 and 2.

Glossary

Curriculum A course of study, usually mandated by the state and thus required of schools to achieve in their students.

Labour Management An approach to managing an organisation whereby adherence to systems and processes are paramount to ensure consistency and uniformity in a production cycle. Generally associated with work in the first and second industrial revolutions.

Standardised testing regime A circumstance in education systems where a standardised test, usually focused narrowly to aspects of literacy and numeracy achievement, is used to inform the performance of respective schools.

Talent Talent is the term given to the highly skilled people that are employed in the modern knowledge-based workplace and it is through their endeavours that outcomes commensurate to a Knowledge Economy era are achieved.

Talent Management An approach to leadership that focuses on identifying, enabling and supporting human brain power to innovate, create and solve problems associated with aspects of consumption and production. Associated with work in a fourth industrial revolution era.

Taylorism (Taylorist)   An approach to work that was developed to suit the first industrial revolution. Conformity, uniformity and standardisation were the central focuses of production outputs, and managers worked to ensure workers complied with established means.

Notes

1 www.nap.edu.au/information/faqs/naplan–general
2 www.myschool.edu.au/
3 www.australiancurriculum.edu.au/about-the-australian-curriculum/

References

Ajzen, I. (1991). The theory of planned behavior. *Organisational Behavior and Human Decision Processes, 50*, 179–211.

Apple, M. W. (2001). The rhetoric and reality of standards-based school reform. *Educational Policy, 15*(4), 601–610. https://doi.org/10.1177/0895904801015004005

Berry, B. (2011). *What we must do for our students and our public schools: Now and in the future.* Teachers College Press.

Buske, R. (2018). The principal as a key actor in promoting teachers' innovativeness – Analysing the innovativeness of teaching staff with variance-based partial least square modeling. *School Effectiveness and School Improvement, 29*(2), 262–284.

Coe, R. (2002). *It's the effect size, stupid: What effect size is and why it is important.* Annual Conference of the British Educational Research Association, University of Exeter, England.

DeWitt, P. (2018). *John Hattie isn't wrong. You are misusing his research.* Education Week. https://blogs.edweek.org/edweek/finding_common_ground/2018/06/hattie_isnt_wrong_you_are_misusing_his_research.html

Dinham, S. (2016). *Leading learning and teaching.* ACER.

Duncan, G., Magnuson, K., & Murnane, R. (2016). Reforming preschools and schools. *Academic Pediatrics, 16*(3), Supplement, S121–S127.

Gepp, A., & Kumar, K. (2019). How to improve teaching using blended learning. In L. N. Makewa (Ed.), *Theoretical and practical approaches to innovation in higher education* (pp. 80–90). IGI Global. https://doi.org/10.4018/978-1-7998-1662-1.ch005

Hanushek, E. A. (2016). What matters for student achievement. *Education Next, 16*(2), 18–26.

Harrington, M. (2013, June 26). *Funding the National Plan for School Improvement: An explanation.* Background note, Parliamentary Library.

Hattie, J. (2012). *Visible learning for teachers: Maximising impact on learning.* Routledge.

Horn, M., & Staker, H. (2015). *Blended: Using disruptive innovation to improve schools.* Jossey-Bass.

Howes, C. S., & Taylor, R. W. (2020, January 13). *Building technical, commercial and soft skills in evolving organisations.* International Petroleum Technology Conference. https://doi.org/10.2523/IPTC-20078-Abstract

Kaestle, C. (n.d.). *Testing policy in the United States: A historical perspective.* The Gordon Commission on the Future of Assessment in Education. www.ets.org/Media/Research/pdf/kaestle_testing_policy_us_historical_perspective.pdf

Kelley, T. R., Knowles, J. G., Holland, J. D., & Han, J. (2020). Increasing high school teachers self-efficacy for integrated STEM instruction through a collaborative community of practice. *International Journal of STEM Education, 7*, 1–13. https://doi.org/10.1186/s40594-020-00211-w

Lamorte, W. W. (2018). Behavioral change models: The theory of planned behaviour. Retrieved October 7, 2019, from http://sphweb.bumc.bu.edu/otlt/MPH-Modules/SB/BehavioralChange Theories/BehavioralChangeTheories3.html

Leithwood, K. (2013). Leadership and student learning: What works and how. In C. Wise, P. Bradshaw, & M. Cartwright (Eds.), *Leading professional practice in education* (pp. 25–37). Sage Publications Ltd.

Li, C., & Lalani, F. (2020). The COVID-19 pandemic has changed education forever. This is how. The World Economic Forum COVID Action Platform. www.weforum.org/agenda/2020/04/corona virus-education-global-covid19-online-digital-learning/

Lynch, D. (2012). *Preparing teachers in times of change: Teaching school, standards, new content and evidence.* Primrose Hall.

Lynch, D., Smith, R., Yeigh, T., & Provost, S. (2019). A study into 'organisational readiness' and its impacts on school improvement. *International Journal of Educational Management*, 393–408.

Macklin, P., & Zbar, V. (2017). *Driving school improvement: A practical guide.* ACER Press.

Marzano, R. J., Waters, T., & McNulty, B. A. (2005). *School leadership that works: From research to results.* ASCD.

Masters, G. N. (2009). *A shared challenge: Improving literacy, numeracy and science learning in Queensland primary schools.* ACER.

McGunagle, D., & Zizka, L. (2020). Employability skills for 21st-century STEM students: The employers' perspective. *Higher Education, Skills and Work-Based Learning*, 1–22.

Ministerial Council on Education, Employment, Training and Youth Affairs [MCEETYA]. (2009). *Melbourne Declaration on Educational Goals for Young Australians.* Commonwealth of Australia.

Moir, S., Hattie, J., & Jansen, C. (2014). Teacher perspectives of 'effective' leadership in schools. *Australian Educational Leader, 36*(4), 36–40.

North, K., & Gueldenberg, S. (2011). *Effective knowledge work: Answers to the management challenge of the 21st century.* Emerald Group Publishing.

Pastor, M. T. (2020). Getting better-skilled future professionals by teaching transversal skills: Establishing an educational company to teach transversal skills to children. Published thesis: Degree Program in International Business Bachelor's Thesis. Autumn 2020. www.theseus.fi/bitstream/handle/10024/335709/THESIS%20MANUEL%20TEROL%20PASTOR.pdf?sequence=2&isAllowed=y

Rios, J. A., Ling, G., Pugh, R., Becker, D., & Bacall, A. (2020). Identifying critical 21st-century skills for workplace success: A content analysis of job advertisements. *Educational Researcher, 49*(2), 80–89. https://doi.org/10.3102/0013189X19890600

Robinson, K. (2017). *Out of our minds: The power of being creative.* Capstone.

Robinson, V., Hohepa, M., & Lloyd, C. (2009). *School leadership and student outcomes: Identifying what works and why: Best evidence synthesis.* www.educationcounts.govt.nz/publications/series/2515/60170

Schiemann, W. A. (2012). *The ACE advantage: How smart companies unleash talent for optimal performance.* Society for Human Resource Management.

Schiemann, W. A. (2014). From talent management to talent optimisation. *Journal of World Business, 49*(2), 281–288.

School Improvement Unit [SIU]. (2017). Annual report. Queensland: A state of learning. Findings from the 2017 school reviews. https://schoolreviews.education.qld.gov.au/res/Documents/2017-annual-report-full-report.pdf

Stephenson, J. (1999). Corporate capability: Implications for the style and direction of work-based learning. Retrieved July 1, 2020, from http://hdl.voced.edu.au/10707/120693

Sun, J., & Leithwood, K. (2015). Direction-setting school leadership practices: A meta-analytical review of evidence about their influence. *School Effectiveness and School Improvement, 26*(4), 499–523. https://doi.org/10.1080/09243453.2015.1005106

Taylor, J. (2020, March 14). Coronavirus and the NBN: Will your broadband be up to speed if you have to work from home? *The Guardian.* www.theguardian.com/technology/2020/mar/13/corona virus-and-the-nbn-will-your-broadband-be-up-to-speed-if-you-have-to-work-from-home

Thomson, S., De Bortoli, L., Underwood, C., & Schmid, M. (2019). *PISA 2018: Reporting Australia's Results.* Volume I, Student Performance. Australian Council for Educational Research (ACER). https://research.acer.edu.au/ozpisa/35

UNESCO, IBE. (2015). The curriculum in debates and in educational reforms to 2030: For a curriculum agenda of the twenty-first century. IBE Working Papers on Curriculum Issues No. 15.

Vrasidas, C. (2015). The rhetoric of reform and teachers' use of ICT. *British Journal of Educational Technology, 46*(2), 370–380.

Willis, R. L., Lynch, D., Fradale, P., & Yeigh, T. (2019). Influences on purposeful implementation of ICT into the classroom: An exploratory study of K-12 teachers. *Education and Information Technologies, 24*(1), 63–77.

Wolff, R., & Booth, M. (2017). Bridging the gap: Creating a new approach for assuring 21st century employability skills. *Change: The Magazine of Higher Learning, 49*(6), 51–54.

Yeigh, T., Lynch, D., Turner, D., Fradale, P., Willis, R., Sell, K., & Lawless, E. (2020). Using blended learning to support whole-of-school improvement: The need for contextualisation. *Education and Information Technologies*, 1–27. https://doi.org/10.1007/s10639-020-10114-6

3 Educational disruption

Why all the fuss about Blended Learning?

Relevant Australian Professional Standards for Teachers: 1.2; 1.5; 2.6; 3.4; 3.6; 4.5; 5.1; 5.4; 6.2; 6.3; 6.4; 7.4

Chapter synopsis

As this book has continually emphasised, the power of technology to disrupt virtually every area of human endeavour is enormous and continues to increase, and education is certainly not immune to this impact. Rather, in many ways, education is more susceptible to technological disruption than most other areas, due to the way multiple stakeholders and socio-political elements are required to operate in accordance with one another to support effective teaching and learning across various levels of social change. As we have seen in relation to the positioning and reform history of education, as detailed in Chapters 1 and 2, this has created a situation in which the traditional concepts and principles of education have become less relevant to modern schooling, and because of this many modern educators are seeking alternative approaches to teaching and learning that are better able to respond to technological disruption. It is also important to note that these alternative approaches are increasingly technology-dependent in relation to the coronavirus or COVID-19 pandemic, and this has caused many schools and school systems to move even more strongly to the use of online learning as a major focus for teaching and learning (Newcomb, 2020).

In this chapter we look at **Blended Learning** as an intentional response to technological disruption, specifically designed to harness its positive potential in a way that supports student learning. From this perspective Chapter 3 will provide clear insights into the intention of Blended Learning as a modern pedagogical approach, with a particular emphasis on the goals of Blended Learning to encourage student-directed learning as an important pedagogical outcome. Important elements of Chapter 3 include:

- Further defining and positioning Blended Learning as a historical development.
- Analysing Blended Learning as a distinct form of pedagogy that is driven by concepts of mastery learning, student agency, personalised learning and improved relationships.
- Describing the relationship between Blended Learning and **twenty-first-century skills**.
- Describing different models of Blended Learning and explaining why these represent pedagogical design elements, rather than simply being strategies for infusing technology into education.
- Demonstrating how the implementation of a Blended Learning program needs to be guided by clear goal-driven design principles and an iterative process.
- Evaluating what high-quality Blended Learning might look like.

Introduction

The way we are learning is changing. This has taken place quickly and in a pervasive manner, with the use of technology to drive and support learning becoming increasingly important to the way teaching and learning occurs. During the past decade or so we have seen the rise of Massive Open Online Courses (MOOCs) and digital learning solutions, along with the use of Learning Management Systems (LMS) as solutions for supporting online learning, increased use of Information Communication Technology (ICT) in schools and classrooms, the application of 'big data' algorithms (Aguilar, 2018) to support more targeted learning and the incorporation of mobile e-learning solutions. Each and all of these affect the way schools operate and students learn, and altogether have created an international focus on the role of educational technology in terms of how to use these technologies to support school improvement and how to evaluate their success in doing so (Research and Markets Report, 2017). The impact of technology in this broad fashion has been both disruptive and innovative for education, and has also highlighted the need to apply technology to the specific strengths, limitations and needs of schools within the education community. In this respect Blended Learning has formed as a distinct pedagogical approach that is designed to harness the power of technology in innovative and positive ways that address the specific needs of schools in a flexible manner. It is therefore important to explore what Blended Learning is, as well as why it is considered a valuable application of technology for education, which is the purpose of this chapter.

The concept behind Blended Learning is, ostensibly, to combine the best elements of face-to-face (F2F) and online modes of instruction in ways that place the learner at the centre of the teaching/learning process. This requires a transitional arrangement for education, at the heart of which lies a conceptual transformation from thinking about learning in terms of a time-based system that attaches the learning to specific time frames (primary before secondary, year-7 before year-8, etc.), to thinking about learning in terms of specific learning competencies that attach the learning to a mastery-based system that provides for flexible learning. The goal for this transition is to increase successful learning for students (Christensen Institute, 2019) and to prepare them to engage in **digital entrepreneurship** as a particular skill set for thriving in the twenty-first century (Kraus et al., 2018; Nambison, 2018).

This transitional expectation began to emerge with the advent of the Web 2.0, which was premised on user-generated content as opposed to the simple consumption of content as had occurred in the Web 1.0 (Alexander, 2008; Zdravkova et al., 2012). In this respect the Web 1.0 was still aligned with more traditional teaching approaches, in which the teacher acts as a sort of gatekeeper, deciding what content students receive (Reigeluth et al., 2016), and who is often constrained by what the state includes in mandated curricula (Reys et al., 2003). The student's role in this more traditional use of technology is to accept and engage with this content on the terms provided by the teacher and state (Suskie, 2018). This situation progressed with the advent of user-created content in Web 2.0 structures, leading to more ICT-leveraged **personalised learning**, which assumes a greater inclusion of student-created understanding and product. This focus on personalised learning continued to gain sophistication and scope with the advent of the Web 3.0, which focuses on the so-called 'semantic web', in which systems make meaning and recommendations through large data and metadata sets in order to personalise the experience even more (Devedzic, 2004; Khribi et al., 2009).

The use of technology to frame and motivate sophisticated personalised learning is seen as particularly important for modern education because of the increasing prominence of the **gig economy** as an artefact of technological disruption, wherein workers are viewed more as entrepreneurs than traditional employees (Wood et al., 2019). There are three core assumptions that Blended Learning uses to assist this transition:

- The assumption that all students should be enabled to advance their learning upon mastery of the relevant, specified criteria (student-directed learning).
- The assumption that explicit and measurable learning objectives are what empower student learning (data-driven learning).
- The assumption that the purpose of assessment is to develop a meaningful and positive learning experience for students (assessment as learning).

These assumptions represent a highly student-centred approach to learning, and positions Blended Learning as a type of **connectivism learning theory** (Goldie, 2016), that is, a technology-driven approach to learning that is intensely focused on the individual and the self-directed connections they make in order to personalise and direct their learning outcomes, often referred to as **entrepreneurship education** (Wood et al., 2019). In this respect the purpose of Blended Learning is to provide a pedagogical framework that encourages and supports learning that is progressively student-directed, and in support of this purpose we can identify the following as important characteristics of Blended Learning:

- That Blended Learning operates in response to the imperatives of the Knowledge Economy, as this economy has led to increased educational competition globally.
- That Blended Learning represents a distinct pedagogical approach, designed specifically to repurpose technological innovation to the needs and purposes of modern education and prepare learners to work and thrive in the technology-driven economies of the twenty-first century.
- That Blended Learning uses ICT to increase both the accessibility and scalability of teaching and learning.
- That Blended Learning is a highly student-centred pedagogical approach, requiring a re-think of the role of both the learner and teacher.
- That teaching and learning arrangements will occur somewhere along a continuum involving an intentional mixture of online and F2F learning for students.

From this perspective we will explore different aspects of Blended Learning and the key Knowledge Economy issues that impact students, teachers and schools, and how these aspects require the transitional arrangements we have identified. We begin by examining more closely the nature of technological disruption and how this has affected education in ways that require the use of a technology-driven pedagogy, such as Blended Learning, to respond to these issues.

The need to respond to global competition

According to Lynch (2017), Blended Learning is important for education today because it is the way classrooms of the future will need to work. As noted in Chapters 1 and 2, this is largely due to the way technological disruption has brought about increased educational competition globally, and how this has, in turn, required governments to improve the efficiency of education in line with the demands this competition places on education systems.

As also discussed in Chapters 1 and 2, technological disruption has placed increasing pressure on schools and teachers to improve the learning outcomes of their students (OECD, 2013), forcing governments to focus on the quality of teaching and learning and how to provide accountability for their learning outcomes. This is largely occurring because nations realise that their future economic prosperity depends on having an education system that is internationally competitive (Bonin, 2017; Hanushek & Woessmann, 2011; Rothstein, 2010) and capable of preparing students to participate in the digital economies of the twenty-first century (Wood et al., 2019).

From this perspective a global body of information devoted to describing, comparing and evaluating the learning outcomes of different countries and their education systems has taken shape (e.g., English Proficiency Index; International Association for the Evaluation of Educational Achievement; Programme for International Student Assessment [PISA]; Trends in International Mathematics and Science Study [TIMSS]; World's Top 20 Project), spurred-on by the advantages that high-performing schools generate in trade and socio-economic terms (Carr, 2011; Darling-Hammond & Snyder, 2015; Marginson, 2006; Ocloo et al., 2014; OECD, 2013; Scheerens, 2013; Shirrell, 2016). In conjunction with this, the publishing of so-called education league tables often causes education systems to question their effectiveness when academic performance falls below that of other schools, school systems and nations (Ball, 2013; Blum, 2015; Good to Great Schools, 2016). The use of information in this way is a product of the Knowledge Economy that, when taken altogether, creates an international imperative for education systems to plan for positive educational change in terms that are accountable, measurable, effective and sustainable. Such imperatives have resulted in calls for schools, universities and other education providers to assist schools to improve, and in doing so, develop clear measures of teacher quality and school improvement (e.g., AITSL, 2015; Bonin, 2017; Darling-Hammond & Snyder, 2015; Ingvarson et al., 2014; Lynch et al., 2016; TEMAG, 2014).

Blended Learning and school improvement

The notion that teacher quality and school improvement should be operationalised and then measured has generated consternation in some practitioner quarters (Thompson, 2013; Yeigh & Lynch, 2017), and particularly so when such measures are used as the catalyst for addressing educational change at both the system and school level (William, 2009). In this regard some commentators argue that attempts to operationalise and measure such things encourage a **teach-to-the-test mentality**, and thereby serve to de-professionalise teachers. This outcome is seen as particularly unhelpful when the goal is ultimately to improve the instructional capacity of schools and teachers from an accountability perspective (Klenowski & Wyatt-Smith, 2012; Thompson & Harbaugh, 2013).

In response to this imperative, most education systems rely on teacher professional learning (PL) for generating improved teaching quality (Ingvarson et al., 2014; Leahy & William, 2009). However, a problem exists in that this often involves programs that tend to adopt a fairly generic, one-size-fits-all approach that fails to take into account the peculiarities of individual teachers and the students they teach. In particular, such programs are not able to account for the highly variable nature of teacher quality or for the differential impact that other school factors – such as the impact of technological disruption or the ability of school leadership to successfully lead for change – can contribute (Coelli & Green, 2012; Dhuey & Smith, 2014; Grissom et al., 2015; Heck & Hallinger, 2014; Orphanos & Orr, 2014).

Most countries nonetheless seek measures by which they can monitor and evaluate the quality of their teaching, as well as that of their school leaders. This generally takes the form of professional standards and criteria, by which the characteristics viewed as important to quality teaching and effective leadership can be formally defined. As an example, the current imperative for identifying these things in Australia (AITSL, 2012, 2015) highlights teacher quality in the form of specific teaching standards (AITSL, 2011), which seek to articulate quality teaching practices as the basis for improved student learning outcomes. In relation to school leadership, AITSL (2014) also provides clear descriptors concerning the professional standards expected for principals in the categories *leading improvement* and *innovation and change*. In relation to educational disruption and the purpose of Blended Learning, we note that these standards stipulate that principals are expected to lead educational networks by trialling and exploring new ideas for the system, as well as by acting as a guide, coach and mentor to staff and colleagues. They are to further evaluate the personal and organisational effects of change through regular feedback from stakeholders and, importantly, through evidence of impact on student outcomes, as well as develop an 'innovative and outward-focused role' as a leader influencing school excellence across the system (AITSL, 2014, p. 17). Overall these AITSL standards highlight the importance of educational innovation as the basis for quality teaching and clear direction.

School leadership and student achievement

Key indicators of educational proficiency generally include standardised tests, such as the National Assessment Program – Literacy and Numeracy (NAPLAN) in Australia, which is carried out each year for the purpose of monitoring and evaluating educational achievement nationally (Australian Curriculum, Assessment and Reporting Authority [ACARA]: www.acara.edu.au/). Analysing the data from this program allows us to understand the relationships that exist between school leadership and student achievement, as a preliminary means of identifying the characteristics of school leadership that seem to be important to school improvement outcomes. In this respect, the role of principals and other school leaders is also highlighted as crucial for leading change in relation to school improvement programs (Darling-Hammond & Snyder, 2015; Shirrell, 2016), identifying this role as fundamental to school improvement in general.

When we combine the role of school leaders in managing change for improvement with Blended Learning, we begin to see the larger picture that is necessary for modern teaching and learning. As noted above, Blended Learning is designed to respond to the disruptive influence of technology in ways that employ ICT for the purpose of improving teacher effectiveness and student learning. This purpose assumes the notion of school improvement, and requires school leaders to take a central role in directing and guiding the change required for school improvement in relation to Blended Learning related knowledge, skills and capabilities. The key role played by leaders in implementing whole of school Blended Learning is explored further in Chapter 5.

In this respect it is also important to note that research indicates Blended Learning improves student achievement via increased learner agency (Maxwell & White, 2017), and that this, in turn, improves student engagement (Truitt & Ku, 2018). There is also research showing that Blended Learning can increase student self-regulation, especially when using the rotation model (Cheng et al., 2019). We have yet to see large-scale analyses concerning the overall efficacy of Blended Learning, but this is due to its relatively new development, and is precisely why further Blended Learning research needs to be conducted. Importantly, the outcomes we do have invite additional research into the current emphasis on Blended Learning within a contextualised framework designed to support school improvement in relation to the imperatives of the Knowledge Economy (Yeigh et al., 2020). What we can also say at the current time is that when viewed as a distinct pedagogy aimed at supporting school improvement, Blended Learning appears necessary as an important teaching and learning framework, and especially so within the renewed emphasis on online and distance learning that is currently taking place in response to the coronavirus (COVID-19) pandemic. From this perspective it is important that we now take a closer look at what is involved in Blended Learning, how it can be modelled, how it relates to what are known as the twenty-first-century skills, and how the implementation of Blended Learning requires goal-driven design principles and an iterative process that are based on formative and ongoing evidence. Key questions around this could include reflections about what kinds of changes in the teacher's role are required to operate within a Blended Learning environment; how the role of students might change in a Blended Learning environment; how Blended Learning can be used to support school improvement; and what aspects of change should the principal be particularly responsible for.

Defining Blended Learning

In terms of defining Blended Learning, we have to consider both what the straightforward term means and what it might also imply, and each of these aspects need to be considered in relation to how the actual practice of Blended Learning takes place.

The straightforward term, 'blended learning' suggests that students are learning via a combination of face-to-face (F2F) and online activities, but the implications of this are that students will have a degree of control over the time, place and pace of their learning, and that the online part of their learning will take place within actual school settings.

Student control is a necessary part of Blended Learning because Blended Learning is postulated on the knowledge that students don't all learn at the same pace – sometimes a student is able to speed through a learning activity and really understand it quickly, while at other times she or he may need longer to grasp a concept, or even need a completely different pathway to follow in order to master that bit of their learning. This seems a critical part of Blended Learning because it lays the foundation for student ownership of their own learning. In relation to Blended Learning, student ownership means that students are empowered with the skills, information and tools that they need to manage their own learning, providing a sense of personal agency (Lotrecchiano et al., 2013). Personal agency is essential to Blended Learning because it largely determines the degree of quality learning that will take place within a Blended Learning program. In this respect it is important to understand that student agency is what actually promotes high expectations within a Blended Learning environment.

Situating Blended Learning

Connecting student learning to actual school settings is also important because this links the online learning to what's happening in the classroom, ensuring that the learner's online experience is informing what's happening in the classroom and vice versa. In this respect an important conceptual understanding for Blended Learning is that it is actually the 'space' that exists between online learning and face-to-face classroom learning, allowing it to be adaptive to individual school contexts in relation to the amount of F2F versus online learning that may be required. When understood from this perspective, Blended Learning can be seen as a modern pedagogy in which the classroom and online learning elements inform and direct one another in a reciprocal relationship. At the heart of this relationship lies the fundamental role of the teacher and the student, and thus a core purpose of Blended Learning is to change the nature of these roles in a manner that differentiates and personalises student learning in accordance with its situated positioning for a particular school context.

In this regard we note that a current issue with Blended Learning is that the data systems and software needed to make this reciprocal relationship completely seamless don't yet exist in some cases and are not sufficiently provided in others. This issue can be divided into four domains for planning and analysis purposes: physical infrastructure, digital infrastructure, user dispositions to EdTech, and user competencies with EdTech. Each organisation or institution will find varied readiness in each of the four domains specific to its context and developmental phase. Thus, whereas the notion of Blended Learning seems ideally suited as a modern pedagogy, as well as especially necessary in the current pandemic climate, we need to recognise that it's still early days yet, so our ability to design the 'ultimate Blended Learning environment' is still developing. We can still design incredibly engaging and highly useful Blended Learning approaches with existing technology, however, which is the focus of this book. In this manner we urge you to create your own list of the Blended Learning elements you might want to use as you move through this book, recognising that the most important aspect of Blended Learning continues to be the passion and leadership that the teacher brings to the design table. That will be the best way to ensure you get what you need from this book in terms of your own ideas about how you might implement Blended Learning.

The role of technology

Inherent to Blended Learning is the use of technology to assist learning. This happens in a number of ways, but there are a couple of issues we need to be aware of with respect to technology as an aspect of Blended Learning: First, that it is not the use of technology itself that defines what Blended Learning is and, second, that the primary importance of technology is its ability to 'scale-up' the learning process while at the same time lower the costs normally associated with large-scale learning. Thus, the use of technology neither defines nor determines the nature of Blended Learning, but rather operates as a means by which certain aspects of Blended Learning – in particular the online aspects of learning – are delivered.

Blended Learning seeks to increase student-centred learning via the assistance of ICT (Horn & Staker, 2017). An important feature of ICT is its ability to integrate teaching and learning in ways that release teachers from much of the mundane tasks involved in teaching, while at the same time engaging students in more self-directed learning. This sort of integration promotes student-centred learning because it aligns student learning with the overall mission and goals of the school, effectively mobilising the major components that affect this learning in service of the school's educational purposes (Patrick & Sturgis, 2015; Vanderlinde & van Braak, 2010). This involves a process that takes place over time, however, and it is important to note that ICT support for increasing student-centred learning is initially developed and scaffolded by a school's teachers, in conjunction with the school leadership team and ICT support staff (Arnett, 2019). Chapter 6 of this book looks at using a reference framework known by its acronym SAMR to further explore this aspect.

In this respect a key role for technology within a Blended Learning environment is to support the personalisation of learning, generally as attached to a particular mastery-based program or unit of work. The importance of this role goes back to the work of Bloom (1984), who highlighted what he called the '2 sigma problem', which has to do with the advantages bestowed upon learning when personalisation is increased. In this respect Figure 3.1 displays learning outcome differences between normal 'lecture-based' classroom teaching (which is often the norm in many classrooms even today), group-based mastery teaching and one-on-one individual tutoring. What this graph shows is that the more personalised learning becomes, the more student achievement outcomes increase, as indicated by the different achievement score distributions shown for each teaching strategy. The importance of 'sigma' in this respect is that it represents one full standard deviation (SD) in the distribution means, with a group-based mastery teaching strategy delivering one full SD above the lecture-based strategy, and an individual tutoring strategy delivering two full SDs above the generally used lecture-based approach. Of importance is that these findings underscore the emphasis placed upon personalised learning as an important goal for Blended Learning.

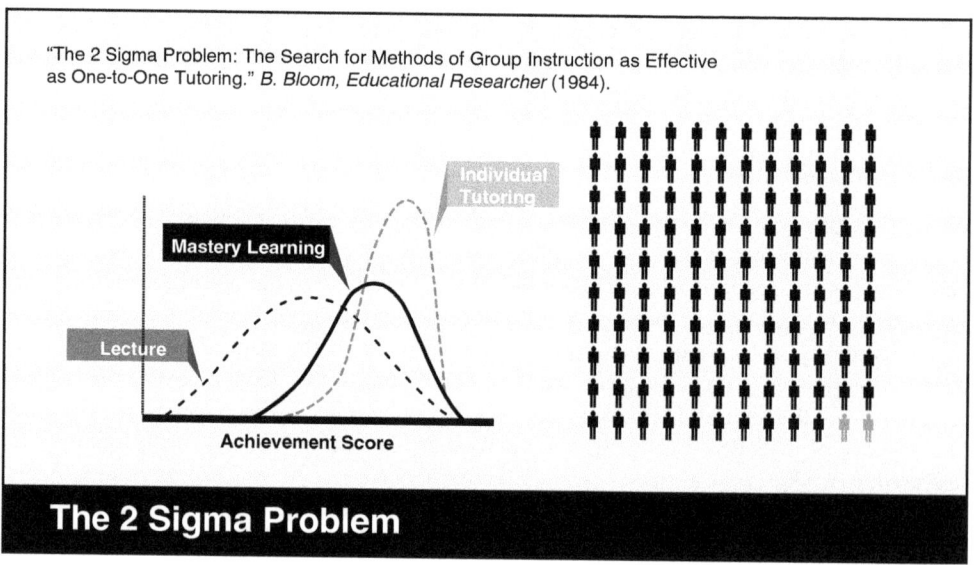

Figure 3.1 Impact of personalised learning as a teaching strategy (used with permission).

Blended Learning as a continuum of personalised learning

In defining what Blended Learning is, we also need to explore Blended Learning as a continuum-based design 'space'. To assist your initial understanding of Blended Learning in this manner, we ask you to look at Figure 3.2, which depicts the Blended Learning 'space' as occurring within a set of continuums: one representing face-to-face teaching and learning in relation to online teaching and learning, and the other representing the engagement modes (synchronous versus asynchronous) that can accompany these teaching and learning positions. Notice the inclusion of a 'replacement' identifier as a key function of this mapping process, and that this function can take place in a way that sustains more traditional instruction or in a way that replaces more traditional instruction. This suggests that when we design Blended Learning in a way that includes teaching and learning elements that occur more online and in an asynchronous fashion, we are applying Blended Learning in a more disruptive manner, and when we design Blended Learning in a way that includes teaching and learning elements that occur more F2F and in a synchronous fashion, we are applying Blended Learning in a more traditional manner.

It is important to note that the particular arrangement of the various elements shown in Figure 3.2 represent only one way these elements could be organised. Examining this figure more closely, we can see there are many different aspects of Blended Learning

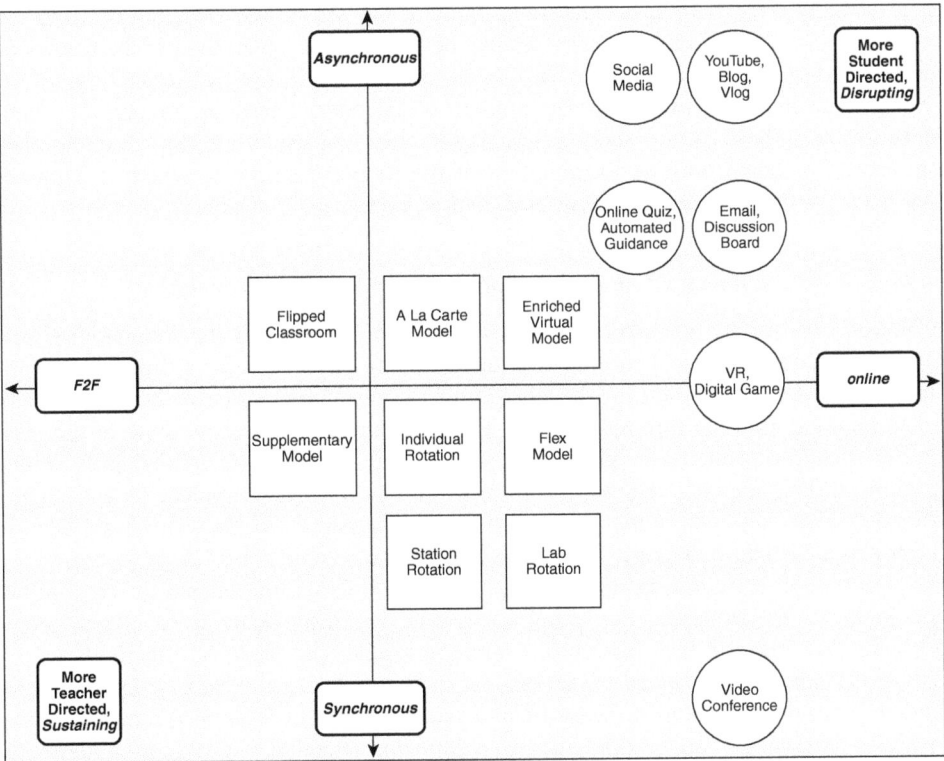

Figure 3.2 Overview of Blended Learning as a continuum (created by the authors).

that we need to take into account when defining what it is, how much it encompasses and to what extent it transforms the process of teaching and learning. In this respect Blended Learning can be viewed as a continuum that uses technology to connect classroom learning and online learning, and is designed to promote student ownership and agency in relation to learning.

Modularity theory as a conceptual framework for Blended Learning

The replacement function identified for Blended Learning in Figure 3.2 also reinforces the idea that a primary aspect of Blended Learning as an instructional pedagogy is its ability to transition the nature of teaching in relation to traditional classroom teaching and learning. It also raises the issue of **modularity theory** as applied to education (Price, 2018). This is because, as also shown in Figure 3.2, modularity theory illustrates how Blended Learning can be used to combine the interdependent elements of teaching and learning, as aspects of traditional school-based learning, in ways that repurpose these aspects to new and innovative applications: for example, using technology to repurpose the teaching and learning functions that normally occur face-to-face in a physical environment to the use of a 'flipped' classroom (see below). In this sense, modularity theory provides a generalised framework for the underlying assumption that Blended Learning is a transformative pedagogy designed to promote pedagogical innovation through the process of repurposing. This is an important concept for Blended Learning because it recognises that pedagogical evolution can occur within the recognisable boundaries of traditional education, while at the same time changing the roles and functions of this education to new purposes that better meet the imperatives of the Knowledge Economy.

We now need to examine specific models of Blended Learning, in order to better understand how these various concepts and principles can be implemented at the classroom level. We begin with an examination of the flipped classroom, which is a foundational principle for Blended Learning as a distinct pedagogical system.

The flipped classroom as a foundational principle of Blended Learning

The notion of a flipped classroom is simple, and provides one of the foundational principles upon which Blended Learning is structured. The basic idea for a flipped classroom is that what used to be done in the classroom is now done online at home, and what used to be done at home through practice and problem-solving is now done in the classroom, so that the teacher can guide student learning through this critical part of their engagement. This concept represents the most common way to implement and support a Blended Learning environment, and is thus fundamental to the notion of Blended Learning as a distinct pedagogy. Figure 3.3 provides a graphic overview of how a flipped classroom works. Note that in this representation the online components of learning take place in the home, whereas the learning practice, working through problems, project work, etc., take place in the classroom, where the teacher can be most effective.

Using the notion of a flipped classroom, let us now take a brief look at some common Blended Learning models as a means of understanding and evaluating the different ways in which this strategy can be implemented within the Blended Learning continuum. We begin with the station rotation model, and then proceed to look at the lab rotation and flex models of Blended Learning. As will be discussed further in Chapter 6, these are all sub-models of a more generic Blended Learning model known more simply as the

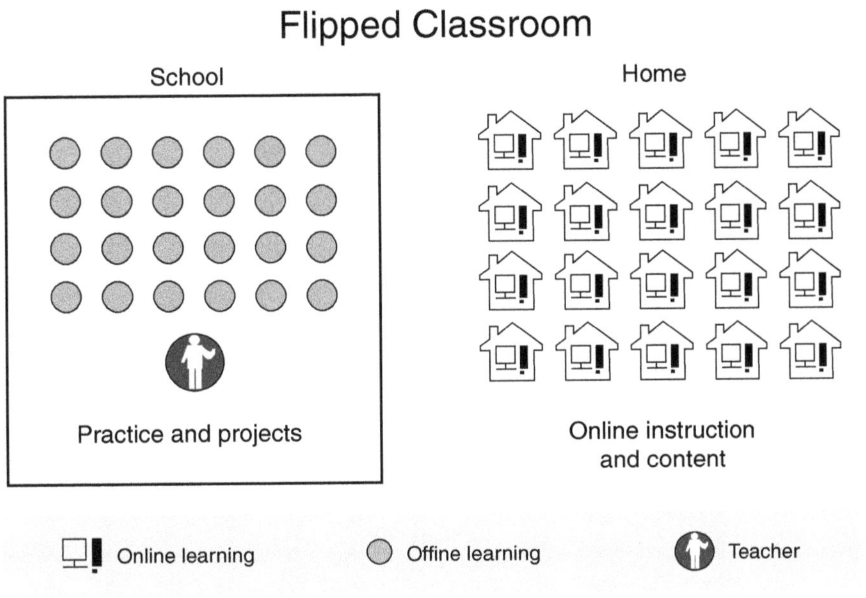

Flipped Classroom

Figure 3.3 Conceptual overview of a flipped classroom (from the Christensen Institute, used with permission).

rotation model. We introduce you to them here to provide conceptual continuity across the evolving construction of Blended Learning that is being developed in this book, focusing more on their procedural elements for the current chapter.

Station rotation model

As shown in Figure 3.4, the station rotation model implements Blended Learning by having students rotate between different stations. In this model some students might start with teacher-led instruction, but then move to collaborative activities and stations – essentially project work with other students. They then move yet again into a laboratory situation, where they work on computers to perform online learning. The aims of this model are to capitalise on the teacher's ability to conduct small group instruction and to encourage group-based collaboration. The online instruction part of station rotation allows students to forge ahead a bit, developing new skills and knowledge or strengthening existing skills and knowledge. We might view this model as incorporating a 'partially flipped' classroom principle, in that the online learning, while separate from regular classroom learning, still takes place within the school setting rather than at home. The teacher's guidance of learning practice and problem-solving still remains a prominent feature for the model however.

Lab rotation model

Lab rotation can take a variety of different forms, but the basic idea is similar across all of them and thus Figure 3.5 provides a generic picture of the lab rotation model. Note that direct instruction across different disciplines is prominent in this model, but then

Station Rotation

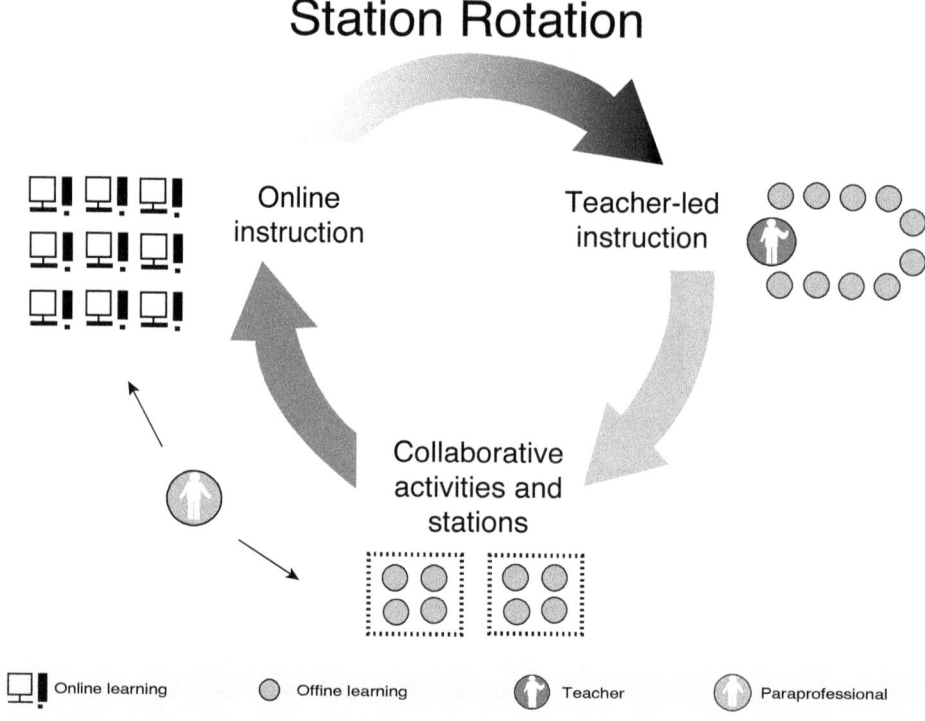

Figure 3.4 Graphic overview of the station rotation model of Blended Learning (from the Christensen Institute, used with permission).

students rotate out of these more traditional classes into a laboratory situation at specific times, where they work online and in a way that helps to integrate their discipline learning. This is quite similar to the station rotation model, but whereas in that model students rotate within a single classroom, in the lab rotation model they rotate to an entirely separate learning environment dedicated to the online learning components of their studies. In this model, we would use ongoing student data to group students for learning, and to determine what – and how often – they needed to use the lab to practice and develop specific skills. Lab rotation remains a 'partially flipped' example of flipping the classroom, however, even though it incorporates multiple rotations that can involve several different curriculum areas. Note also the need for collecting progressive data in order to make decisions about the rotations involved.

Flex model

The flex model of Blended Learning, shown in Figure 3.6, can again take various forms, including one that uses virtual reality to transport student awareness into different settings. However, the main way in which the flex model differs from a rotation approach is that in a flex approach students aren't required to follow a preordained time structure or pace for their learning. Instead, each learner negotiates what is commonly referred to as a 'playlist',

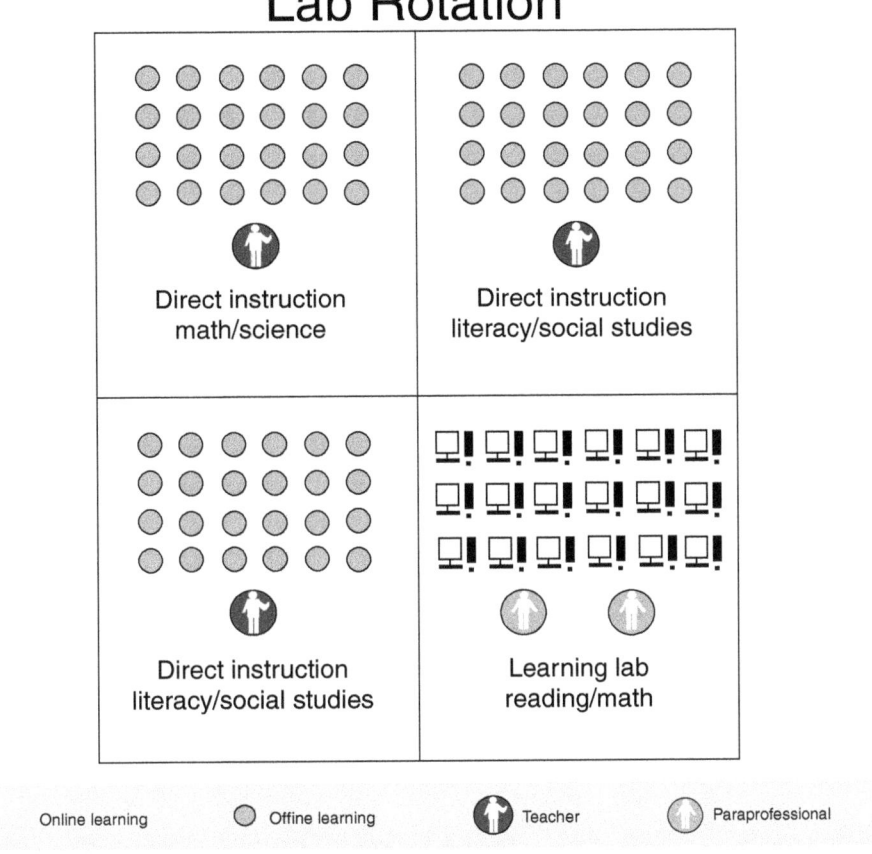

Figure 3.5 Generic structure of the lab rotation model of Blended Learning (from the Christensen Institute, used with permission).

which determines what they need to learn and when they need to learn it. The process for constructing this involves giving students a mastery quiz at the beginning of a course or unit of work (i.e., a formative assessment) to find out what they know and need to know. This provides a clear basis for individual playlists in the first instance, but it also provides a 'jump-point' for students who have already mastered the necessary knowledge and skills being taught by the unit of work, allowing these students to immediately move ahead to the next relevant level of learning.

The important driver for the flex model is that students are encouraged to go as fast as they feel a need to, as well as to follow different learning pathways, depending on their individual levels of learning readiness and need. Importantly, and similar to the lab rotation model, the use of formative assessment allows these decisions to be made by data-driven decisions that seek to position the learner in relation to their individual ability and need, rather than limit their learning via the use of a more rigid learning framework. This gives students a great deal of control over the time, place and pace of their learning,

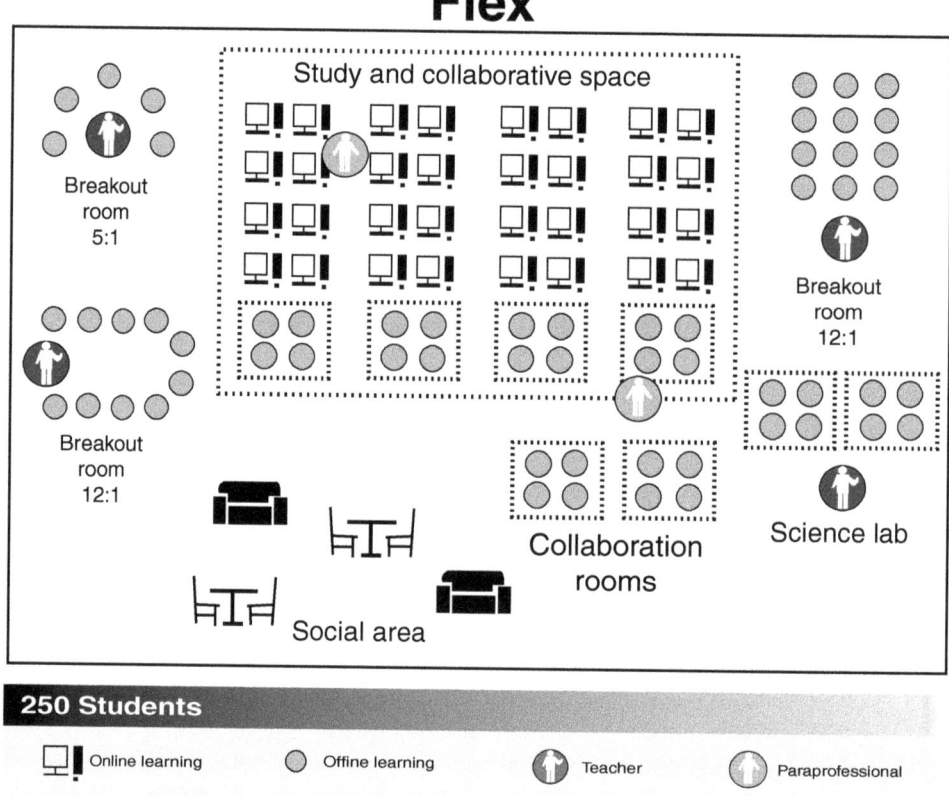

Figure 3.6 Components of the flex model of Blended Learning (from the Christensen Institute, used with permission).

and thus lends itself to many of the characteristics of high-quality Blended Learning. In this respect the flex model represents a proficiency-based (mastery-based) approach to learning, and because of this provides a good way to foster student agency as a primary aspect of the learning process.

High-quality Blended Learning

The ultimate goals of Blended Learning are to increase student engagement with learning and to improve student learning outcomes. Of course, we can't expect that this will occur simply because we have implemented some sort of Blended Learning approach in relation to our teaching. Rather, we need to ensure that the Blended Learning we design is characterised by high-quality elements that embody the core assumptions of Blended Learning to a high degree. These assumptions are that all students should be enabled to advance their learning upon mastery of the relevant, specified criteria; that explicit and measurable learning objectives are what empower student learning; and that the purpose of assessment is to develop a meaningful and positive learning experience for students.

Keeping these assumptions in mind, we can see that high-quality Blended Learning will require that the learning is personalised, mastery-based, student-centred and based on high expectations from the teacher.

From the perspective provided by these assumptions we can identify high-quality Blended Learning as learning that is designed to encourage and support a student-centred pedagogy by differentiating the learning, promoting mastery and student agency, encouraging self-directed student engagement, and seeking to improve relationships between the students and their school, the students and their teacher and between one another. As with any reformative innovation, Blended Learning can be done well or it can be done poorly, but if you are truly interested in adopting a Blended Learning pedagogy at your school or for your own teaching, we hope you will find the flexible mindset implicit to Blended Learning to be a catalyst for instructional change, and use it to implement clear goal-driven teaching plans that seek to address the needs of your students in a way that will maximise both their learning and your teaching.

Technology and COVID-19

As this book goes to press, the impact of the coronavirus pandemic (COVID-19) is spreading globally, with an infection rate that has been sudden and staggering. The shock from this pandemic has been felt by everyone, and seems viscerally palpable as we write this book. However, and of particular importance to our discussion here, the world's response to COVID-19 has largely seen nations shutting down their borders, implementing clear social distancing measures, ramping-up hygiene protocols and imposing self-isolation where necessary. This has resulted in schools and classrooms being closed for the most part, turning to home schooling and distance education as the new 'norm' for teaching and learning during the 'shutdown' phase of our COVID-19 response. This has, in turn, resulted in multiple issues around online teaching and learning, including learning engagement, resourcing, assessment and teacher capabilities (NSW Government, 2020). It has also raised particular questions around the quality of online learning experiences (Newcomb, 2020) and the preparedness of teachers to deliver online learning (Thomson, 2020), as well as ignite debates about the negative impact of online learning for disadvantaged students (Davey, 2020).

The COVID-19 pandemic has interrupted our lives and created a myriad of challenges to consider as we try to adjust to new working arrangements while still continuing our professional duties as educators. According to Price (2020) this may provide an opportunity for moving more closely to a competency-based educational approach, and Blended Learning would seem particularly suitable as a vehicle for supporting this. We can do no more than highlight the broad scope of this pandemic at the present time, however, as this situation continues to unfold and the world prepares for a possible 'second-wave' of infection. It does seem that the impact of this pandemic will be long lasting, and we therefore encourage you to reflect on the impact of this virus in relation to your developing sense of professional identity, especially how you will interact with the ongoing need to engage with technology as a core skill set for teaching. In this respect the importance of Blended Learning appears magnified as a result of the COVID-19 pandemic, in that it is specifically designed to allow for a range of online teaching and learning experiences. There may, therefore, be no better time to engage with this type of pedagogy than the present, and it seems that the future will demand the very sort of skill sets that this type of pedagogy provides.

Chapter summary

The implementation of high-quality Blended Learning can remove barriers to learning, because this approach offers flexible ways to learn new skills, and can be adapted for learning to occur whenever and wherever best suits the needs of a school, the teacher and the learner. Designing effective Blended Learning remains a challenging task, yet the inherent malleability of this approach, in particular the way it can be adapted for individual learning contexts, allows Blended Learning to provide meaningful and engaging learning experiences that can motivate and connect students. Designing effective Blended Learning requires clear planning and the use of formative information, which we will explore in greater detail in the final chapter of this book. At this point, however, we can say that this planning will need to consider how to integrate the use of technology to support student learning and school improvement from a strategic perspective, how to support teachers in their use of ICT, the role of school leadership in leading for change in relation to applied technology, issues around the monitoring and evaluation of technology integration and issues concerning learning equity at the macro level of educational systems and policy. We will continue to explore these sorts of design considerations as we progress through this book, beginning with a look at what research tells us about effective schools in Chapter 4.

Glossary

Blended Learning   A distinct, technology-driven pedagogy designed to harness the power of technological disruption in positive ways that can assist modern teaching and learning to address the imperatives of the Knowledge Economy.

Connectivism learning theory   Learning theories describe how people learn in terms of their ability to grasp, process, retain and make meaning of the instructional information they receive as part of the teaching and learning process. Connectivism learning theory is a theoretical framework for understanding this process in a digital age, where the learning inherently involves the use of the Internet, social media, ICT and other elements of information literacy.

Entrepreneurship education   An approach to education that focuses on empowering students with the knowledge, motivation and skill sets required to achieve socio-economic development and entrepreneurial success as a primary focus for their learning.

Gig economy   An extension of the Knowledge Economy in which people use the Internet, ICT and social media to undertake temporary, flexible working 'gigs' as the basis of their employment.

Modularity theory   According to the Christensen Institute, modularity theory provides 'a framework for explaining how different parts of a product's architecture relate to one another and consequently affect metrics of production and adoption' (https://www.chris tenseninstitute.org/interdependence-modularity/). Modularity theory is important because it allows us to design teaching and learning models that suit individual school circumstances, without having to change every aspect of the existing model to do so.

Personalised learning   An educational approach seeking to customise individual student learning according to the strengths and limitations of the student and their situation. Elements of customisation include modifying learning area content, adjusting the learning focus in relation to capabilities and/or cross-curriculum priorities, and aligning individual learning goals with appropriate content.

Social digital entrepreneurship   A corollary of entrepreneurship education based on the use of social media to develop, fund and promote business in the twenty-first century. A key goal of digital entrepreneurship is to minimise the need for infrastructure, initial investment and risk normally associated with doing business.

Teach-to-the-test mentality   A phrase used to refer to the tendency for schools and education systems to focus on instructional approaches that directly target standardised achievement tests in response to the accountability imperative of the Knowledge Economy.

Twenty-first-century skills   A series of 'portable' skill sets that many educators believe are crucial for today's students to be successful in the Information Age that increasingly characterises the Knowledge Economy. These skill sets are generally categorised into three areas (learning skills; literacy skills and life skills), and tend to include an entrepreneurial focus (collaboration, creative thinking, leadership, information literacy, communication, etc.).

References

Aguilar, S. J. (2018). Learning analytics: At the nexus of big data, digital innovation, and social justice in education. *TechTrends, 62*(1), 37–45.

AITSL (Australian Institute for Teaching and School Leadership). (2011). *Accreditation of initial teacher education programs in Australia.* Ministerial Council for Education, Early Childhood Development and Youth Affairs.

AITSL (Australian Institute for Teaching and School Leadership). (2012). *Australian professional standards for teachers.* Retrieved October 30, 2019, from www.aitsl.edu.au/australian-professional-standards-for-teachers

AITSL (Australian Institute for Teaching and School Leadership). (2014). *Global trends in professional learning and performance and development: Some implications and ideas for the Australian education system.* Retrieved October 30, 2019, from www.aitsl.edu.au/docs/default-source/default-document-library/horizon_scan_report.pdf

AITSL (Australian Institute for Teaching and School Leadership). (2015). *Initial teacher education: ITE reform.* Retrieved October 30, 2019, from www.aitsl.edu.au/initial-teacher-education/ite-reform

Alexander, B. (2008). Web 2.0 and emergent multiliteracies. *Theory into Practice, 47*(2), 150–160.

Arnett, T. (2019). *One major barrier to high-quality blended learning.* Retrieved September 11, 2019, from www.christenseninstitute.org/blog/one-major-barrier-to-high-quality-blended-learning/?_sft_topics=k-12-education

Ball, S. (2013). *The education debate.* The Policy Press.

Bloom, B. S. (1984). The 2-sigma problem: The search for methods of group instruction as effective a one-to-one tutoring. *Educational Researcher, 13*(6), 4–16.

Blum, S. D. (2015). The game of school. Retrieved November 14, 2019, from www.susanblum.com/learning-versus-schooling-a-blog-about-both/category/game-of-school

Bonin, H. (2017). The potential economic benefits of education of migrants in the EU. *EENEE Analytical Report No. 31.* Publications Office of the European Union.

Carr, K. J. (2011). Commercialisation Australia: Program guidelines. Retrieved August 31, 2019, from www.commercialisationaustralia.gov.au/AboutUs/Documents/Commercialisation%20Australia%20Ministerial%20Program%20Guidelines%20No1%20of%202011.pdf

Cheng, L., Ritzhaupt, A. D., & Antonenko, P. (2019). Effects of the flipped classroom instructional strategy on students' learning outcomes: A meta-analysis. *Educational Technology Research and Development, 67*(4), 793–824. https://doi.org/10.1007/s11423-018-9633-7

Christensen Institute. (2019). *Disruptive innovation.* Retrieved November 10, 2019, from www.christenseninstitute.org/disruptive-innovations/

Coelli, M., & Green, D. A. (2012). Leadership effects: School principals and student outcomes. *Economics of Education Review, 31*(1), 92–109. https://doi.org/10.1016/j.econedurev.2011.09.001

Darling-Hammond, L., & Snyder, J. (2015). Professional capacity and accountability: An introduction. *Education Policy Analysis Archives, 23*(14), 1–9. https://doi.org/10.14507/epaa.v23.2005

Davey, M. (2020). *'Confusing and stressful': The debate around children and coronavirus as Australian schools reopen*. Retrieved May 3, 2020, from www.theguardian.com/world/2020/apr/27/confusing-and-stressful-the-debate-around-children-and-coronavirus-as-australian-schools-reopen

Devedzic, V. (2004). Education and the semantic web. *International Journal of Artificial Intelligence in Education, 4*(2), 165–191.

Dhuey, E., & Smith, J. (2014). How important are school principals in the production of student achievement? *Canadian Journal of Economics/Revue canadienne d'économique, 47*(2), 634–663. https://doi.org/10.1111/caje.12086

Goldie, J. G. S. (2016). Connectivism: A knowledge learning theory for the digital age? *Medical Teacher, 38*(10), 1064–1069. https://doi.org/10.3109/0142159X.2016.1173661

Good to Great Schools. (2016). *Direct instruction: A principal's perspective*. Retrieved September 16, 2017, from https://goodtogreatschools.org.au/

Grissom, J. A., Kalogrides, D., & Loeb, J. (2015). Using student test scores to measure principal performance. *Educational Evaluation and Policy Analysis, 37*(1), 3–28. https://doi.org/10.3102/0162373714523831

Hanushek, E. A. &., & Woessmann, L. (2011). The economics of international differences in educational achievement. In E. Hanushek, S. Machin, & L. Woessmann (Eds.), *Handbook of the economics of education* (pp. 89–200). Elsevier.

Heck, H. R., & Hallinger, P. (2014). Modeling the longitudinal effects of school leadership on teaching and learning. *Journal of Educational Administration, 52*(5), 653–681. https://doi.org/10.1108/JEA-08-2013-0097

Horn, M. B., & Staker, H. (2017). *The blended workbook: Learning to design the schools of our future*. Jossey-Bass. Retrieved August 14, 2019, from www.wiley.com/en-au/The+Blended+Workbook:+Learning+to+Design+the+Schools+of+our+Future-p-9781119388074

Ingvarson, L., Reid, K., Buckley, S., Kleinhenz, E., Masters, G., & Rowley, G. (2014). *Best practice teacher education programs and Australia's own programs*. Department of Education.

Khribi, M. K., Jemni, M., & Nasraoui, O. (2009). Automatic recommendations for e-learning personalization based on web usage mining techniques and information retrieval. *Journal of Educational Technology & Society, 12*(4), 30–42.

Klenowski, V., & Wyatt-Smith, C. (2012). The impact of high stakes testing: The Australian story. *Assessment in Education: Principles, Policy and Practice, 19*(1), 65–79. https://doi.org/10.1080/0969594X.2011.592972

Kraus, S., Palmer, C., Kailer, N., Kallinger, F., & Spitzer, J. (2018). Digital entrepreneurship: A research agenda on new business models for the twenty-first century. *International Journal of Entrepreneurial Behavior & Research*. https://doi.org/10.1108/IJEBR-06-2018-0425

Leahy, S., & William, D. (2009). From teachers to schools: Scaling up professional development for formative assessment. In J. Gardner (Ed.), *Assessment and learning* (2nd ed., pp. 49–71). SAGE.

Lotrecchiano, G. R., McDonald, P. L., Lyons, L., Long, T., & Zajicek-Farber, M. (2013). Blended learning: Strengths, challenges, and lessons learned in an interprofessional training program. *Journal of Maternity and Child Health, 17*, 1725–1734. https://doi.org/10.1007/s10995-012-1175-8

Lynch, D., Smith, R., Provost, S., & Madden, J. (2016). Improving teaching capacity to increase student achievement: The key role of data interpretation by school leaders. *Journal of Educational Administration, 54*(5), 575–592. https://doi.org/10.1108/JEA-10-2015-0092

Lynch, M. (2017). *Implementing blended learning in higher education*. Retrieved August 13, 2019, from www.thetechedvocate.org/implementing-blended-learning-higher-education/

Marginson, S. (2006). Dynamics of national and global competition in higher education. *Higher Education, 52*(1), 1–39. https://doi.org/10.1007/s10734-004-7649-x

Maxwell, C., & White, J. (2017). *Blended (r)evolution: How 5 teachers are modifying the Station Rotation to fit students' needs*. Clayton Christensen Institute for Disruptive Innovation. Retrieved October 10, 2019, from www.christenseninstitute.org/publications/stationrotation/

Nambison, S. (2018). Digital entrepreneurship: Toward a digital technology perspective of entrepreneurship. *Entrepreneurship Theory and Practice, 41*(6), 1029–1055. https://doi.org/10.1111/etap.12254

Newcomb, T. (2020). *'Why do I want digital experiences for my kids if it looks like this?' — Experts fear parent Backlash against online learning.* Retrieved March 30, 2020, from www.the74million.org/article/why-do-i-want-digital-experiences-for-my-kids-if-it-looks-like-this-experts-fear-parent-backlash-against-online-learning/?utm_source=Ed%20Digest&utm_medium=email&utm_campaign=4%2F10%2F20

NSW Government. (2020). *COVID-19 and public schools in NSW.* Retrieved March 20, 2020, from https://education.nsw.gov.au/news/latest-news/coronavirus-nsw-education

Ocloo, C. E., Akaba, S., & Worwui-Brown, D. K. (2014). Globalization and competitiveness: Challenges of small and medium enterprises (SMEs) in Accra, Ghana. *International Journal of Business and Social Science, 5*(4), 287–296.

OECD (The Organisation for Economic Co-operation and Development). (2013). *Perspectives on global development 2013: Industrial policies in a changing world.* OECD Publishing. https://doi.org/10.1787/persp_glob_dev-2013-en

Orphanos, S., & Orr, M. T. (2014). Learning leadership matters: The influence of innovative school leadership preparation on teachers' experiences and outcomes. *Educational Management Administration & Leadership, 42*(5), 680–700. https://doi.org/10.1177/1741143213502187

Patrick, S., & Sturgis, C. (2015). *Maximising competency: Education and blended learning.* Incol Competency Works. Retrieved June 1, 2019, from http://bit.ly/cwcompetency blended

Price, R. (2018). *Packing for the journey: Can lifelong learning fit in a college-sized suitcase?* Retrieved February 17, 2020, from www.christenseninstitute.org/blog/packing-for-the-journey-can-lifelong-learning-fit-in-a-college-sized-suitcase/?_sft_topics=interdependence-modularity

Price, R. (2020). How competency-based education can help the nation recover from COVID-19. Retrieved May 2, 2020, from www.christenseninstitute.org/blog/how-competency-based-education-can-help-the-nation-recover-from-covid-19/?utm_source=Ed±Digest&utm_medium=email&utm_campaign=5/1/20

Reigeluth, C. M., Beatty, B. J., & Myers, R. D. (2016). *Instructional-design theories and models, volume IV: The learner-centered paradigm of education.* Routledge.

Research and Markets Report. (2017). *Global E-learning market analysis & trends – Industry forecast to 2025.* Retrieved February 2, 2020, from www.researchandmarkets.com/

Reys, R., Reys, B., Lapan, R., Holliday, G., & Wasman, D. (2003). Assessing the impact of "standards"- based middle grades mathematics curriculum materials on student achievement. *Journal for Research in Mathematics Education, 34*(1), 74–95.

Rothstein, J. (2010). Teacher quality in educational production: Tracking, decay, and student achievement. *Quarterly Journal of Economics, 125*(1), 175–214. https://doi.org/10.1162/qjec.2010.125.1.175

Scheerens, J. (2013). *What is effective schooling? A review of current thought and practice.* International Baccalaureate Organisation. Retrieved October 30, 2018, from www.ibo.org/globalassets/publications/ib-research/continuum/what-is-effective-schooling-report-en.pdf

Shirrell, M. (2016). New principals, accountability, and commitment in low-performing schools. *Journal of Educational Administration, 54*(5), 558–574. https://doi.org/10.1108/JEA-08-2015-0069

Suskie, L. (2018). *Assessing student learning: A common sense guide* (3rd ed.). Jossey-Bass.

TEMAG (Teacher Education Ministerial Advisory Group). (2014). Action now: Classroom ready teachers. Retrieved October 30, 2018, from www.studentsfirst.gov.au/teacher-education-ministerial-advisory-group

Thompson, G. (2013). NAPLAN, My School and Accountability: Teacher perceptions of the effects of testing. *The International Education Journal: Comparative Perspectives, 12*(2), 62–84.

Thompson, G., & Harbaugh, A. (2013). A preliminary analysis of teacher perceptions of the effects of NAPLAN on pedagogy and curriculum. *Australian Education Researcher, 40*(3), 299–314. https://doi.org/10.1007/s13384-013-0093-0

Thomson, S. (2020). What PISA tells us about our preparedness for remote learning. *Teacher* (Australian Council for Educational Research), April, 2020. Retrieved May 3, 2020, from www.teachermaga zine.com.au/columnists/sue-thomson/what-pisa-tells-us-about-our-preparedness-for-remote-learning?utm_source=CM&utm_medium=Bulletin&utm_content=21April

Truitt, A. A., & Ku, H.-Y. (2018). A case study of third grade students' perceptions of the station rotation blended learning model in the United States. *Educational Media International, 55*(2), 153–169. https://doi.org/10.1080/09523987.2018.1484042

Vanderlinde, R., & van Braak, J. (2010). The e-capacity of primary schools: Development of a conceptual model and scale construction from a school improvement perspective. *Computers & Education, 55*(2), 541–553. https://doi.org/10.1016/j.compedu.2010.02.016

William, D. (2009). *Assessment for learning: Why, what and how?* Institute of Education, University of London.

Wood, A. J., Graham, M., Lehdonvirta, V., & Hjorth, I. (2019). Good gig, bad gig: Autonomy and algorithmic control in the global gig economy. *Work, Employment and Society, 33*(1), 56–75. https://doi.org/10.1177/0950017018785616

Yeigh, T., & Lynch, D. (2017). Reforming initial teacher education: A call for innovation. *Australian Journal of Teacher Education, 42*(12), 112–127. https://doi.org/10.14221/ajte.2017v42n12.7

Yeigh, T., Lynch, D., Turner, D., Fradale, P., Willis, R., Sell, K., & Lawless, E. (2020). Using blended learning to support whole-of-school improvement: The need for contextualisation. *Education and Information Technologies*. https://doi.org/10.1007/s10639-020-10114-6

Zdravkova, K., Ivanovic, M., & Putnik, Z. (2012). Experience of integrating web 2.0 technologies. *Educational Technology Research and Development, 60*(2), 361–381.

Appendix: Online resources

Robinson, K. (2010). *Bring on the revolution!* www.ted.com/talks/sir_ken_robinson_bring_on_the_revolution
(Makes the case for a radical shift from standardised schools to personalised learning – creating conditions where the natural talents of children can flourish.)

Monique Markoff. (2014). *Blended learning and the future of education.* https://youtu.be/Mb2d8E1dZjY
(Provides clear insights for implementing blended learning.)

Koller, D. (2012). *What we're learning from online education.* www.ted.com/talks/daphne_koller_what_we_re_learning_from_online_education
(Discusses using free online courses as a way to research how people learn)

Haines, K. (2016). *Blended learning and technology integration.* https://youtu.be/KD8AUfGsCKg
(Discusses the role of technology in blended learning.)

KIPP_*Student empowerment* (9 mins): www.blendedlearning.org/directory/
(Testimonial for the use of blended learning.)

Individual rotation with teach to one (5 mins): www.blendedlearning.org/directory/
(Explains how to use the rotation model of blended learning.)

4 What does the research evidence say about effective schools?

Relevant Australian Professional Standards for Teachers: 1.5; 2.6; 3.2; 3.6; 4.5; 6.2; 6.4

Chapter synopsis

Effective schools achieve educational and social outcomes for students. At the core of this statement is both a performance and growth, or value add, consideration. Both should be required regardless of socio-economic factors or geographic location of the school. This is important because the established approach to determining effective schools has been on a set of narrow, often standardised test measures. In this respect the approach to effective schooling by policymakers and education system leaders has largely focused on teacher performance and principal accountability.

While the important effect of teaching practices on learning outcomes is indisputable, reform efforts that consider the complex nature of schools and take a broader view of important conditions and factors that improve classroom practice offer more comprehensive approaches. This chapter will unpack what is meant by the notion of an effective school, which further discussions will then locate within a Knowledge Economy context. The chapter explores the school construct, which is a global phenomenon, and research into effective schools, before generating a model to explain how key elements of each are exploited in the organisation of the school to create the effective Blended Learning school.

Introduction

To this point in the book, we have detailed major changes having taken place in society over recent decades leading to a fundamental change in work and home life, and introduced Blended Learning as a distinct pedagogical approach designed to accommodate these changes. At the heart of such change is the coupling of human ingenuity with technological innovation. This has triggered a series of four industrial revolutions which, in turn, have redefined how modern-day lives are lived and how work is undertaken.

In Chapter 2, the case for education reform was argued, based on what we identified as an ineffectual reform rhetoric conspiring with false education dichotomies to generate a malaise in the system of education. This has resulted in schools continuing to function as they have always done. As an insight into how to deal with such challenges, the concept of Talent Management was introduced as a Knowledge Economy construct for how teachers – the Talent factor in a system of schooling – can be positioned and supported by their school leader for teaching and learning improvements. Important for this chapter is the capacity and customisation benefits that Blended Learning sets up for the teacher.

In summary, the three opening chapters have collectively argued that society has undergone a fundamental change that now impacts every aspect of modern-day life. Given that schools prepare young people for future society, our central proposition is, quite simply, that if schools and their teachers are to prepare young people for modern society, then they have to change accordingly. But as we have pointed out in Chapter 2, there are inherent challenges in reforming and changing schools. The powerful nature of the status quo is but one. Blended Learning, we argue, is the vehicle through which to undertake a transformation of the traditional schooling logic and deal with associated challenges that manifest in a Knowledge Economy, but in order to implement this appropriately a clear understanding of the evidence surrounding effective schooling is required.

In this chapter, we examine and locate the premise of the 'effective school' in our overall Blended Learning thesis. To achieve such a goal, we review the school effectiveness literature to provide an account of the key elements at play to establish a set of positions on the effective school. These positions we then locate within the context of the Knowledge Economy to formulate a set of considerations for establishing Blended Learning in a school. With this point in mind, we illustrate several key points by outlining an original implementation model. We turn first to the basic definition of the school for key points of reference.

The concept of a school

A school can be defined as an educational institution which has the expressed purpose of preparing young people for future adult life in a society (Balci, 2007). Schools are located in nearly every locality in every country around the globe and are essentially grouped into three categories: centres for early childhood, primary (or elementary) schools and high schools (to overall educate children generally aged from 5 through 18 years of age). Each has a school leader, known as the head, director or principal, and is supported by a range of teachers who are assigned to a student cohort by age-related and study area criteria.

Generally, each school type is focused on delivering a systemically developed and mandated syllabus which is embedded in a government policy position (Logan & Watson, 1992; Lynch, 2012). These syllabi are organised into discrete study areas such as mathematics, English and science. In Australia, for example, schooling is the responsibility of state governments. Thus, while the federal government, directly or indirectly, ultimately funds schools in Australia, it is the state governments that have legislative responsibility for the provision of schools and for mandating the study curriculum. A similar circumstance exists in other countries including the United Kingdom and the United States of America.

Specific societal issues which governments value are embodied in a mandated study syllabus and taught in all schools. Indigenous perspectives, sex education and religious education are three examples in the Australian context. In 2015 state governments in Australia agreed to move towards implementation of a national curriculum but, to date, not all states have adopted it in their schools. To understand this reluctance to forego control of schooling is to understand and appreciate the key role that schools and their curriculums play in creating and influencing future society. Early chapters have highlighted, for example, the economic gains that a highly educated society generates (Hanushek & Woessman, 2020). But schools are important also in establishing the norms through which a society operates. These norms inform a young person's initiation into the culture of a society and in turn, defines for them how they should think about certain things and how they are to act and interact within the society (Sisman, 2011).

As we have previously noted, schools across the globe have a distinctly similar appearance and operational logic. Most operate a 9am to 3pm timetable, enact a curriculum through the appointment of a teacher to an age-related classroom cohort, and operate through orchestrated long-held traditions and rituals such as classes, uniforms, school mottos, salutations, student assemblies and textbooks. These similarities in schooling are the product of early European colonisation and their establishment, for better or for worse, of schooling systems globally (Logan & Watson, 1992). In recent times various additional functions, such as 'daycare' and 'before and after school care', as well as various social welfare services, have coalesced around the school to ensure students are 'looked after' while busy parents work. The establishment of support services within and around schools such as welfare and policing services – known as community or full-service schools – is an example of how schools are a convenient and powerful organising element within modern society (Anderson et al., 2019; Richardson, 2009)

In summary, our initial point for this chapter is that schools are key instruments of the state and fundamental to the society in which young people will grow into. They exist to prepare young people for future life and the outcomes of such a process have significant impacts (positive if successful and negative if unsuccessful) on the society in which such young people graduate.

Having made these introductory comments about schools, we now examine the concept of the effective school.

The effective school

There are a plethora of studies into school effectiveness, having their genesis in literature from the 1960s, which has chiefly argued for the codification and professionalisation of schools (Balci, 2007; Hargreaves & Fullan, 2012; Jansen, 1995). Further, and interestingly, most studies focus on and thus implicate the key role played by the school leader in achieving the effective school (Döş & Savaş, 2015; Fullan, 2016; Hattie, 2009). According to Klopf et al. (1982), an effective school can be defined as 'an optimum learning environment in which students' cognitive, affective, psychomotor, social and aesthetic development is optimally ensured is formed' (Balci, 2007, p. 10). Cheng (1996), cited in Rai and Prakash (2014), view school effectiveness as:

> a concept often used in the literature of school management and improvement and often confused with school efficiency that means the capacity of a school to maximise its functions or the degree to which a school can perform school functions given a fixed amount of school input, whereas effectiveness can be described as the extent to which the desired level of outputs is achieved.
>
> (2014, p. 41)

Put simply, the effective school is easily understood as an educational entity that has the capacity to achieve learning outcomes in every student and which are consistent and in-line with expectations as laid out in associated curriculum documents and corresponding community expectations. As Chapter 2 indicated, this is a difficult agenda, with school performance in countries such as Australia declining in terms of various standardised tests and despite a focus on these for over a decade. These test measures are essentially public proxies for confidence in individual schools. This decline can thus be perceived as a mismatch between the system of schooling and the profile of learners presenting for education, coupled with the complexities of modern life and exponential change (Hattie, 2009; Lynch et al., 2019).

Murman and Pauly (1981) observed, and interestingly this is an observation made in many recent leadership studies (see, for example, Hargreaves & Fullan, 2012; Hattie, 2009, 2012), that:

> We have learned a great deal from quantiative research on the determinants of school effectiveness. The most important lesson is that schools make a difference ... [and that] teachers are a critcal resource.
>
> (1981, p. 25)

In 2009, John Hattie released his book *Visible Learning: A Synthesis of Over 800 Meta-analyses Relating to Achievement,* where he noted five domains of influence in the learning life cycle of the student. Chief among them are, not surprisingly, the school leader and the teacher. Taken together, studies such as Hattie (2009), Lynch et al. (2019), Brundrett (2013) and Marzano et al. (2005) indicate that the improvement of teaching and learning in a school requires the orchestration of a plan of action that places an emphasis on what the teachers and their school leader do. In Chapter 5, we define this orchestration as leaders having developed states of alignment, capability and engagement [ACE] in teachers, and thus rendering them 'readied' and positioned for appropriate actions.

Returning to the school effectiveness concept, we can understand the effective school as one that has the capacity to deliver a mandated curriculum that meets the learning profile of each and every student. Such performance is benchmarked to curriculum expect-ations, is fluid and sensitive to changing societal conditions and is moderated by assessment regimes that objectively compare performance across classrooms and schools and which are tied to a 'fit' to the society in which such graduates will work and live. In this arrangement, the effective school has engineered an approach, in terms of its organ-isational logic, its pedagogic device structures and its performance monitoring regimes, such that it can assure each student will achieve success in terms of learning outcomes achieved.

How the effective school is positioned in a Knowledge Economy?

In order to answer this fundamental question, we have developed a conceptual model. This model, which we term the *blended learning implementation schema* (see Figure 4.1), iden-tifies the key elements involved and illustrates how each interacts and thus informs the other. The commentary which follows refers to this model in order to explain and illustrate our key points.

All schools operate in, and thus are influenced by and focused to, the context of their existence. This notion of 'context' comes to represent the peculiarities of the school community at both the macro (global and national level) and micro (town, community school level), as well as the societal circumstance in which schools are working to graduate their students into. In this case, the Knowledge Economy comes to represent this latter point. Students feature prominently in the model, in that the product of the model is to service the learning needs of *each* student. Note the emphasis upon 'each' student. This personalisation of learning, and through which Blended Learning creates the required capacities, is a key feature of the Blended Learning curriculum-approach

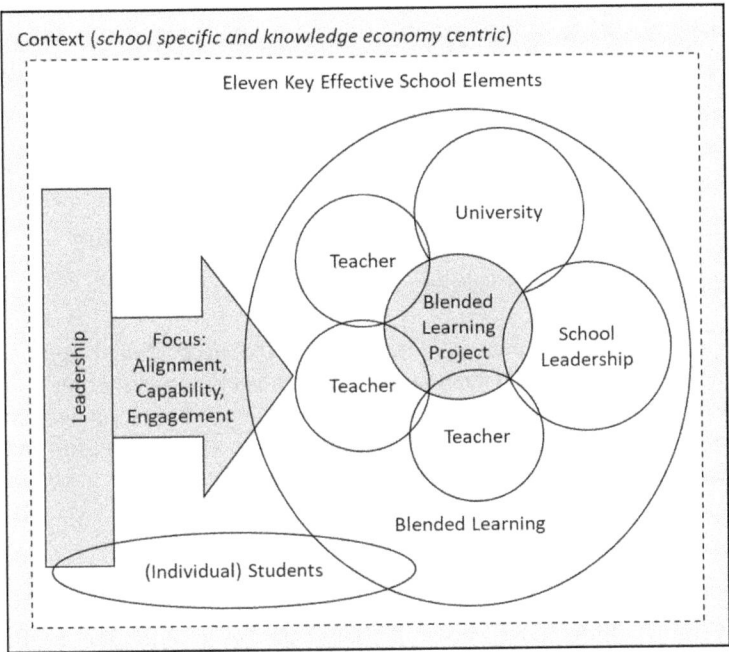

Figure 4.1 Blended learning implementation schema.

logic. We examine personalised learning briefly in a section which follows and in more detail in Chapters 3 and 7.

Recall from Chapter 1 that the Knowledge Economy, by virtue of an interplay between consumer demand, technological innovation and convergence coupled to human ingenuity, has created a world in which change is the new normal. In contrast to the previous industrial economies, working in the Knowledge Economy puts a premium on familiarity with networked knowledge rather than with scarcity. In the Knowledge Economy, the more networks individuals have, the higher the value of relationships (Burlacu, 2011). People steeped in a 1980s industrial era mindset, for example, tend not to comprehend this new mode of operating. In short, first, second and third industrial revolution mindsets (i.e., pre-1990) affirm the emergent world as 'the same' as it always was, but with more 'problems' to grapple with. People with this mindset often seek to package and deliver the old more effectively and are wary of the change that threatens what they know (Hanushek & Woessman, 2020). The contrasting mindset asserts that the world, because of the effects of new technologies, the structure of a new kind of labour market, the universalism of popular culture, the need for self-assertion and patently different life prospects for young people, is radically different, and the approaches to learning and employment, therefore, must also be radically different (Lynch, 2012). One can appreciate that school leaders and their teachers in the effective school would view the world in this way.

We note that operating as an effective school is also conditioned upon the curriculum that is mandated by the state. If the curriculum is content-heavy and uses assessment based on the recall of facts, then the teacher is likely to revert to traditional teaching methods and use didactic methods to impart knowledge – to 'fill up the empty vessel with knowledge' – and therefore work to maintain the status quo of schooling. By contrast, a curriculum that is embedded in problem-solving, teamwork and experimentation, and works to create mindsets that take risks, value collaboration and ideation will, in effect, prepare students for a Knowledge Economy and its profile of ongoing exponential change and thus work to transform the school. A curriculum such as this will focus on the individual and generate a curriculum approach that is based on **personalised learning**.

Personalised learning: a new dimension in effective schooling

We can understand personalised learning as

> instruction in which the pace of learning and the instructional approach are optimised for the needs of each learner. Learning objective, instruction approaches and instruction content (and its sequencing) may all vary based on learning needs. In addition, learning activities are made available that are meaningful and relevant to learners, driven by their interests and often self initiated.
>
> (USDE, 2016, p. 7)

The logic of personal learning is a significant departure from the traditional schooling logic, where students are organised in age-related cohorts and taught a static curriculum. While various policy documents talk about catering to individual needs, the reality is that the traditional schooling logic has little in the way of scope and capacity for dealing with individuals. Further, the teaching mindset is about promoting students from one grade to another and filtering them out to work or on to further higher learning (Lynch, 2012).

In a Blended Learning environment, technology creates the required capacities through a myriad of electronic devices and software applications that can be customised to meet a specific learner profile needs. This does not come to mean students are put on 'autopilot'. Rather, the teacher has a key role in designing learning programs that are focused explicitly on achieving predefined learning outcomes in each student. The student, in effect, has their learning managed and its design is customised to their individual profile.

This means that a student in the effective Knowledge Economy school will need to have their own learning plan. Their learning profile will be ascertained and monitored, and the program of learning customised to meet their needs. The teacher, while primarily concerned with instruction, will evolve themselves, into what Lynch and Smith (2010) term, the **Learning Manager**. The term Learning Manager is a transition from the teacher construct of the first through third industrial revolution to the education practitioner that is appropriate for a Knowledge Economy. Learning Managers in this perspective have the pedagogic skills for developing sound academic knowledge and skills, as well as developing in students elements such as personal resilience, social competence, complex reasoning skills (such as critical thinking and comparing and contrasting), and habits of mind that underscore personal work ethics, knowledge sharing and cooperation techniques that a Knowledge Economy curriculum requires. These students will be well networked and will work within and without their school community forging partnerships with industry, employer groups and other entities to further the scope and potential for learning. But importantly, the Learning Manager mindset focuses on a set of learning design considerations for the individual student and uses Blended Learning to create the required classroom capacities. This comes to represent a coupling of evidence-based practice with technological capacities. Important to our developing argument, the ability to work as a Learning Manager is an aspect of Talent.

Having outlined the focus that falls upon the individual student in a Blended Learning environment, we now return to the theory around effective schools to explain and locate the conditions in which Blended Learning must be positioned for learning outcome effects.

The conditions for effective schooling

For optimal teaching and learning effects, the school is required to locate itself within, and then operate under, the influence of eleven key school effectiveness elements. To explain this logic, we draw upon the work of Griffith (2003), which has served the test of time in both findings and assertions, and is reproduced as Table 4.1.

Griffith (2003, p. 31) identifies eleven key elements which collectively represent the attributes of the effective school. These elements are a product of 'effective leadership' which is enacted by the head and their leadership team. The leader we talk of here is the Transformational Leader. This type of leader is said to demonstrate high levels of interpersonal skills, such as trust, which deepens their commitment to the school and places a premium on student achievement. The Transformational Leader is one who empowers teachers to improve from within and engages staff to think about continuous improvement (Thomas et al., 2020). The Transformational Leader is represented in Figure 4.1 as 'Leadership'. We examine the Transformational Leader in greater detail in Chapter 5. Our key point here is that the school leader is a key player in any school reform and improvement program and thus central and pivotal to the overall agenda and strategy. Put simply, an ineffectual Transformational Leader compromises the chance of Blended Learning success.

This then brings us to the strategy of the leader. We can understand this strategy as developing states of alignment, capability and engagement (ACE) in teachers and by

Table 4.1 Attributes of effective schools (adapted from Griffith, 2003, p. 31)

Key element	Exemplified by
Outstanding leadership	Firm, purposive; participative; frequent monitoring, sense-making; 'maverick' orientation
Shared vision and goals	Unity of purpose; consistency in practice; collegiality and collaboration
Concentration on teaching and learning	Optimise learning time; academic emphasis; focus on achievement
Purposeful teaching	Efficient organisation; clarity of purpose; structure lessons
High expectations	
Monitoring performance	Pupil performance; school performance
Learning environment	Orderly atmosphere; attractive work environment
Clear and fair discipline	
Rights and responsibilities	Responsibilities of position; control of work
Learning organisation	Staff development and training; staff innovation and problem-solving; staff input to decisions
Parent involvement in children's education	

direct association in the students for whom the school serves. We can understand *alignment* as the extent to which staff agree to and have a knowledge of (a) the goals and the associated strategies of the school as well as (b) the espoused values and expectations of stakeholders. *Capability* is the extent of skills, technologies and associated processes that staff rely upon to effectively and efficiently complete their jobs, while *engagement* is the extent to which staff are working towards the goals and aspirations of the school. The approach that the Transformational Leader uses to enact and sustain each state is known as Talent Management, a concept introduced in Chapter 2 and further explored in Chapter 5. We will also explain the ACE logic in greater detail in Chapter 5.

At this stage in the discussion, the conditions for establishing the effective school have been articulated and the key role of leadership highlighted. Both of these are established and thus referenced to the context in which the school serves. This chiefly refers to the Knowledge Economy, but it also takes into consideration the microelements of the school and its community. This now brings us to the need for a mechanism to transition the school to Blended Learning and importantly activate the Talent for teaching and learning outcomes. The 'business end', if you like, of the model and what comes to represent the aspirations of a reimagined school.

The delivery of effective schooling is a specific product of the work of the teacher, however their capacity is mediated by other variables such as 'the community', 'parents' and 'student predispositions' (Hattie, 2009). The key point, however, is that although it is the teacher who makes the fundamental difference for students, they are reliant on the effective school for optimal effects in their students (Hattie, 2011, 2012). This effectiveness is delivered through leadership.

The mechanism in our model, and the thesis of this book, is the use of Blended Learning as the pedagogic approach which works to prepare and position teachers as the required Talent that is specifically positioned to deliver effective schooling in relation to the imperatives of the Knowledge Economy. This preparation and positioning of teachers – the creation of Talent – occurs through a learner-mediated partnership (Stephenson, 1999), comprising a university, teachers working in teams and the school's leadership, focused on a Blended Learning project that has been designed to build teacher capability. We term this arrangement the Blended Learning capability building model. We explain this model in greater detail in Chapter 5, but a key point to note is that the model exploits teamwork and professional learning, focused through teachers working on 'real-time, real work' Blended Learning based projects, which are supported through a formalised coaching, mentoring and feedback regime. Of importance to the current chapter is that this arrangement is orchestrated by school leadership.

Chapter summary

Schools are an important construct in modern society. They prepare young people for future life and play a part in developing and contributing to the fabric of society. Schools have a history, a set of traditions which, shown repeatedly over time, causes them to be reluctant to change, despite exponential change happening around them. We argue Blended Learning is a mechanism through which schools and their teachers are able to transition to a new paradigm in teaching and learning; one that is a better fit to the Knowledge Economy of today.

This chapter has focused on the effective school and reveals the key role played by school leaders in creating and sustaining the conditions for schools to achieve at optimal levels. This notion of achievement is centred on the capacity that the school has to deal with each student as an individual and, in doing so, optimises their learning outcome performance. By association, the teacher transforms from content deliverer to Learning Manager and works to apply evidence-based teaching and learning strategies for the benefit of individual students. This individualised notion is known as personalised learning.

Returning to the theme of schools and their reluctance to change in Chapter 1, we have introduced and explained in this chapter a model or schema for how Blended Learning is implemented in a Knowledge Economy circumstance. The outlined schema was explained to reveal a series of key school effective elements which interact with school leadership and teachers, operating in what Stephenson (1999) calls a 'learning mediated' partnership. Taken together, this chapter has highlighted a set of underlying conceptual ideas about the relationship between school leadership and effective schooling which we bring to bear on discussions about Blended Learning in the chapters that follow. We continue this examination in Chapter 5 by exploring the key role played by school leaders in leading for change.

Glossary

Effective school   An educational entity that has the capacity to achieve learning outcomes in every student and which are consistent and in line with expectations as laid out in associated curriculum documents and correspondingly community expectations.

Learning Manager   This term is used to signal a refocusing of the industrial era teacher, from a content provider to an educational practitioner commensurate to a Knowledge Economy era, where their focus is upon a new set of knowledge and skills aimed at preparing student mindsets and skill sets for conditions of social change that pervade local and global societies in the twenty-first century.

Personalised learning   Instruction in which the pace of learning and the instructional approach are optimised for the needs of each learner.

School   A school can be defined as an educational institution which has the expressed purpose of preparing young people for future adult life in a society.

Schooling   A formalised process of educating young people, generally organised into early childhood, primary or elementary and high schools, and organised according to long held traditions and rituals, predominated in face-to-face classroom routines.

References

Anderson, J. A., Chen, M. E., Min, M., & Watkins, L. L. (2019). Successes, challenges, and future directions for an urban full service community schools initiative. *Education and Urban Society, 51*(7), 894–921.

Balci, A. (2007). *Effective school and school improvement theory, practice and research*. Pegem A Publishing.

Brundrett, M. (2013). The importance of teachers, teaching and school leaders: The 'silver thread' of the reform agenda for English schools. *Education 3–13, 41*(5), 459–461. https://doi.org/10.1080/03004279.2013.848511

Burlacu, S. (2011). Characteristics of knowledge-based economy and new technologies in education. *Administratie Si Management Public, 16*, 114–119.

Cheng, Y. C. (1996). *School effectiveness and school-based management: A mechanism for development*. The Falmer Press.

Döş, İ., & Savaş, A. C. (2015). Elementary school administrators and their roles in the context of effective schools. *SAGE Open, 5*(1), 1–11.

Fullan, M. (2016). *The new meaning of educational change* (5th ed.). Routledge.

Griffith, F. (2003). Schools as organisational models and implications for examining school effectiveness. *Elementary School Journal, 104*(1), 29–47.

Hanushek, E., & Woessman, L. (2020). Education, knowledge capital and economic growth. In S. Bradley & C. Green (Eds.), *The economics of education* (pp. 171–182). Academic Press.

Hargreaves, A., & Fullan, M. (2012). *Professional capital: Transforming teaching in every school.* Teachers College Press.

Hattie, J. (2009). *Visible learning: A synthesis of over 800 meta-analyses relating to achievement.* Routledge.

Hattie, J. (2011). Challenge of focusing education reform. *The Australian.* Retrieved July 7, 2011, from www.theaustralian.com.au/business/news/rethinking-education-the-challenge-of-focusing-reform/story-fn8ex0p1-1226069556190

Hattie, J. (2012). *Visible learning for teachers: Maximising impact on learning.* Routledge.

Jansen, J. (1995). Effective schools? *Comparative Education, 31*(2), 181–200. https://doi.org/10.1080/03050069529100

Klopf, G., Schelden, E., & Brennan, K. (1982). The essentials of effectiveness: A job description for principals. *Principal, 61*(4), 35–38.

Logan, G., & Watson, T. (1992). *Soldiers of service.* AEBIS Publishing.

Lynch, D. (2012). *Preparing teachers in times of change: Teaching school, standards, new content and evidence.* Primrose Hall.

Lynch, D., & Smith, R. (2010). *Rethinking teacher education: Teacher education in a knowledge age.* AACLM Press.

Lynch, D., Smith, R., Yeigh, T., & Provost, S. (2019). A study into 'organisational readiness' and its impacts on school improvement. *International Journal of Educational Management, 33*(2), 393–408.

Marzano, R. J., Waters, T., & McNulty, B. A. (2005). *School leadership that works: From research to results.* ASCD.

Murmane, R. J. (1981). Interpreting the evidence on school effectiveness. *Teachers College Record, 83,* 19–35.

Murman, R., & Pauly, E. (1981). *How the financing of the public schools affects their ability to education.* Final Report of Research. National Institute of Education. https://files.eric.ed.gov/fulltext/ED227592.pdf

Rai, A., & Prakash, A. (2014). In pursuit of effective schools: From western perspective. *I-Manager's Journal on Educational Psychology, 7*(4), 41–49.

Richardson, J. (2009). *The full-service community school movement: Lessons from the James Adams Community School.* Springer.

Sisman, M. (2011). *The pursuit of excellence in education, effective schools.* Pegem A Publishing.

Stephenson, J. (1999). *Corporate capability: Implications for the style and direction of work-based learning.* Research Centre for Vocational Education and Training, University of Technology.

Thomas, L., Tuytens, M., Devos, G., Kelchtermans, G., & Vanderlinde, R. (2020). Transformational school leadership as a key factor for teachers' job attitudes during their first year in the profession. *Educational Management Administration & Leadership, 48*(1), 106–132.

US Department of Education [USDE]. (2016). *Future ready learning: Reimagining the role of technology in education.* Office of Educational Technology.

5 Exploring the key role played by school leaders in relation to educational change

Relevant Australian Professional Standards for Teachers: 3.2; 3.4; 3.6; 3.7; 4.5; Professional standards expected for Principals: *Leading improvement*; *Innovation and Change* (AITSL, 2014)

Chapter synopsis

This chapter will examine the essential role of school leadership in delivering meaningful change and improvement in schools. While it is clear the greatest effects in student achievement come from the quality of teaching, the behaviours and actions of school leaders is increasingly understood as a prerequisite to quality teaching. The effects leaders have on student learning will be explored by discussing how school leadership is being defined by governments and educational authorities. Recent studies have made explicit what actions school leaders should undertake to positively impact student results. The chapter will further examine some shortfalls with current thinking on educational change. While incremental improvements can be achieved, there are many forces working at maintaining the status quo in schools. The rapidly changing world demands more than incremental change and school leaders need to apply the best of what is known to bring about significant change. The chapter will conclude by presenting a methodology for school leaders to apply that will provide insights into a school's readiness for change referencing a growing understanding of Talent Management theory, in particular, how meaningful change can be enacted in complex environments with highly skilled professionals.

Introduction

Chapter 1 outlined a profile of exponential change having occurred in society through four industrial revolutions. It concluded by stating that technological innovation and convergence has transformed every aspect of modern society and life, placing significant pressures on schools and teachers to realign the 'what' and 'how' of education to better fit students to this changed global profile. Chapter 1 further revealed that despite a profile of profound and fundamental societal change, the organisation and positioning of schools remains relatively unchanged. This theme, of change needed in schools and teaching, continued into Chapter 2, where it was revealed that a rhetoric of change abounds, yet the results of change attempts appear to coalesce around teachers doing largely the same things in their classrooms and lamenting yet another education fad. Perhaps these are harsh words, and we do admit that there are pockets of innovation occurring in some schools, but these examples are in the vast minority and therefore we view this situation as a fundamental puzzle given the world in which schools now operate.

In this chapter, we explore the key role that school leaders play in transforming schools. The central goal of the chapter is to explain and locate the school leader as the main agent in a change agenda focused on introducing Blended Learning. The chapter commences with a brief review of the literature around school leadership. This exposé seeks to highlight the potency of effective school leaders, and to identify the attributes that effective leaders bring to successful change agendas. In order to scaffold the school leader into the Blended Learning agenda, and to explain how the effective school leader plans and executes their Blended Learning agenda, the concept of Talent Management is then reintroduced from Chapter 2. From this perspective we present the argument that effective school leaders are focused on nurturing and positioning their school staffing 'Talent' by creating states of **alignment**, **capability** and **engagement** (ACE), thus enabling their teachers to innovate, create and problem solve as key knowledge workers in a Knowledge Economy circumstance.

To conclude this chapter, we examine the premise of a new leadership mindset. The simple message is that the strategies and insights revealed in this chapter represent and require a new mindset for effect, a mindset that comes to see the world differently and to consider new things in a new light (Kaser & Halbert, 2009). We commence our outlining with an insight into effective school leadership.

Impact of school leadership

The central tenet of this book is locating Blended Learning into the curriculum of the school so as to generate required teaching capacities, but significantly, to engineer a schooling logic that best meets the profile of a society enmeshed in a fourth industrial revolution context, or what is commonly referred to as a Knowledge Economy. Our central argument is that in order to generate such change, leadership must be activated to achieve school improvement. Leadership, we argue, is a key focus in all school change agendas because, as Leithwood et al. (2008) note, 'there is not a single documented case of a school successfully turning around its pupil achievement trajectory in the absence of talented leadership' (p. 29). This view is also supported by Robinson et al. (2008), who found that 'the more leaders focus their relationships, their work, and their learning on the core business of teaching and learning, the greater their influence on student outcomes' (p. 21). In summary, school management, leadership, and improvement are particularly important when it comes to school reform with leadership considered second only to classroom instruction as an influence on student learning (Hargreaves & Fullan, 2012; Hattie, 2009; Louis et al., 2010; Lynch et al., 2019).

The emphasis on leadership has been influenced by a wide range of studies which demonstrate leadership impact on student outcomes. For example, Macklin and Zbar (2017) argue that improvement stands or falls on school leadership and what it does. Further, Leithwood (2013) found that certain practices which were useful for most successful leaders, were also important where instructional improvement was the goal, that is, 'setting directions, developing people, redesigning the organisation and managing the instructional program' (p. 636).

The importance of school leadership to school improvement requires further empirical research as well. In this respect, groundbreaking research work by Marzano et al. (2005) found that only 69 of 5,000 studies into school leadership over the previous 35 years had closely examined 'the quantitative relationship between school leadership and the academic achievement of students' (p. 6), and these studies provided clear indications of the behaviours needed for leaders to influence student outcomes. Of importance is that these influential leadership behaviours were those required for what is known as second-order change (Marzano et al., 2005, p. 113), that is, change that is perceived as a break from the past. Second-order-change behaviours were shown to make a notable difference to student learning and included: affirmation, change agency, flexibility, ideals and beliefs, intellectual stimulation, knowledge of curriculum, instruction and assessment, monitoring and evaluating, and inspiring and leading innovation (Marzano et al., 2005, pp. 42–43).

In their meta-analysis of research on school leadership and student outcomes, Robinson, Hohepa and Lloyd (2009, p. 656) revealed five key dimensions of leader impact on student outcomes (effect size in brackets):

- Establishing goals and expectations (0.42)
- Resourcing strategically (0.31)
- Planning, coordinating, and evaluating teaching and the curriculum (0.42)
- Promoting and participating in teacher learning and development (0.84)
- Ensuring an orderly and supporting environment (0.27).

These dimensions are consistent with the view that leaders play an important role in the improvement of teaching quality and student learning by facilitating 'organisational readiness' for change (Lynch et al., 2019; Schiemann, 2014). In analysing the dimension with the largest effect, 'promoting and participating in teacher learning and development' (p. 39) with an effect size of 0.84, it is interesting to note that this involves the leader participating in and with teacher learning and development. Dinham (2016, p. 153) notes that these findings have also been reflected in several studies in the United Kingdom and Australia. This focus on the leader's role working with teachers to promote school improvement demonstrated by better student performance also suggests that working with teachers to promote their alignment, capability and engagement optimises student academic performance (Lynch et al., 2019). We explore these three states in greater detail in a section which follows.

It is also interesting to note, however, that in a recent study Moir et al. (2014) suggested teachers preferred **Transformational Leadership**. Transformational Leadership is a term which has appeared predominantly in education writings since the 1980s (Leithwood et al., 1996; Thomas et al., 2020). This type of leader is said to demonstrate high levels of interpersonal skills, such as trust, which deepened their commitment to the school and who place a premium on student achievement. The Transformational Leader is one who empowers teachers to improve from within and engages staff to think about continuous improvement. In simple terms, this type of school leader seeks to make things better by promoting genuine collaboration between teachers and members of the community (Thomas et al., 2020).

We further note that an environment of continuous school improvement does not occur by chance. Lynch et al. (2019), Hargreaves and Fullan (2012) and Hallinger and Heck (2010) all argue that improvement largely depends on the leadership provided by the head-of-school, and this remains constant whether this leadership occurs in new schools or in reforming and re-activating existing schools. The energy and input of the school leader is a decisive influence in initiating, enhancing and sustaining school improvement (Kaser & Halbert, 2009). Moreover, according to Elmore (2004, p. 113), incentives that focus only on accountability have virtually no relationship to 'the knowledge and practice of improvement'. Taken together, one can appreciate that Transformational Leadership represents a leadership approach or 'style' that is able to capture the requisite skills for Talent Management. This marks Transformational Leadership as an appropriate form of leadership for leading the change management elements that normally take place in conjunction with a school improvement initiative, whether this involves Blended Leaning or any other type of change basis. For this reason, we will examine Transformational Leadership in more detail prior to moving onto the relationship between this leadership style and Talent Management.

Transformational school leadership

According to Yahaya and Ebrahim (2016), and Wang and Howell (2010), understanding the transformational school leader requires a review of their distinctive attributes. For example, one set of transformational attributes has to do with the strategic organisation of key elements within the school, which can be understood as 'transactional' attributes. Another is how the leader acts, presents him-or-herself to situations and thus is perceived by their teachers. This set of attributes comes to represent a characteristic approach to staff, representing 'approach to leadership' attributes. When taken together, these attribute 'sets' allow Transformational Leaders to provide deeper levels of connection and higher levels of commitment, performance, and morality for both themselves and their teachers (Burns, 1978, 2003). Table 5.1 illustrates these two sets of transformational attributes.

Having completed a brief exposé into the effects of the school leader and the notion of a Transformational Leader, the task now is to locate such insights into a strategy for preparing, enabling and supporting teachers into a Blended Learning schooling context. The key point here is that, by looking at the range of leadership responsibilities which influence student learning, research supports the position that for changes to occur in schools, and in turn for improvement to occur in student learning, school leaders need to influence the 'organisational readiness' of the school's staff (Lynch et al., 2019; Schiemann, 2012). Following Schiemann (2012), this means 'optimisation of the Talent' amongst the teaching body, and it involves the leader working with staff as a Transformational Leader by developing the required states of alignment, capability and engagement that optimisation requires in each member. We argue that these elements are the cornerstone of how Talent is managed effectively in relation to preparing a school for improvement, managing for successful change during the improvement implementation, and ensuring that the improvement is sustainable. In this regard, the notion of Talent Management lies at the heart of being a Transformational Leader when it comes to successful and sustainable school improvement.

Table 5.1 Attributes of the Transformational Leader

Set one: *Transactional attributes*	Set two: *Approach to leadership*
• Building trust and rapport • Organisational diagnosis • Dealing with the process • Using resources • Managing the work • Building skill and confidence in others	• The leadership of other teachers through coaching, mentoring, leading working groups • The leadership of developmental tasks that are central to improving learning and teaching • The leadership of pedagogy through the development and modelling of effective forms of teaching

(Adapted from Wang & Howell, 2010; Yahaya & Ebrahim, 2016)

Talent management as a means to create effective sustainable change

In Chapter 2, we introduced the concept of Talent Management. The Talent Management logic is a repositioning of the school's leadership and management functions, from a pre-occupation with managing static systems and processes, as traditional schooling seeks to maintain, towards identifying, nurturing and positioning the Talent that resides within an organisation for overall strategic effect. From this perspective, we can understand Talent as a natural aptitude that someone holds, an inner quality that emerges effortlessly when cultivated within the appropriate circumstances. Talent can be viewed as the confluence of collective competencies, knowledge, experiences, values and beliefs, energies and behaviours which manifest in an individual, and when actively positioned within the organisation spawns innovation, enables unique problems to be solved and new possibilities to be identified and acted upon (Schiemann, 2012, p. 37). In essence, Talent Management represents an overall transformation of the workplace, wherein the manager's focus moves from labour oversight and supervision to talent enablement, placing a premium on the potentials that 'knowledge work' offers in a Knowledge Economy era. The case has been made that this is now needed in schools (North & Gueldenberg, 2011), which in the current circumstances surrounding this book, we see as entirely applicable.

Having made these introductory statements about Talent Management, we now make a set of key contextual statements to locate Talent Management in the agenda of transforming a school through Blended Learning. These are intended as 'seed' statements here because they are being introduced in order to pave the way for the more detailed Blended Learning preparations that are provided in Chapter 7 of this book. However, it is important to include these ideas here as well, because this will allow the reader to more clearly understand how the various relationships between teachers, school leaders, school students and educational researchers correspond and interact with one another in support of a successful Blended Learning program.

Talent management and Blended Learning

Blended Learning, as outlined in Chapters 3 and 6, comes to represent a strategic initiative that is designed to couple the traditional classroom teaching logic with technological innovation as represented by information communication technologies. This coupling is, in effect, a transition mechanism whereby the traditions of explicit instruction or 'chalk-and-talk' pedagogies are enhanced, and greater capacities generated by strategically harnessing technology. In this manner, Blended Learning comes to represent the best of the analogue (first through third industrial revolutions) and digital worlds (fourth industrial revolution), but with a distinctive agenda to move schools into a new teaching and learning paradigm. This paradigm was presented in Chapter 3.

Talent Management is basically about how the school head or principal establishes, engenders and sustains continuous improvement in a school within a Knowledge Economy circumstance. Talent Management is enmeshed in a leadership mindset that places a premium on identifying, enabling and nurturing talent within the school so as to optimise improvement effects and, importantly, deal with the logistics and contingencies that manifest in all change agendas. Essentially, it is about how everything that is needed, is orchestrated for effect on school improvement and in a circumstance where staff are motivated and engaged to participate at an optimal level (Lynch et al., 2019). In addition, Talent Management seeks to establish the required conditions for teachers to create, innovate and problem-solve: to create conditions in which staff feel they can make mistakes but learn from them, and importantly, position themselves as key players in a major improvement agenda (Lynch et al., 2019).

In line with the ACE model of school readiness, the premise of Talent Management is built on the school leader establishing in all staff (because together they represent the global resource – that is, the capacity-package for the school), states of 'alignment', 'capability' and 'engagement'. In more direct terms this is an inter-related combination of:

Alignment: the extent to which staff agree to and have a knowledge of (a) the goals and the associated strategies of the school as well as (b) the espoused values and expectations of stakeholders. This element is expressed in terms of 'strategic plan' and 'processes within the school'.

Capability: the extent of skills, technologies and associated processes that staff rely upon to effectively and efficiently complete their jobs. This element is expressed in terms of 'staff capability factors' and 'resources available for staff to do their job'.

Engagement: the extent to which staff are working towards the goals and aspirations of the school. This can be understood as staff actually doing what they say they are doing. This element is expressed in terms of staff satisfaction with the school as a workplace and 'their commitment to the school'.

Importantly, Talent Management requires each component of school readiness (ACE) to be achieved at an optimal level in all staff before a change agenda can be first implemented and then sustained (in this case a whole-of-school Blended Learning initiative). The initiating process is essentially through alignment, because it is alignment that galvanises the potentials of Talent to 'the plan' (in schools, to the improvement agenda) and the associated processes that will need to be engineered to achieve it. Because a school has teaching and non-teaching staff, and thus different contributions being made to the improvement agenda, the scope and substance of what the leader is aligning staff to will differ for teaching and non-teaching staff, and in a teaching improvement sense will have more significance to key players such as teachers. Yet the technological side of Blended Learning will also require the specific efforts of support staff, especially IT specialists, for its associated implementation considerations. Our key message, however, is that the overall staff complement represents the school's global resource, and if not aligned accordingly will result in pockets of sub-optimal performance and invariably conflicting agendas, miscommunications and misaligned processes. Ultimately this situation amounts to an ineffective and unsustainable project. Put another way: a successful Blended Learning agenda begins to live and thrive via aligning the collective talents of a school's overall staff.

What does an aligned Blended Learning school look and feel like?

A school that is aligned is one where all staff members know what the school plans to achieve and why, and, further, where the staff understand, and thus accept and appreciate, that new organisational elements must come into play. That 'change' means they will have to personally change what they do to deal with it. In simple terms, the alignment phase is where everyone has 'bought into' the improvement agenda that has been planned. In this sense building alignment is not just about telling staff the agenda, rather it requires the seeding, collaborative building, nurturing and ongoing tending of a central proposition (the plan) to achieve full alignment effect. We can characterise the aligned school as having the following attributes:

- Staff can articulate clearly what the school is aiming to achieve and demonstrate an excitement about what it means for them, their work and the school more generally.
- Staff conversations transition from day-to-day 'gripes and snipes' to pieces that seek clarification, offer up suggestions and possibilities, and generally speak in positive terms about what could or should be.
- Staff begin to locate the 'proposition for change' in terms of themselves and in doing so, begin to formulate conceptions of how they will position themselves to be part of the agenda. Staff in effect come to terms with their existing 'self-interest' and thus see 'their new place' or 'their new fit'.
- As alignment consolidates in the school, the rhetoric of what 'can' and/or 'should be' gives way to tangible actioning of things that contribute to achieving the plan/agenda. This level of alignment is reflected as 'capability' and 'engagement' elements. But they too have to be built and sustained.

Building states of alignment

Schools are busy places and basically continue to operate irrespective of any desire for a new plan of action. Couple this with long-established mindsets and ways of 'doing business', staff turnover, one begins to appreciate just how hard it is to create alignment and then, of course, sustain it. It is a bit like trying to repair a leaking hose while the tap is turned fully on. It requires some clever thinking and a great deal of perseverance. All of which is time-consuming, but inherently about innovating and problem-solving, which further implicates the role of the leader.

One can understand the building of alignment as a function chiefly of the school's leadership. Effective leaders explain, motivate and enthuse their staff to consider new ideas and new propositions and, in doing so, they aim to galvanise staff to agreement and acceptance of a plan of action for change. There are a plethora of readings available on leadership, change management and the like. Each offers a perspective on the role of leaders, and thus we encourage further reading in these areas to fully appreciate what it means to be an effective school leader. Our view is that the Transformational Leader comes to represent the required leader attributes for sustainable change agendas, and that Blended Learning as a whole school project is an appropriate example of how this can be applied to the ACE model of school readiness. In this respect, the following steps are given to help clarify the procedural elements of leading for alignment:

The first step in building alignment as a leader is to personally reflect on the following questions and seek personal clarity and resolution to them:

1. Why are you seeking to implement Blended Learning? What is the compulsive agenda that motivates you to embark on such a plan?
2. Do you fully understand this compulsive agenda and appreciate where Blended Learning will take you (and the school)? What are your reference points (a data profile?) for such an agenda, and are they going to stand up to scrutiny?
3. What are your strengths as a leader? What are your weaknesses? Who around you will attend to the things that you are not good at? Who will constitute your leadership team?
4. What is the talent you have as a whole school? How will you unlock this talent and enable it to flourish?

The second step is to establish the conditions and arrangements for you as the leader to lead, and for 'designated others' to attend to the day-to-day, routine yet critical, elements of school management. In simple terms, decide who will be the 'Blended Learning Program Leader' and 'who' (and how) this person will attend to the day-to-day management considerations. This latter point is an important consideration because it's the day-to-day elements that will distract and cloud the performance of your Blended Learning plan. When the established system of things begins to fail, the blame falls on the new initiative, the focus of concern then moves and alignment comes undone. If you as the principal are not going to act as the Blended Learning Program Leader, then you need to ensure that you symbolically present yourself at key meetings to give the project authority and status, and to signal the project's overall importance. Having said that, Blended Learning is a whole-of-school, central pedagogic strategy, and our advice is that the principal should lead this strategy, given its importance.

The third step is to appreciate that you now have to 'sell' the agenda for change to your staff. While 'sell' is a crude term in this context, the reality is that alignment is an acceptance and an agreement by each staff member to go on 'a journey' with you. In effect, you have a proposition to present to them (note how it is not presented as a fait accompli by calling it 'the plan'). Your objective at the start is to get staff to see it as a 'viable proposition'. You will want their input to achieve it and hence 'the plan' is still to be finalised and confirmed. So, it's a proposition (at this stage), and you want them 'to buy into it' completely. There are many published examples of how to manage a change agenda in schools. Seek personal development in leadership if required and position yourself to hear regular feedback on your performance and the 'plan's' progress. Accept feedback as part and parcel of ultimate achievement. Don't process feedback personally. It is very important to realise everyone is now in the same boat and feedback is thus how engagement and capability are ultimately built. In summary, the following are important outcomes for this step:

- Achieve clarity on the intention and the outcome of change. Generate the 'compulsive agenda for change' (using existing data/trends to do this is a good strategy).
- Invest personal leadership time to achieve deep change in staff.
- Create avenues for staff to provide feedback on progress and opportunities for them to increase their understanding of what is planned and its implications.
- Identify and develop key (talented) teachers as 'change agents' as they will be a powerful resource in such agendas. This circumstance comes to represent 'other staff' taking the lead on 'sub projects', and in doing so, you begin to build the required **capabilities** and 'engagement' factors of readiness. This also paves the way for an associated mentoring program to further support the change agenda via increased collaboration, which we will discuss in more detail in Chapters 7 and 8.

With these points in mind, the following are appreciable indicators of leading for alignment:

- Alignment takes time to be achieved. Do not rush alignment.
- Staff will always process a change agenda in terms of what it will mean for them. If they cannot see a 'place in the sun' or they think they have no way of re-establishing themselves in the new agenda, you effectively place yourself in a battle of many (staff) wills. The trend in schools to date has been that staff will simply out-wait the

leader: and they invariably win when pushed. The leadership must consider the current 'theories of action' of the people who will experience the change. They must 'engage' the teachers in the change process when it is a significant or transformative change that. A purely rational argument may well result in teachers 'bypassing' the change necessary (Robinson, 2017).

- Staff are rational people when they are engaged in critical conversations about what might be and why, especially when such 'opportunities' are well thought out, logical and focused to achieving clarity. The more 'vocal staff' are best met in informal one-on-one situations. You need to invest time in these types of people because they invariably are able to garner an audience of discontent and you will often find once 'won over' they can become some of your strongest 'agents for change'. This reinforces the point about Transformational Leaders collaborating with staff on decision making.
- Staff asking questions, no matter how 'loaded' they may seem, needs to be accepted as an established way of staff seeking to know more about the agenda. Treat questions as an insight and an opportunity to plan your next steps in alignment.

If you've already started the change agenda and it's not working, start again. Start again by going back to the first step, as outlined in an earlier section. Constantly check on the school's current state of alignment. Engagement provides a good way of checking on current alignment, and we discuss this element in a later section. First, however, we need to explain how to extend from alignment to capability.

Building states of capability

Capability is at the heart of all 'Talent' and thus 'the ongoing concern' of the school leader. As we outlined in Chapter 2, Stephenson (1999) defined capability as 'an all-round human quality, an integration of knowledge, skills, personal qualities and understanding used appropriately and effectively – not just in familiar and highly focussed specialist contexts but in response to new and changing circumstances' (1999, p. 2). While Talent is the foundation for knowledge work, it is capability that enables Talent to rise to a particular challenge and to succeed in unknown territory. While professional learning is a common occurrence in schools and a requirement of most teacher registration authorities, many such programs focus narrowly on information updates or train only to specific competencies. In many ways, professional learning in schools today can be described as highly transactional learning and development activities, exampled by a preoccupation with behaviour management, understanding system priorities and curriculum design and development (Lynch et al., 2015). This type of learning is in contrast to capability building, where the focus is on harnessing knowledge and skills that enable performance in unknown or fast-evolving circumstances. We use Cochran and Ferrari's (2009) 7 Skills of Knowledge Workers (see Table 5.2) to represent the agenda for building the capabilities of teachers for establishing and maintaining Blended Learning in a school.

How are capabilities best developed?

Lynch (2012) and Lynch et al. (2018) cite research into a community of practice-type arrangement comprising a partnership with a university that has been used in teacher education regimes designed to increase the collective capacity of both individual teachers and the school as a whole. In this arrangement, the university provides Blended Learning

Table 5.2 The 7 Skills of Knowledge Workers

Thinking Skills – the ability to work with information effectively to solve problems, perform tasks, and design solutions	1. *Critical thinking* – drawing appropriate conclusions based on data 2. *Systems thinking* – seeing the big picture, including how parts of a system affect and influence one another 3. *Analysis skills* – breaking down information and technologies into pieces to understand and categorise individual parts; identifying the root cause of a problem 4. *Problem-solving* – identifying solutions to complex issues 5. *Creativity* – using imagination to combine existing knowledge into new knowledge to fulfill a need 6. *Design* – planning out the implementation of solutions to learning and performance problems
Communication – the ability to understand and share ideas effectively	1. Understanding and interpreting complex information from multiple sources through diverse media 2. Communicating effectively and appropriately in a variety of formats, including visual, verbal, and written, both face-to-face and in digital formats
Teamwork and Leadership – the ability to work with others to achieve a common goal	1. Collaborating and working effectively with others to achieve goals 2. Motivating others through appropriate strategies 3. Working effectively with team and individual strengths to maximise the effectiveness of the whole 4. Leading people to positive outcomes through persuasion, empathy, and effective management
Lifelong Learning and Self-Direction – continual self-improvement through the constant gathering of knowledge	1. Developing general skills like those in this list 2. Developing field-specific skills 3. Gaining formal education to increase ability to sustain success in the knowledge society
Technology Use – use of technology to accomplish goals or tasks	1. Selecting the right tools and technologies for tasks and problem solving 2. Using tools and technologies to appropriately complete tasks and solve problems. 3. Learning quickly how to use a new technology and be willing to adapt new technologies continuously
Ethics and Professionalism – An ethical person makes him or herself personally accountable for their own actions and work	1. Having good work habits and performing assigned work consistently 2. Interacting with others in a professional manner 3. Working effectively and professionally with people of diverse backgrounds
Personal Management – manage habits to maintain health (physical, mental, emotional, and spiritual)	This management should seek to maintain proper balance in all areas of life (family, work, personal, community). It includes the effective management and use of time to accomplish work and achieve goals.

(Reproduced from Cochran & Ferrari, 2009)

based expertise, specialist learning modules and associated supervision and access to accreditation as applicable. The teacher, as an individual within an assigned 'Teaching Team', has opportunity to provide input to the learning regime through a Blended Learning development project, so it meets their specific needs and the profile of their 'classroom cohort', while the school leader provides opportunities for innovating, creating and problem-solving by proving strategic vision, project organisation and sanctioning, access to resources and mentoring arrangements, as well as 'help as required'. This arrangement requires all three parties to embrace mutual concern for shared values, flexibility, openness, responsibility and continuous learning (Stephenson, 1999). We view these operational relationships in strategic terms and identify them as elements of what we refer to as the 'Blended Learning capability building model', presented here as Figure 5.1.

Note that in this capability building model, professional learning tasks are based on the pursuit of real-time, formative Blended Learning focused projects that are situated within the context of the teachers' work, and formulated collaboratively by the teacher and their fellow team members, the school leader and university (Stephenson, 1999). A coaching, mentoring and feedback regime is introduced to enable, support, generate and consolidate the required learnings. In this arrangement, there is an immediate benefit to the school and the teacher's own work through the completion of 'classroom' related tasks, while drawing upon circumstances where Cochran and Ferrari's (2009) 7 Skills of Knowledge Workers are honed and reflected upon.

We note that at one level this represents a 'community of practice' model, wherein each teacher generates their own agenda of 'problems' that are normally taken on and solved by associated colleagues and professionals working in collaborative teams. The knowledge gained from team solutions, however, is essential for dealing with the practical elements of introducing Blended Learning into the school and the respective teacher's classroom curriculum at the individual level of classroom teaching and learning.

Building states of engagement

Having outlined the processes of building alignment and capability, the leadership agenda now turns to engagement. Engagement as such is primarily a psychological state

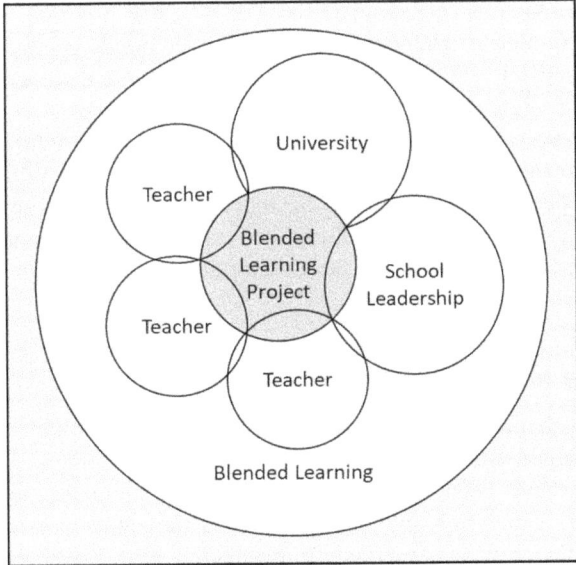

Figure 5.1 The Blended Learning capability building model (created by the authors)

which captures the extent to which staff are working towards the goals and aspirations of the school. It is chiefly indicative of a staff member's commitment and motivation, and it references capability and alignment states in order to gauge these.

Engagement can be understood as staff actually doing what they say they are doing. According to Schaufeli (2013), engagement 'is defined as a blend of three existing concepts: (1) job satisfaction; (2) commitment to the organisation; and (3) extra-role behaviour, that is, discretionary effort to go beyond the job description' (2013, p. 5). Or, as Harter et al. (2002, p. 269) argue, 'an individual's involvement and satisfaction with as well as enthusiasm for work'. With this latter point in mind, engagement can be understood as teachers having been successfully 'aligned' to a Blended Learning agenda and feeling as if they have or will be able to acquire the necessary capabilities. Engagement, therefore, is the litmus test of the success or otherwise of a Blended Learning change agenda.

The state of engagement has to do with the individual and as such is mediated by the values and beliefs personally held but, importantly, engagement also involves the quality of influences and experiences that each individual becomes party to. Returning to the capability building model outlined previously in this chapter, one can appreciate that engagement is engendered in such an arrangement primarily because of two inter-related occurrences. The first of these is peer pressure. Working in a team has the effect of building an interdependence within members and, by direct association, it sets up obligations to perform. There is, in effect, no free-riding in teams (Yahaya & Ebrahim, 2016). In relation to this, it is also important to note that coaching, mentoring, and feedback (CMF) reinforces these obligations as team norms, and more will be discussed about this in Chapter 7. The second occurrence, however, is self-interest. In a world of accountability, coupled with a professional logic that strives for success in their charges, teachers are sensitive to strategies that will enable them to achieve their professional goals. For others, the chance of advancement or acknowledgement of abilities is an attractive proposition. Either way, acknowledging and harnessing self-interest is an aspect of engagement (Azevedo & Akdere, 2011). The use of a CMF regime, as outlined in the capability building model for Blended Learning, further builds engagement as it captures peer pressure and self-interest and uses both to focus the development of capability and build and strengthen alignment.

In summary, engagement is about the individual teacher and how they view themselves in relation to the Blended Learning improvement agenda. While it is a state that needs to be developed and sustained in the individual, it is also an indication of how well the change agenda is being adopted and delivered, and as such measures of engagement can also be used as a proxy for determining at what level alignment and capability are operating in relation to this agenda.

A new leadership mindset for Talent Management

To this point in the chapter, leadership has been highlighted as a key and central ingredient in a whole-of-school Blended Learning initiative. Further, the attributes of the Transformational Leader have been delineated and a set of strategies outlined for building states of alignment, capability and engagement in the collective Talent of a school. Taken together, a blueprint has emerged from which a plan for change can be successfully initiated. Missing to this point, however, has been an identification of the mindset required of the school leader, in order to embrace the logic and potentials of Blended

Learning, Also important for this chapter is the need for this mindset to be able to understand what the inherent considerations that inform Knowledge Economy aligned change agendas such as Blended Learning come to represent.

Kaser and Halbert (2009) identify six distinct mindsets 'that characterise the way successful leaders operate and make sense of the world'. These leaders are

- Motivated by intense moral purpose
- Knowledgeable about current models of learning'
- Consistently inquiry orientated
- Able to build trusting relationships
- Evidence informed
- Able to move to wise action (2009, p. iii)

In effect, Kaser and Halbert argue that because the world has changed, and continues to change fundamentally, the school leader of today needs to be someone who is strategically preparing his/her school and its students for the future. Thinking about the logic of moving schools from being traditional to one that embraces Blended Learning, they make the point that the leadership mindset required is, therefore, one that is focused on leading away from managing a system of 'sorting' and toward 'leading for learning' (Kaser & Halbert, p. 13).

Table 5.3 outlines the difference between the two concepts.

The underpinning logic in all this, as Dweck (2006, p. 238, cited in Kaser & Halbert, p. 14) explains, is that 'mindset change is not about picking up a few pointers here and there. It's about seeing things in a new way'. The inherent change agenda, which has been outlined in this chapter, and the Blended Learning logic the book is presenting require of the leader a mindset that is conditioned and focused to see that a changed world requires a changed approach. Such solutions are not available to buy, nor are they neatly packaged in the next education fad. The Knowledge Economy is about ongoing exponential change, and with it, new knowledge to create and unpack and new opportunities to explore and harness.

Our central message in this chapter has been about the key role that the leader plays in schools and with it the need for a leadership mindset that is focused on change and identifying, supporting and enabling required Talent. In effect, this operates to build enduring states of alignment, capability and engagement through a Transformational Leadership approach and a learning-focused mindset. We will next explore these ideas in relation to the research concerning effective Blended Learning in Chapter 6.

Table 5.3 A leadership mindset that is focused away from sorting to learning

From sorting	To learning
A focus on instruction and teaching	A focus on deeper forms of learning
Summative assessment for grading and reporting	Formative assessment to provide feedback and learner self-regulation
Teaching in isolation	Teaching teams working as learning communities
External centralised pressure	Local internal commitment, capacity building and responsibility

(Adapted from Kaser & Halbert, 2009, p. 13)

Glossary

Alignment   The extent to which staff agree to and have a knowledge of (a) the goals and the associated strategies of the school as well as (b) the espoused values and expectations of stakeholders.

Capability   The general physical or mental power, ability or condition of being capable, being able or fit to make happen, with mind or senses, a state of being ready to do something. Capability is thus about preparedness for work into the future. Capability is a contrast to competence in that competence is personal traits, characteristics or skills in the present and thus relies on capability when it is called upon to be changed, redeveloped or upgraded.

Capabilities   An all-round human quality, an integration of knowledge, skills, personal qualities and understanding used appropriately and effectively – not just in familiar and highly focused specialist contexts but in response to new and changing circumstances.

Engagement   The extent to which staff are working towards the goals and aspirations of the school.

Transformational School Leadership   An approach to changing or reforming a school whereby the leader focuses on providing deeper levels of connection and higher levels of commitment, performance and morality for both themselves and their teachers.

References

AITSL (Australian Institute for Teaching and School Leadership) (2014). Global trends in professional learning and performance & development: Some implications and ideas for the Australian education system. Retrieved October 30, 2017, from www.aitsl.edu.au/docs/default-source/default-document-library/horizon_scan_report.pdf

Azevedo, R. E., & Akdere, M. (2011). Examining agency theory in training and development: Understanding self-interest behaviors in the organisation. *Human Resource Development Review, 10*(4), 399–416. https://doi.org/10.1177/1534484311412150

Burns, J. M. (1978). *Leadership*. Harper & Row.

Burns, J. M. (2003). *Leaders who changed the world*. Penguin Viking.

Cochran, G. R., & Ferrari, T. M. (2009). Preparing youth for the 21st century knowledge economy: Youth programs and workforce preparation. *Afterschool Matters, 8*, 11–25.

Dinham, S. (2016). *Leading learning and teaching*. ACER.

Dweck, C. S. (2006). *Mindset: The new psychology of success*. Ballantine Books.

Elmore, R. (2004). *Reform from the inside out*. Harvard University Press.

Hallinger, P., & Heck, R. H. (2010). Leadership for learning: Does collaborative leadership make a difference? *Educational Management Administration & Leadership, 38*(6).

Hargreaves, A., & Fullan, M. (2012). *Professional capital: Transforming teaching in every school*. Teachers College Press.

Harter, J., Schmidt, F., & Hayes, T. (2002). Business-unit-level relationship between employee satisfaction, employee engagement, and business outcomes: A meta-analysis. *Journal of Applied Psychology, 87*, 268–279.

Hattie, J. C. (2009). *Visible learning: A synthesis of over 800 meta-analyses relating to achievement*. Routledge, Taylor & Francis.

Kaser, L., & Halbert, J. (2009). *Leadership mindsets: Innovation and learning in the transformation of schools*. Taylor & Francis Group.

Leithwood, K. (2013). Leadership and student learning: What works and how. In C. Wise, P. Bradshaw, & M. Cartwright (Eds.), *Leading professional practice in education* (pp. 25–37). Sage Publications Ltd.

Leithwood, K., Harris, A., & Hopkins, D. (2008). Seven strong claims about successful school leadership. *School Leadership and Management, 28*(1), 27–42.

Leithwood, K., Tomlinson, D., & Genge, M. (1996). Transformational school leadership. In K. Leithwood, J. Chapman, D. Corson, P. Hallinger, & A. Hart (Eds.), *International handbook of educational leadership and administration* (pp. 463–471). Kluwer International Handbooks of Education, vol. 1. Springer.

Louis, K. S., Leithwood, K., Wahlstrom, K., & Anderson, S. (2010). *Investigating the links to improved student learning: Final report of research findings*. The Wallace Foundation.

Lynch, D. (2012). *Preparing teachers in times of change: Teaching school, standards, new content and evidence*. Primrose Hall.

Lynch, D., Fradale, P., Sell, K., Turner, D., & Yeigh, T. (2018). Towards an effective model for whole of school blended learning: A conceptual paper. *International Journal of Innovation, Creativity and Change, 4*(1), 29–51.

Lynch, D., Madden, J., & Doe, T. (2015). *Creating the outstanding school*. Oxford Global Press.

Lynch, D., Smith, R., Yeigh, T., & Provost, S. (2019). A study into "organisational readiness" and its impacts on school improvement. *International Journal of Educational Management, 33*(2), 393–408.

Macklin, P., & Zbar, V. (2017). *Driving school improvement: A practical guide*. ACER Press.

Marzano, R., Waters, T., & McNulty, B. (2005). *School leadership that works*. Association for Supervision and Curriculum Development.

Moir, S., Hattie, J., & Jansen, C. (2014). Teacher perspectives of 'effective' leadership in schools. *Australian Educational Leader, 36*(4), 36–40.

North, K., & Gueldenberg, S. (2011). *Effective knowledge work: Answers to the management challenge of the 21st century*. Emerald Group Publishing.

Robinson, V. (2017). *Reduce change to increase improvement*. Corwin.

Robinson, V. M. J., Lloyd, C. A., & Rowe, K. J. (2008). The impact of leadership on student outcomes: An analysis of the differential effects of leadership types. *Educational Administration Quarterly, 44*(5), 635–674.

Robinson, V., Hohepa, M., & Lloyd, C. (2009). *School leadership and student outcomes: Identifying what works and why: Best evidence synthesis iteration*. Ministry of Education.

Schaufeli, W. B. (2013). What is engagement? In C. Truss, K. Alfes, R. Delbridge, A. Shantz, & E. Soane (Eds.), *Employee engagement in theory and practice* (pp. 1–37). Routledge.

Schiemann, W. A. (2012). *The ACE advantage: How smart companies unleash talent for optimal performance*. Society for Human Resource Management.

Schiemann, W. A. (2014). From talent management to talent optimisation. *Journal of World Business, 49*(2), 281–283.

Stephenson, J. (1999). Corporate capability: Implications for the style and direction of work-based learning. Retrieved June 1, 2020, from http://hdl.voced.edu.au/10707/120693

Stephenson, J. (1999). *Corporate capability: Implications for the style and direction of work-based learning*. RCVET Working Paper, 99–14. Research Centre for Vocational Education and Training. http://pandora.nla.gov.au/pan/22468/20021106/www.uts.edu.au/fac/edu/rcvet/working%20papers/9914Stephenson.pdf

Thomas, L., Tuytens, M., Devos, G., Kelchtermans, G., & Vanderlinde, R. (2020). Transformational school leadership as a key factor for teachers' job attitudes during their first year in the profession. *Educational Management Administration & Leadership, 48*(1), 106–132.

Wang, X., & Howell, J. M. (2010). Exploring the dual-level effects of transformational leadership on followers. *Journal of Applied Psychology, 56*(3), 1–11. https://doi.org/10.1037/a0020754

Yahaya, R., & Ebrahim, F. (2016). Leadership styles and organisational commitment: Literature review. *The Journal of Management Development, 35*(2), 190–216.

6 What does the research evidence say about Blended Learning?

Relevant Australian Professional Standards for Teachers: 1.2; 1.5; 2.6; 3.4; 3.6; 4.5; 5.1; 5.4; 6.2; 6.3; 6.4; 7.4

Chapter synopsis

This chapter investigates the current state of research evidence regarding Blended Learning in general, whether it produces desirable student learning outcomes, and what the research literature says regarding the efficacy of various models of Blended Learning. Specifically, this chapter will:

- establish the prevalent parameters guiding current Blended Learning research;
- outline the most commonly employed models of BL and their associated outcomes in relation to these specific parameters;
- investigate the factors most associated with both successful and unsuccessful implementation of Blended Learning in the field;
- describe implications for leadership that arise from the evidence as found in the literature.

Introduction

The preceding chapters have detailed the role education plays in a Knowledge Economy, made a case for educational reform, and investigated the theory of disruption as it has been manifested in education. Further, this book has summarised the current research regarding effective schools and the role of school leaders in creating them through formal change processes. In short, to this point the book has established the context and circumstances for changing pedagogy, as well as the ability of Blended Learning to support this change in the form of a distinct pedagogical approach aimed at harnessing the disruptive power of technology in positive ways. As noted in Chapter 3, Blended Learning occurs along a continuum of ICT-driven pedagogical support and provides a number of specific models designed to help teachers implement this support in effective ways. In this chapter we expand on the applicability of Blended Learning by examining other pedagogical models available for consideration within the Knowledge Economy that exist in addition to Blended Learning. In relation to this chapter, the question facing governments, school leaders and citizens is whether there is sufficient evidence to support the contention that Blended Learning can deliver the desired gains in student outcomes across the range of student profiles found in education, particularly public education. In this chapter we look at the research evidence supporting and questioning Blended Learning as a viable solution to the challenges facing educators and leaders in their quest to improve student outcomes.

Parameters informing Blended Learning research

Blended Learning is a fairly recent development in education; at the time of this writing there are still competing definitions in the published literature for what Blended Learning comprises, although groups such as the Christensen Institute's Blended Learning Universe organisation have worked towards reaching consensus. In this respect Blended Learning can be defined as 'any formal education program in which a student learns at least in part through online learning, with some element of student control over time, place, path and/or pace' (Horn et al., 2015, p. 34). In the main, research into Blended Learning falls within a fairly consistent set of parameters, including learning modes and models, required resources, roles and responsibilities and student learning outcomes. In Chapter 3 we noted that these parameters occur within a continuum, something we will look at more closely in Chapters 7 and 8. In this chapter, however, we want to more simply establish the nature and scope of the evidence supporting Blended Learning as an efficacious form of technology-driven pedagogy.

Defining Blended Learning

In Chapter 3 we outlined a variety of Blended Learning models and in doing so located the potentials that Blended Learning has come to represent in terms of disrupting traditional approaches to schooling. Previous chapters have made clear the urgent need to transform schools from their industrial revolution histrionics into an education system compatible with the imperatives of the Knowledge Economy. The challenge is thus how to achieve such a goal. Our central argument is that Blended Learning comes to represent an inherent strategy for this, due to its natural ability to respond to Knowledge Economy imperatives, as well as to the impact of modern changes relating to COVID-19 and technology in general. When it comes to defining Blended Learning, however, we begin by noting that computers in the classroom can simply facilitate substituting digital forms for traditional practice: word processing, researching online when writing papers, and drilling skills (Christensen et al., 2011; Ossiannilsson, 2018). Technology, then, at least in its current common range of implementations, has not yet demonstrated sufficient efficacy in enabling change in teacher practice. This is one reason why research attempting to understand the effective use of technology for teaching and learning has centred on a concept called 'Blended Learning' (Willis et al., 2018), and even though competing definitions of Blended Learning have proliferated, there has more recently been a trend to formalise the definition of Blended Learning as a discrete pedagogical approach, hence the need for further research such as represented in this book.

Michael Horn and Heather Staker (2015), following on their earlier initial collaboration with Clayton Christensen of Harvard University, define Blended Learning as 'any formal education program in which a student learns at least in part through online learning, with some element of student control over time, place, path and/or pace' (p. 34). They stress that the formal nature of the learning distinguishes it from informal learning or gaming, for example, that a student might do individually. From this perspective the perceived need for increased skills and knowledge, and the realisation that integrating digital technologies into classrooms and educational programs can improve both the quality and success of education, has been broadly held. The different modalities along the continuum of Blended Learning are formally connected one to another for an individual or class, creating a cohesive whole, rather than simply grouping a disjointed series of learning experiences together, and that the selected modes are deliberately chosen (Staker & Horn, 2012). Other researchers define Blended Learning as a range of ICT and associated pedagogies that essentially supplement but do not replace physical classroom learning (Means et al., 2013; Singh, 2003; Welker & Berardino, 2005).

To some, the term 'Blended Learning' can be used interchangeably with 'differentiated instruction' or even personalised learning (Ossiannilsson, 2017). In the realm of Blended Learning this is being achieved through a heightened focus on student-centred learning. We note that student-centred learning does not necessarily rely on a blended approach or technology to be present or even successful, yet blended courses by their very nature shift responsibility to the learner, as through technology much of the learning takes place independently, in small student groups, and outside of the traditional classroom (Caulfield, 2012; Horn & Staker, 2015).

A context for the introduction of Blended Learning

A number of common schemata also attempt to describe bringing classroom technology integration such as Blended Learning into practice. Although these schemata are widely used, however, there remains inconsistent interpretation of such models (Hamilton et al., 2016). For the purpose of this discussion, consider the following sample schema, the **SAMR model**. SAMR is an acronym for 'substitution, augmentation, modification, and redefinition', an ascending hierarchy of how analogue tasks are ported to a digital environment. Whilst the SAMR model can be useful as an example, it is by no means without aspects that can be improved, such as an emphasis on product rather than process (Cardullo et al., 2018; Hamilton et al., 2016). For example, if a traditional analogue task was to write an essay using pen and paper, 'substitution' would involve using a word processor, 'augmentation' could include embedding links or perhaps a QR code to external sites, 'modification' would extend this to directly embedding video clips into a blog post, while 'redefinition' might go as far as doing away with the essay format entirely and instead asking the students to create and maintain a series of vlogs to convey the same information.

Using the SAMR model as a reference, it would appear that much of what transpires in schools is firmly still in the 'substitution' phase (Romrell et al., 2014; Singh, 2003). This is due to many factors such as school culture (Erdogan, 2011), teacher ICT competence and beliefs (Chia-Pin et al., 2014; Cummings, 2008; Inan & Lowther, 2010), varying levels of ICT infrastructure (Chun et al., 2015), and the support schools provide teachers in changing their practice (Li & Ma, 2010). Simply having access to ICT, whether in the form of a lab or even as a 1:1 program where every child has a device, is no guarantee of increased student outcomes (Carrasco & Torrecilla, 2012). Because they do not supplant traditional teaching, only supplement and reinforce traditional pedagogy, computers can simply add cost and complexity while failing to change practice (Christensen et al., 2011; Horn et al., 2015). Lectures, quizzes/tests, and writing assignments in which students acquire content knowledge and then reiterate it to demonstrate understanding remain common in many forms of online learning (Christensen et al., 2011; Szpunar et al., 2014). Some teachers that have attempted to meaningfully integrate ICT have reported that it requires more work on their part and can result in a diminished classroom dynamic. Students, on the other hand, have reported that such approaches are more flexible, independent and convenient, yet also report experiencing confusion, diminished social aspects, and increased required effort (Welker & Berardino, 2005). Given the relatively new frontier this embodies, particularly in primary and secondary schools, this mixed reporting is perhaps to be expected. It also invites further investigation, aimed at teasing-out important characteristics of effective Blended Learning and further delineating how this particular pedagogy can be implemented effectively.

The Blended Learning continuum

Blended Learning models range from those that sustain or supplement traditional face-to-face teaching and learning to those that radically transform teaching approaches. At the conservative end of the spectrum there are supplementary models comprising a nearly exclusively face-to-face pedagogy, with ICT tools leveraged to improve targeted areas. An example of this would be a teacher directing a student to a website or game-like app that allows the student to practise a specific skill such as multiplication or division. The selection of the site or app may be deliberate on the teacher's part, but it is not necessarily systematic or consistent. Indeed, the lack of systematic integration is an area of study for researchers attempting to understand how tech-use decisions are made by teachers (Lawless & Pellegrino, 2007). These decisions can be influenced by peer-recommendation, attendance at a conference, or by chance discovery, behaviour that falls within the parameters described by **Concerns-based adoption models** (Straub, 2009), which seek to identify and address the stages of concerns that arise as individuals and groups engage in change or development.

As suggested in Chapter 3, Blended Learning can occur along a continuum, indicating that a spectrum of Blended Learning practices is available. At the transformative end of the spectrum there are models in which online systems replace all of a brick-and-mortar schooling experience, with no physical face-to-face engagements. Staker and Horn (2012) created a simple diagram to illustrate this, inviting other researchers to add or modify, as they themselves did in subsequent iterations (Horn et al., 2015). Figure 6.1 is our expanded version of Staker and Horn's original, delineating a range of models along this **Blended Learning continuum**. Note, however, that neither 'supplemental' nor 'no physical presence' are included in our continuum (as discussed by Staker & Horn, 2015), as both fall outside the scope of Blended Learning, belonging instead to traditional face-to-face or full online learning, respectively.

Blended Learning models

Within this continuum there are a number of specific Blended Learning models we need to examine in some detail. As mentioned in Chapter 3, a fundamental Blended Learning model, the 'rotation model', provides the essential elements for several of sub-models of Blended Learning, including station rotation and lab rotation, with each of these based on the fundamental process of a flipped classroom. We noted the procedural differences between these sub-models in Chapter 3, but here point out that, progressing through these differences in order, discretion over the schedule/timing of the rotation moves progressively from the teacher and towards the student(s) across these sub-models. The first sub-model included in this group is called the 'station rotation model', the second sub-model within the rotation model is the 'lab rotation model', and here we also mention a final example in the rotation category known as the 'individual rotation model'. The individual rotation model features the highest level of personalisation of the models

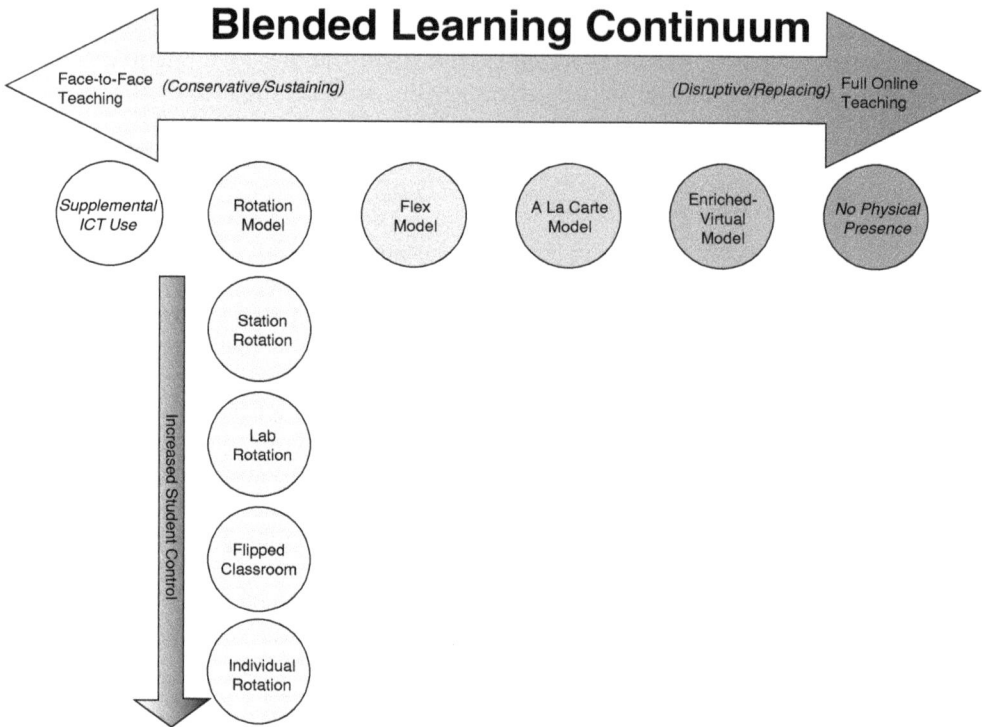

Figure 6.1 The Blended Learning continuum (adapted from Horn, Staker, & Christensen, 2015).

included here, because in this model not all students will rotate through all of the stations or learning modes, instead participating in those that best meet their needs, whether self, algorithm or teacher-determined (Powell et al., 2015; Staker & Horn, 2012). There have been many studies conducted over the time during which the individual rotation model has proliferated, which consistently show increased learning for students using this model. Support for this model is also indicated by a body of research suggesting the individual rotation model has the potential, with refinement, to be an effective addition to a school or teacher looking to implement Blended Learning (Chung Kwan & Khe Foon, 2017; Kim et al., 2014; Lo & Hew, 2017; Schultz et al., 2014; Xuesong et al., 2017; Yanjie & Manu, 2017; Yanjie et al., 2017).

It is also important to note that the underlying principle of a **flipped classroom** can itself be viewed as an additional sub-model within the rotational set, acting as a sort of 'macro-rotation' model that oscillates broadly between the learner's home and school. The use of a flipped classroom has shown promise as an effective approach to Blended Learning, and may be the most familiar model to many educators (Chung Kwan & Khe Foon, 2017; Steele et al., 2014; Yanjie et al., 2017). As noted in Chapter 3, the notion of a flipped classroom provides an important, basic premise for Blended Learning in general, in that within a Blended Learning environment in-class time spent with the teacher can be better used to clarify, extend, and apply new knowledge to problems, instead of using class time to acquire basic knowledge or information through lecture, videos, or reading. Extending our discussion of Blended Learning models from Chapter 3, we now examine the flex model in more detail, as well as highlight two additional models in terms of their potential for increased personalisation of learning.

The flex model

The next model to consider is the 'flex model'. In addition to the teacher of record, other adults on-site are available to provide face-to-face interaction as needed when using this model. This allows, for example, for a limited number of specialists to support a large number of students, scaffolding for learning that include aspects of apprenticeship, mentoring and entrepreneurial preparation. The flex model can be applied in school contexts where, for example, there are not enough teachers to offer certain courses, or perhaps not enough student interest to offer a full course. Instead, the school can allow time for students to pursue individual interests that fall within certain credit categories, with a limited number of teachers on hand to facilitate the class, giving face-to-face support to the students on an as-needed basis. This requires teachers to view themselves not as content teachers, but as teachers of how to learn, how to problem solve, how to find information. It is possible that teachers with a constructivist philosophy would find engaging in the flex model easier than a traditional content-focused instructor (Crawford & Jenkins, 2018; Horn et al., 2015). There would also be a corresponding responsibility on the student to take learning into their own hands, which would require a range of skills such as strong time budgeting, research, and project management. The basic structure of this model was illustrated visually in Chapter 3 (Figure 3.6).

The a la carte model

The next Blended Learning model is the 'a la carte model', once known as the 'self-blend model'. Within the Blended Learning continuum, this model operates more towards the online areas of the continuum, with courses not taken face-to-face being taught primarily online, and the teacher also conducting instruction online. This marks an important distinction from the flex model (Horn et al., 2015), and we can see a current example of this in the educational offerings provided by the company Pamoja, who administer international courses that allow schools (for a fee) to expand their offerings globally, with fully developed courses staffed by teachers around the world (Oliver et al., 2014). Importantly, students may complete the courses at home or on campus, depending on how the school wishes to structure its iteration of this model, and hence the 'a la carte' designation. There are two challenges that are easy to spot in this model however. First, the teacher-of-record is not an employee of the school. There are contractual obligations, of course, when partnerships are established, but school administration does not have the same day-to-day input possible with traditional faculty; should issues arise, intermediary participants will come into play in a way not seen with the usual school model. The second challenge is that the on-site teacher and online teacher-of-record need to communicate and cooperate with one another in a timely, consistent, efficient manner, and this can provide challenges in its own right.

Enriched virtual model

The last of the models included within the Blended Learning paradigm that we will discuss is the 'enriched virtual model'. In this model the majority of learning occurs remotely, online, and with only supplemental face-to-face support offered at a brick-and-mortar campus. Most the examples of this model arose from companies that started as strictly online companies but later saw the need for some additional face-to-face support (Staker & Horn, 2012). Note, however, that students in this model are not choosing online or face-to-face engagement on a course-by-course basis. Rather, it is a whole-school experience, differentiating this model from the a la carte model. This model is also different to a straightforward flipped classroom approach, because the students do not often attend face-to-face sessions and in fact may not attend the brick-and-mortar campus every day of the week (Horn et al., 2015).

The centrality of personalised learning

As would be expected in such a model, the student bears substantial responsibility for managing their learning, but it is incumbent upon the instructors to maintain an immediacy of interaction with their students, in order to personalise the learning and take responsibility for it (Woods & Baker, 2004). Indeed, this model could be argued to offer the highest degree of personalisation, and we note that, at its core, personalised learning is one of the major outcomes that Blended Learning seeks to achieve (Childress & Benson, 2014; Christensen et al., 2011; Horn et al., 2015; Khribi et al., 2009; Liang et al., 2006; Marache-Francisco & Brangier, 2013; Nedungadi & Raman, 2012; Patrick et al., 2013; Powell et al., 2015; Shian-Shyong et al., 2008; Song et al., 2012; Spector et al., 2016; Tzu-Chi et al., 2013; Xuesong et al., 2017).

In the context of Blended Learning, personalisation is achieved through variation of the path, place, and pace of learning, with as much agency given to the students as possible. Tables 6.1 and 6.2 summarise the commonalities and differences, respectively, between the models we have reviewed here, using path, place and pace of learning as differentiators between them.

Table 6.1 Summary of Blended Learning model commonalities

	Path	*Place*	*Pace*
Common aspects across all models	Leverage ICT to better determine student strengths and areas of growth, extend teacher impact, inform actions	Both in-person and online engagements employed	Both synchronous and asynchronous engagements employed
	Deliberate selection of ICT matched to need(s) of students or small groups of students	Content acquisition can occur outside classroom; application can occur in class	
	Blending individual and collaborative learning modes	Locates learning in genuine contexts with authentic audiences	
	Gradual release of locus of responsibility to students		
	Publishing of student work, seeking authentic audience		
	Teacher acts as facilitator, coach, and resource specialist		

(Created by the authors)

Table 6.2 Blended Learning model comparison

Model	Path	Place	Pace
Rotation: Station, Lab, Flipped Classroom, Individual Rotation	Teacher retains control, but multiple paths presented to students Blended portion of learning increases as you move from station to individual rotation	Teacher retains control Offers benefits to schools on a budget or working within strict State guidelines	Teacher retains control Typically, a fixed schedule
Flex	Allows students to seek paths not possible in brick-and-mortar location Fundamental shift away from onsite teacher as provider of content, to learning facilitator	Teacher-of-record site-based rather than online Small team of on-site teachers can support students	Flexible schedule Student has more control
A La Carte	Specific courses taken online Expands student offerings at schools with limited faculty, or for very specific student needs	Teacher of record is online Locus of responsibility shifts away from brick-and-mortar location Communication/ cooperation between on-site and online teachers critical	Flexible schedule but online offerings might have fixed aspects, depending upon provider
Enriched Virtual	Often developed by purveyors of online courses to meet defined needs High degree of personalisation possible Whole-school, rather than course-by-course basis	Closest model to fully online learning Supplemental face-to-face support	Flexibility depends upon provider Student can have high degree of control

(Created by the authors)

Impact of Blended Learning on student outcomes

Given the relatively recent development of Blended Learning, it is not surprising that there are few meta-analyses involving hundreds of studies to assist our 'big picture' understanding of this pedagogy. Much original research regarding the impact of Blended Learning on student outcomes is still in process, and these are often case studies or highly context-specific studies. That said, each of the models described in the previous section does have research that supports their implementation to some degree or other. For example, the rotation model has demonstrated improvements resulting from increased agency and control (Maxwell & White, 2017) and student engagement (Truitt & Ku, 2018). It has also been useful when used for topics such as sexual health in which student confidentiality or privacy play an important role (Coyle et al., 2019), by allowing students to explore potentially fraught topics in relative security. The same sources indicate, however, that technical issues and student self-management can be an issue for this model. Similarly, flipped classrooms have demonstrated a small but statistically significant improvement in student achievement outcomes, yet, as with the rotation model, the level of student self-regulation is critical (Cheng et al., 2019). Research on the flex model is mostly found in tertiary contexts, but the model appears to improve attitude towards learning, with no negative impact on performance, compared to traditional methods (Yudt & Columba, 2017). The flex model derives its beneficial impact by allowing the teacher to work with individual students to improve targeted areas since the teacher is no longer solely responsible for content delivery (Stecyk, 2018), something that we think should port into a K-12 context. In secondary schools, a la carte models have shown promise in assisting at-risk students by allowing a flexible approach to credit recovery, such as the a la carte model employed by the Spokane, WA, public school system (Powell et al., 2015). The enriched virtual model has also seen success as a way to reach at-risk students, by providing them the support they need to transition to fully online models (Powell et al., 2015).

All of these studies suggest that Blended Learning in its various forms can and does have a positive impact on student learning. We note, however, the caveat that there needs to be a match between the model of Blended Learning employed and the teaching and learning context within which it is implemented. This represents an important aspect of applied Blended Learning that we will explore more thoroughly in Chapters 7 and 8. For now, however, we simply call your attention to the evidence suggesting that Blended Learning is an efficacious pedagogy for education. We will continue here by examining some of the factors that appear to contribute to the success of Blended Learning as a technology-driven approach for modern teaching and learning.

Factors contributing to success or failure when implementing Blended Learning

As noted prior in this book, because of the modern focus on instructional approaches such as student-centred learning and the growth of a knowledge-driven economy and society, a series of core, 'twenty-first century' skills have been identified by organisations such as the European Union and Organisation for Economic Co-operation and Development, for development in both K-12 and higher education, in order to prepare young people for the ever-changing future they face (OECD, 2016; Whitty, 2006). These skills are considered 'portable' in that they involve broadly applicable knowledge and application, such as effective communication, collaboration and teamwork, critical thinking and problem-solving, as well as creativity. Importantly, these skills have also been identified as essential and complementary to basic educational competencies such as literacy and numeracy (ACER, 2019; Jerald, 2009; Kivunja, 2015), requiring a shift to pedagogies that are able to support such skills, as well as promoting teacher motivation to do so.

Teacher motivation is sometimes overlooked regarding initiatives to shift pedagogy, yet it is critical to take this into account, as it is teachers who ultimately decide what they actually do in their classrooms. In particular, the difference between intrinsic and extrinsic teacher motivation significantly influences whether observable change is temporary or sustained (Schechter et al., 2017). In addition, teacher skills involving ICT, robust and updated critical infrastructures, and clear leadership goals are three other areas that have been shown to support or detract from successful outcomes in Blended Learning (Moskal et al., 2013). These areas need to be carefully analysed in order to make data-informed decisions (Kazakoff et al., 2018), especially as school leaders attempt to influence teacher practice. Lastly, school culture (Min, 2019) must also be addressed for successful, sustained moves to a Blended Learning environment. This includes targeting more individualised professional learning for teachers, as well as seeking to support the social interchanges that unite and support teaching culture. Of importance is that school leaders are responsible for managing and leading the changes that need to accompany the implementation of these factors, a necessary component of effective Blended Learning to which we now turn.

Implications for school leaders

The preceding section summarises important factors to consider when undertaking initiatives aimed at harnessing Blended Learning to improve student outcomes. In this regard, and much as teachers can be more successful when they understand each child in their classrooms, an important 'take-away' for school leaders is that it is necessary to understand and leverage the varied motivations in their faculty bodies and provide ongoing, targeted professional learning to address areas for pedagogical improvement in the area of Blended Learning, rather than simply using 'off the shelf' solutions. To do this effectively, it will be additionally important for leaders to maintain clear goals and measurable expectations, and to use regular data collection and analysis regimes to provide actionable, timely feedback to teachers, while also providing transparent accountability to parents and community stakeholders. Of importance is that a common denominator for many of these leadership areas involves the social interactions that bind and support teaching culture in schools, often referred to as **social capital**. Chapter 5 explored many of the key roles played by school leaders in relation to educational change, but here we want to particularly examine the capacity of social capital as a critical factor in the type of leadership for change that needs to accompany the implementation of Blended Learning in schools and other education settings.

School culture and social capital

As acknowledged variously in this book, there exists an imperative for modern education to adopt knowledge and skill-sets appropriate to the integration of ICTs and other forms of a technology-driven pedagogy in schools. However, it can be argued that due to the scope and pace of adoption, one form of disruption that can occur in relation to the implementation of Blended Learning is that it can have a negative impact on the social reality of teachers and schools (Brabazon, 2017; Carnevale & Desrochers, 2002). Bridging this gap – between the need for accelerated development and change, and the social and cultural shift needed to make this change successful – may be more important than ever in the current COVID-19 pandemic. Thus another key challenge that school leaders need to address when implementing Blended Learning will be understanding how to lead for change in ways that accommodate the social interactions that teachers depend on for personal and professional success. Given this, school leaders need to investigate ways to improve the social capital of teachers, in order to equip them with the understanding and resources needed to mediate and facilitate the competencies, knowledge and skills required to prepare students to live and work in the ever-evolving Knowledge Economy (WorldBank, 2003).

Social capital (aka professional capital) became prominent via the work of Pierre Bourdieu, who focused on social capital primarily in terms of social networks and sociability (Bourdieu, 1986; cf. Schaefer-McDaniel, 2014). The idea of social capital is that the quantity and quality of interactions and social relationships that take place within and between groups can be ascertained and have an effect on participation and commitment, with high social capital seemingly essential for the development of core skills and successful instructional approaches (Hargreaves & Fullan, 2012). We view these sorts of skills and instructional approaches as including those needed to teach for student-centred learning within a Blended

Learning environment. Thus, in order to accelerate the development and preparation of young people for a future in which they need to become ever more self-reliant, it is important that schools and school leaders focus on mediating and facilitating the growth of teachers' social capital. This is perceived as necessary to support the development of positive teacher identity in service of preparing students to succeed in the gig economy, which seems to represent the shape of things to come for the modern learner.

James Coleman extended the concept of social capital by asserting that it assists individuals to develop expectations and obligations of trust and reciprocity, as well as establish norms and values in relationships. Of importance to the current discussion is that although Bourdieu had suggested that social capital should also be related to schools, Coleman specifically applied the concept of social capital as an essential component of successful teaching and learning in schools (Coleman, 1990). In this respect Coleman proposed six essential bi-directional, interpersonal relationships essential for building healthy social capital, relationships among students, teachers and parents, as well as between teachers and students, teachers and parents, and students and parents (Coleman, 1990; Schaefer-McDaniel, 2014). In schools these relationships have traditionally been built and maintained in face-to-face environments. However, with the increased use of technology in education this has changed significantly, and these relationships are now often being developed, maintained and reinforced across online, blended and face-to-face settings, emphasising the need for school leaders to understand social capital and support its positive application within technology-driven pedagogies such as Blended Learning.

From this perspective we have begun to see research into social capital in relation to digital and online environments. For example, in their study on the effectiveness of social capital for online learning Lu et al. (2013) investigated which social networking mechanisms facilitate the emergence of social capital and how these mechanisms achieve this. They found that although no single mechanism could be identified, there was nonetheless a 'strong positive effect of social capital on student satisfaction toward online learning and on virtual group learning outcomes' (p. 520) Similar findings have been provided by Steinfield et al. (2007), who investigated the benefits of Facebook on college students' social capital and concluded that positive social capital can be established within online environments. However, as with Blended Learning itself, it is early days yet with respect to conclusive and clearly agreed understandings concerning social capital within digital and online pedagogical environments, and thus this remains an area for ongoing research in relation to Blended Learning. What we do know is that within online environments teachers' professional capital needs to be developed, especially as Blended Learning has seen the convergence of traditional face-to-face and online teaching and learning. In this regard many schools are providing professional learning and development aimed at integrating technologies, adapting pedagogy and implementing online learning programmes in ways that make use of collaboration as the basis for rich teacher and learner interactions (Ayala, 2009). We will now examine the sorts of collaborations, as well as other activities, that school leaders need to be aware of in relation to leading for positive change that aims to support Blended Learning as a modern pedagogical approach.

Leading to support positive social capital

As noted in prior research by the authors, the role of the principal is pivotal when it comes to leading for positive change in schools (Yeigh et al., 2019), and especially when it comes to ensuring that a school is 'ready' to undertake change for improvement at a strategic level

(Yeigh & Lynch, 2018). The importance of strategic leadership has been highlighted by the impact of the COVID-19 pandemic, which has forced schools to move to an almost exclusively online teaching and learning environment (NSW Government, 2020; Schwartz, 2020). Of significance is that this move has been necessarily reactive, and because of this has resulted in multiple issues around online teaching and learning, including learning engagement, resourcing, assessment and teacher capabilities (NSW Government, 2020). It has also raised particular questions around the quality of online learning experiences (Newcomb, 2020) and the preparedness of teachers to deliver online learning (Thomson, 2020), especially in light of the broad variations in teacher ability, resourcing and access to online networks that are apparent both across and within education systems (Schwartz, 2020; Waite, 2020). Important areas of variability include instructional requirements, learner attendance, grading flexibility, learning continuity (ensuring that students are able to move from one grade or year-level to the next) and how to provide for students with special or additional needs (NSW Government, 2020; Schwartz, 2020).

These areas require teachers to work collaboratively and to depend on one another for professional support. There is, therefore, an intuitive logic to the idea that building social capital remains imperative for principals and other school leaders who wish to ensure that the online instruction provided by their school under COVID-19 conditions is firmly embraced by teachers. Indeed, as schools seek to re-open upon subsidence of the COVID-19 pandemic, the use of Blended Leaning will remain (Arnou, 2020), and therefore all these areas of variability will require school leaders to lead for change in ways that connect and empower teachers to work together in the most effective manner possible, that is, in ways that promote positive social capital in support of blended and online instruction. With this in mind, we will end this chapter by identifying some of the areas by which principals can effect positive social capital within an online teaching and learning environment.

Areas for building social capital for blended or online learning

Because social capital for teachers is largely supported through interpersonal relationships that take place between teachers, between teachers and school leaders, between teachers and their students, and between teachers and parents, strategies for encouraging this within a blended or online learning environment require school leaders to plan for how interactions can be arranged between teachers and these other stakeholders via technology. For school leaders this can encompass knowing how to manage a myriad of specific areas, activities and processes, including understanding which technologies to use for connecting teachers with their students and the students' parents (Arnett, 2020), how to approach student grading from a 'do no harm' perspective (Schwartz, 2020), how to support parents to structure time and resources for remote student learning (Arnou, 2020), how to motivate teacher collaboration and problem-solving (Ibrahim & Nat, 2019), how to incorporate evidence-based practices for teachers (Yeigh et al., 2020), how to organise teachers for synchronous and asynchronous online teaching (Allen & Seaman, 2014), and how to support teacher and learner resilience (Waite, 2020). In every case the aim is to support a teaching and learning environment that supports the required learning processes, wherever these may occur along the Blended Learning continuum, in order to achieve the desired learning results for students.

All of these areas are important, and many will be covered in greater detail in Chapters 7 and 8. However, connecting technologies and building teacher and student resilience for the long-haul are areas that seem to stand out as immediate concerns in the current COVID-19 situation. In this regard we note that principals and other school leaders can set up what Arnett (2020) calls 'feedback loops' between schools and families, in order to ensure that teachers, students and parents are working in collaboration to provide quality online learning. One program that can be helpful for designing asynchronous interactions for this is Flipgrid, which allows teachers to introduce learning topics and then follow these through with the learner via discussion threads.

Resourcing will also be important, and ensuring that teachers are able to use a variety of digital resources to support both synchronous and asynchronous learning is essential. We have listed a number of online resources that you may wish to check out at the end of this chapter. School leaders who are aware of these sorts of resources will be better equipped to assist and manage online learning in their schools, and in ways that help teachers and students to connect and interact with one another.

Building resilience is a critical area for school leaders to be aware of when planning for effective online learning. It is also an area that tends to affect all aspects of online learning, especially in relation to the COVID-19-related school shutdowns and partial re-openings that have compelled schools to move into online modes of teaching and learning. In relation to this, school leaders might explore the American-based Digital Learning Collaborative (www. digitallearningcollab.com/), which has created a variety of resources for creating digital teaching and learning programs designed to foster resilience via strategic planning and organisation. Waite (2020) also points out that we can also look the elements school systems have used to respond to prior emergencies as examples of how to build resilience during times of crisis as a conceptual way to think about how to develop resilience. She suggests that important elements of planning for resilience conceptually include identifying and mitigating risks, avoiding redundant thinking (i.e., thinking that aims to simply replicate face-to-face teaching in an online context), and understanding that both education systems and schools operate at multiple levels simultaneously, therefore affording multiple avenues for adaptability.

Waite also suggests several more specific strategies for building resilience that both teachers and school leaders can make use of. These include deliberately mapping student relationships, and then using this 'map' to differentiate student support (e.g., a behavioural method known as **socio-metric evaluation** could be used for this), focusing on the use of educational technology designed to connect students, designing the online learning around a mastery-based approach to merit and award, ensuring that the teaching and learning approach is highly student-centred, setting SMART (specific, measurable, actionable, realistic, and time-related) goals for the online approach, and making sure that this approach remains firmly focused on **learner agency** as a major outcome of the learning. Howell (2020) further stresses the importance of 'systems thinking' when it comes to resilience, noting that complex crises require the kind of multi-layered and open-ended problem-solving that this sort of thinking can provide. This would involve the principal analysing the capabilities and alignment of staff with respect to the overall abilities this affords at any given point in time, and then using this information to help plan for contingencies that may impact on the limitations of the 'system' moving forward. The common denominator across all these concepts and principles is that they use technology to inform, connect, empower and support both teachers and students, thus contributing toward resilience as an outcome of connection and ownership.

Chapter summary

In this chapter we have sought to establish the evidence supporting Blended Learning as an efficacious technology-driven pedagogy. We reiterated what Blended Learning is and highlighted that, as a pedagogy, it is focused on how to use technology in ways that promote student-centred, personalised learning. We examined how to establish some important parameters for implementing Blended Learning, using the Blended Learning continuum to show how different models of Blended Learning can be used to control for the level of personalised learning that takes place. We then reviewed research showing the degree to which Blended Learning can impact student achievement, and examined a series of factors that contribute to the successful implementation of Blended Learning, such as the promotion of portable skill sets and teacher motivation. Following on from this, Chapter 6 identified the critical role that school leaders play in leading the changes that need to occur when implementing Blended Learning, noting in particular the need for principals and other school leaders to understand how to make use of social capital within blended and online learning environments. We concluded the chapter by identifying areas, concepts and specific strategies by which school leaders can plan for successful blended and online learning, as has been necessitated in 2020 by the COVID-19 pandemic event. In Chapter 7 we will progress these understandings by examining how they suggest we should position Blended Learning in relation to a school improvement initiative.

Resources

Here are some further resources you will find helpful to know about as a teacher or school leader. They contain interesting and useful videos, simulations and various practice activities, and are designed to assist in the design of a blended learning environment, where resources that can be used both synchronously and asynchronously are required:

Mastery resources

These are mainly adaptive platforms that give students the opportunity to progressively practise and demonstrate their learning:

Newsela, Lexia CORE5, iReady, Achieve3000, Khan Academy, Quill, Prodigy, ST Math, DreamBox, iReady, Mangahigh

Content knowledge

Use these to introduce new information and reinforce existing knowledge:

Khan Academy, cK-12, Actively Learn, Generation Genius, YouTube educational videos, Crash Course, TEDed. There is also a program called edpuzzle that lets you embed questions within online videos to help custom-tailor student learning.

Glossary

Blended Learning continuum   A continuum-based delineation of how Blended Learning can be used to support a more conservative/sustaining (face-to-face) application of technology for learning, or a more disruptive/replacing (online) application of technology for learning.

Concerns-based adoption models   A model of conceptual development which posits that the types of questions people ask when undergoing change evolve in response to a sequence of concerns that represent the developmental phase of the person adopting the change.

Flipped classroom   Fundamental model and principle of Blended Learning, wherein the traditional, classroom-based approach to teaching and learning is 'flipped', having the student engage with content learning at home, prior to undertaking classroom learning for an area or topic, and then having the teacher assist this learning during face-to-face classroom learning, by actively facilitating student concept learning and problem-solving for the learning.

Learner agency   The idea that the purpose of education is to enable learners to develop independent thinking, as a means of becoming self-sufficient, autonomous individuals who 'own' their knowledge and learning at an intrinsic level.

SAMR model   SAMR is an acronym for substitution, augmentation, modification and redefinition. This model provides an ascending hierarchy of how analogue tasks can be transferred into a digital environment. Using this model, it appears that the current use of technology in schools remains at the most basic (substitution) level of application.

Social capital (aka professional capital)   Refers to the quantity and quality of social interactions within and between social groups, with higher quantity and quality indicating higher value (capitol) for the social interactions. Importantly, social capitol contributes notably to the access individuals have to knowledge and information, their sense of expectation, trust and obligation, and the extent to which they adhere to social norms and codes of behaviour.

Socio-metric evaluation   A method for identifying social and academic relationships amongst children and students. Once identified, these relationships can be used for purposes of group work, seating arrangements, project work and the like. They can also be used for forward planning in relation to online learning arrangements, by using them to help identify which students might require more synchronous versus asynchronous engagement, increased contact time, etc.

References

Allen, I. A., & Seaman, J. (2014). *Grade change: Tracking online education in the United States.* Online Learning Consortium. Retrieved September 20, 2019, from www.google.com/url?sa=t&rct= j&q=&esrc=s&source=web&cd=1&ved=2ahUKEwi5v6rAgL_pAhVUxzgGHaacAHYQFjAAegQIB hAB&url=https%3A%2F%2Fwww.onlinelearningsurvey.com%2Freports%2Fgradechange. pdf&usg=AOvVaw0s9WLk4bugiEgBLbTVR685

Arnett, T. (2020). The online edtech that helps educators make distance learning less distant. *Christensen Institute.* Retrieved May 15, 2020, from www.christenseninstitute.org/blog/the-online-edtech-that-helps-educators-make-distance-learning-less-distant/?utm_source=Ed%20Digest&utm_medium=email&utm_campaign=5%2F8%2F20

Arnou, C. (2020, April 14). *Scenario's voor onderwijs tijdens en na de corona-crisis.* Retrieved April 20, 2020, from https://ppw.kuleuven.be/platforml/Blogs/scenario2019s-voor-onderwijs-tijdens-en-nade-corona-crisis

Australian Council of Educational Research (ACER). (2019). *Literacy and numeracy for the 21st century.* Retrieved May 17, 2020, from www.acer.org/au/discover/article/literacy-and-numeracy-for-the-21st-century

Ayala, S. J. (2009). Blended learning as a new approach to social work education. *Journal of Social Work Education, 45,* 277–288. https://doi.org/10.5175/JSWE.2009.200700112

Bourdieu, P. (1986). The forms of capital. In J. Richardson (Ed.), *Handbook of theory and research for the sociology of education* (pp. 241–258). Greenwood Press.

Brabazon, T. (2017). From digital disruption to educational excellence: Teaching and learning in the knowledge economy. *International Journal of Social Sciences & Educational Studies, 3*(3). https:// doi.org/10.23918/ijsses.v3i3p188

Cardullo, V. M., Wilson, N. S., & Zygouris-Coe, V. I. (2018). Emerging technologies: Perspectives from metacognitive teachers. In M. Khosrow-Pour (Ed.), *Information and technology literacy: Concepts, methodologies, tools, and applications, Vol. 1* (pp. 203–223). IGI Global.

Carnevale, A., & Desrochers, D. (2002). The missing middle: Aligning education and the knowledge economy. *Journal for Vocational Special Needs Education, 25*(1), 3–23. https://eric.ed.gov/?id=EJ903935

Carrasco, M. R., & Torrecilla, F. J. M. (2012). Learning environments with technological resources: A look at their contribution to student performance in Latin American elementary schools. *Educational Technology Research and Development, 60*(6), 1107–1128.

Caulfield, J. (2012). *How to design and teach a hybrid course.* Stylus Publishing.

Cheng, L., Ritzhaupt, A. D., & Antonenko, P. (2019). Effects of the flipped classroom instructional strategy on students' learning outcomes: A meta-analysis. *Educational Technology Research and Development, 67*(4), 793–824.

Chia-Pin, K., Chin-Chung, T., & Meilun, S. (2014). Development of a survey to measure self-efficacy and attitudes toward web-based professional development among elementary school teachers. *Journal of Educational Technology & Society, 17*(4), 302–315.

Childress, S., & Benson, S. (2014). Personalised learning for every student every day. *The Phi Delta Kappan, 95*(8), 33–38.

Christensen, C. M., Horn, M. B., & Johnson, C. W. (2011). *Disrupting class: How disruptive innovation will change the way the world learns.* McGraw-Hill Education.

Chun, L., Chin-Chung, T., & Di, W. (2015). The role of ICT infrastructure in its application to classrooms: A large scale survey for middle and primary schools in China. *Journal of Educational Technology & Society, 18*(2), 249–261.

Chung Kwan, L., & Khe Foon, H. (2017). Using first principles of instruction to design secondary school mathematics flipped classroom: The findings of two exploratory studies. *Journal of Educational Technology & Society, 20*(1), 222–236.

Coleman, J. S. (1990). *Foundations of social theory* (pp. 300–321). The Belknap Press of Harvard University.

Coyle, K. K., Chambers, B. D., Anderson, P. M., Firpo-Triplett, R., & Waterman, E. A. (2019). Blended learning for sexual health education: Evidence base, promising practices, and potential challenges. *Journal of School Health, 89*(10), 847–859.

Crawford, R., & Jenkins, L. E. (2018). Making pedagogy tangible: Developing skills and knowledge using a team teaching and blended learning approach. *Australian Journal of Teacher Education, 43*(1), 8.

Cummings, A. (2008). Spanish teachers' beliefs and practices on computers in the classroom. *Hispania, 91*(1), 73–92. https://doi.org/10.2307/20063625

Erdogan, T. (2011). Turkish primary school teachers' perceptions of school culture regarding ICT integration. *Educational Technology Research and Development, 59*(3), 429–443.

Hamilton, E. R., Rosenberg, J. M., & Akcaoglu, M. (2016). The Substitution Augmentation Modification Redefinition (SAMR) model: A critical review and suggestions for its use. *TechTrends, 60*(5), 433–441.

Hargreaves, A., & Fullan, M. (2012). *The power of professional capital.* Teachers College Press.

Horn, M. B., & Staker, H. (2015). *Blended: Using disruptive innovation to improve schools.* Jossey-Bass.

Horn, M. B., Staker, H., & Christensen, C. M. (2015). *Blended: Using disruptive innovation to improve schools.* Jossey-Bass.

Howell, L. (2020). *Boosting resilience to COVID-19.* Project Syndicae. Retrieved May 20, 2020, from www.project-syndicate.org/commentary/covid19-requires-strengthening-five-resilience-components-by-lee-howell-2020-04

Ibrahim, M. M., & Nat, M. (2019). Blended learning motivation model for instructors in higher education institutions. *International Journal of Educational Technology in Higher Education, 16*(12). https://doi.org/10.1186/s41239-019-0145-2

Inan, F. A., & Lowther, D. L. (2010). Factors affecting technology integration in K-12 classrooms: A path model. *Educational Technology Research and Development, 58*(2), 137–154.

Jerald, C. D. (2009). *Defining a 21st century education.* Center for Public Education.

Kazakoff, E. R., Macaruso, P., & Hook, P. (2018). Efficacy of a blended learning approach to elementary school reading instruction for students who are English Learners. *Educational Technology Research and Development, 66*(2), 429–449.

Khribi, M. K., Jemni, M., & Nasraoui, O. (2009). Automatic recommendations for e-learning personalisation based on web usage mining techniques and information retrieval. *Journal of Educational Technology & Society, 12*(4), 30–42.

Kim, M. K., Kim, S. M., Khera, O., & Getman, J. (2014). The experience of three flipped classrooms in an urban university: An exploration of design principles. *The Internet and Higher Education, 22*(Supplement C), 37–50. https://doi.org/10.1016/j.iheduc.2014.04.003

Kivunja, C. (2015). Teaching students to learn and to work well with 21st century skills: Unpacking the career and life skills domain of the new learning paradigm. *International Journal of Higher Education, 4*(1). https://doi.org/10.5430/ijhe.v4n1p1

Lawless, K. A., & Pellegrino, J. W. (2007). Professional development in integrating technology into teaching and learning: Knowns, unknowns, and ways to pursue better questions and answers. *Review of Educational Research, 77*(4), 575–614.

Li, Q., & Ma, X. (2010). A meta-analysis of the effects of computer technology on school students' mathematics learning. *Educational Psychology Review, 22*(3), 215–243.

Liang, T.-P., Lai, H.-J., & Ku, Y.-C. (2006). Personalised content recommendation and user satisfaction: Theoretical synthesis and empirical findings. *Journal of Management Information Systems, 23*(3), 45–70.

Lo, C. K., & Hew, K. F. (2017). A critical review of flipped classroom challenges in K-12 education: Possible solutions and recommendations for future research. *Research and Practice in Technology Enhanced Learning, 12*(1), 4.

Lu, J., Yang, J., & Yu, C.-S. (2013). Is social capital effective for online learning? *Information & Management, 50*(7), 507–522. https://doi.org/10.1016/j.im.2013.07.009

Marache-Francisco, C., & Brangier, E. (2013). *Process of gamification: From the consideration of gamification to its practical implementation.* Paper presented at the Conference: CENTRIC 2013: The Sixth International Conference on Advances in Human oriented and Personalised Mechanisms, Technologies, and Services, Venice, Italy.

Maxwell, C., & White, J. (2017). Blended (r) evolution: How 5 teachers are modifying the Station Rotation to fit students' needs. *Clayton Christensen Institute for Disruptive Innovation.*

Means, B., Toyama, Y., Murphy, R., & Baki, M. (2013). The effectiveness of online and blended learning: A meta-analysis of the empirical literature. *Teachers College Record, 115*(3), 1–47.

Min, M. (2019). School culture, self-efficacy, outcome expectation, and teacher agency toward reform with curricular autonomy in South Korea: A social cognitive approach. *Asia Pacific Journal of Education.* https://doi.org/10.1080/02188791.2019.1626218

Moskal, P., Dziuban, C., & Hartman, J. (2013). Blended learning: A dangerous idea? *The Internet and Higher Education, 18*, 15–23.

Nedungadi, P., & Raman, R. (2012). A new approach to personalisation: Integrating e-learning and m-learning. *Educational Technology Research and Development, 60*(4), 659–678.

Newcomb, T. (2020). 'Why do I want digital experiences for my kids if it looks like this?' — Experts fear parent backlash against online learning. *The 74.* Retrieved April 22, 2020, from www.the74million.org/article/why-do-i-want-digital-experiences-for-my-kids-if-it-looks-like-this-experts-fear-parent-backlash-against-online-learning/?utm_source=Ed%20Digest&utm_medium=email&utm_campaign=4%2F10%2F20

NSW Government. (2020). *COVID-19 (coronavirus).* Retrieved April 23, 2020, from https://education.nsw.gov.au/covid-19

Oliver, M., Domingo, M., Hunter, J., Pan, L., & Gourlay, L. (2014). *Pre-tertiary engagement with online learning.* https://discovery.ucl.ac.uk/id/eprint/10019278

Ossiannilsson, E. (2017). *Blended learning: State of the nation.* The International Council for Open and Distance Education.

Ossiannilsson, E. (2018). *Blended learning-state of the nation.* Paper presented at the CSEDU (2).

Patrick, S., Kennedy, K., & Powell, A. (2013). Mean what you say: Defining and integrating personalised, blended and competency education. *International Association for K-12 Online Learning.*

Powell, A., Watson, J., Staley, P., Patrick, S., Horn, M., Fetzer, L., Hibbard, L., Oglesby, J., & Verma, S. (2015). Blending learning: The evolution of online and face-to-face education from 2008–2015. Promising practices in blended and online learning series. *International Association for K-12 Online Learning.*

Romrell, D., Kidder, L., & Wood, E. (2014). The SAMR model as a framework for evaluating mLearning. *Online Learning Journal, 18*(2). https://www.learntechlib.org/p/183753/

Schaefer-McDaniel, N. J. (2014). Conceptualizing social capital among young people: Towards a new theory. *Children, Youth and Environments, 14*(1), 153–172. www.jstor.org/stable/10.7721/chilyoutenvi.14.1.0153

Schechter, R. L., Kazakoff, E. R., Bundschuh, K., Prescott, J. E., & Macaruso, P. (2017). Exploring the impact of engaged teachers on implementation fidelity and reading skill gains in a blended learning reading program. *Reading Psychology, 38*(6), 553–579.

Schultz, D., Duffield, S., Rasmussen, S. C., & Wageman, J. (2014). Effects of the flipped classroom model on student performance for advanced placement high school chemistry students. *Journal of Chemical Education, 91*(9), 1334–1339.

Schwartz, S. (2020). States all over the map on remote learning Rigor, Detail. *Education Week* (May, 2020). Retrieved May 7, 2020, from www.edweek.org/ew/articles/2020/05/13/enormous-variation-among-state-online-learning-programs.html?cmp=eml-enl-eu-news1&M=59575597&U=1790648&UUID=5a0962b1730c8128b2846c213757611a

Shian-Shyong, T., Jun-Ming, S., Gwo-Jen, H., Gwo-Haur, H., Chin-Chung, T., & Chang-Jiun, T. (2008). An object-oriented course framework for developing adaptive learning systems. *Journal of Educational Technology & Society, 11*(2), 171–191.

Singh, H. (2003). Building effective blended learning programs. *Educational Technology, 43*(6), 4.

Song, Y., Wong, L.-H., & Looi, C.-K. (2012). Fostering personalised learning in science inquiry supported by mobile technologies. *Educational Technology Research and Development, 60*(4), 679–701.

Spector, J. M., Dirk, I., Demetrios, S., Lan, Y., Evode, M., Amali, W., . . . David, C. G. (2016). Technology enhanced formative assessment for 21st century learning. *Journal of Educational Technology & Society, 19*(3), 58–71.

Staker, H., & Horn, M. B. (2012). Classifying K-12 blended learning. *Innosight Institute.*

Stecyk, A. (2018). Assessment of blended learning mechanisms and models. *European Journal of Service Management, 27*(1, 3/2018), 299–305.

Steele, J. L., Lewis, M. W., Santibañez, L., Faxon-Mills, S., Rudnick, M., Stecher, B. M., & Hamilton, L. S. (2014). *Competency-based education in three pilot programs: Examining implementation and outcomes: Report prepared for the Bill & Melinda Gates Foundation* (pp. 1–12). RAND Corporation.

Steinfield, C., Lampe, C., & Ellison, N. B. (2007). The benefits of Facebook "friends:" Social capital and college students' use of online social network sites. *Journal of Computer-Mediated Communication, 12*(4), 1143–1168. https://doi.org/10.1111/j.1083-6101.2007.00367.x. %J

Straub, E. T. (2009). Understanding technology adoption: Theory and future directions for informal learning. *Review of Educational Research, 79*(2), 625–649.

Szpunar, K. K., Jing, H. G., & Schacter, D. L. (2014). Overcoming overconfidence in learning from video-recorded lectures: Implications of interpolated testing for online education. *Journal of Applied Research in Memory and Cognition, 3*(3), 161–164.

Thomson, S. (2020). What PISA tells us about our preparedness for remote learning. *Teacher* (Australian Council for Educational Research). Retrieved April 22, 2020, from www.teachermagazine.com.au/columnists/sue-thomson/what-pisa-tells-us-about-our-preparedness-for-remote-learning?utm_source=CM&utm_medium=Bulletin&utm_content=21April

Truitt, A. A., & Ku, H.-Y. (2018). A case study of third grade students' perceptions of the station rotation blended learning model in the United States. *Educational Media International, 55*(2), 153–169.

Tzu-Chi, Y., Gwo-Jen, H., & Stephen Jen-Hwa, Y. (2013). Development of an adaptive learning system with multiple perspectives based on students' learning styles and cognitive styles. *Journal of Educational Technology & Society, 16*(4), 185–200.

Waite, C. (2020). Envisioning the 7 habits of highly resilient schools. *Christensen Institute*. Retrieved May 5, 2020, from www.christenseninstitute.org/blog/envisioning-the-7-habits-of-highly-resilient-schools/?utm_source=Ed%20Digest&utm_medium=email&utm_campaign=5%2F15%2F20

Welker, J., & Berardino, L. (2005). Blended learning: Understanding the middle ground between traditional classroom and fully online instruction. *Journal of Educational Technology Systems, 34*(1), 33–55. https://doi.org/10.2190/67FX-B7P8-PYUX-TDUP

Whitty, G. (2006). *Teacher professionalism in a new era*. Paper presented at the first General Teaching Council for Northern Ireland Annual Lecture, Belfast, March 2006. https://www.researchgate.net/profile/Geoff_Whitty/publication/254428419_Teacher_professionalism_in_a_new_era/links/0c960537605f9ce543000000/Teacher-professionalism-in-a-new-era.pdf

Willis, R., Lynch, D., & Fradale, P. (2018). Operationalizing blended learning to the context: Towards clarity in implementation. *International Journal of Innovation, Creativity and Change, 4*(2), 17.

Woods, R. H., & Baker, J. D. (2004). Interaction and immediacy in online learning. *The International Review of Research in Open and Distributed Learning, 5*(2). https://doi.org/10.19173/irrodl.v5i2.186

WorldBank. (2003). *Lifelong learning in the global knowledge economy*. https://elibrary.worldbank.org/doi/abs/10.1596/978-0-8213-5475-9

Xuesong, Z., Jibao, G., Hefu, L., Jyh-Chong, L., & Chin-Chung, T. (2017). An experiential learning perspective on students' satisfaction model in a flipped classroom context. *Journal of Educational Technology & Society, 20*(1), 198–210.

Yanjie, S., & Manu, K. (2017). How to flip the classroom? Productive failure or traditional flipped classroom pedagogical design? *Journal of Educational Technology & Society, 20*(1), 292–305.

Yanjie, S., Morris, S. Y. J., Maiga, C., & Weiqin, C. (2017). "HOW" to design, implement and evaluate the flipped classroom: A synthesis. *Journal of Educational Technology & Society, 20*(1), 180–183.

Yeigh, T., & Lynch, D. (2018). School leadership and school improvement: A correlational analysis of school readiness factors. *School Leadership and Management*. https://doi.org/10.1080/13632434.2018.1505718

Yeigh, T., Lynch, D., Turner, D., Provost, D., & Willis, R. (2019). Organisational readiness and strategic leadership for school improvement. *International Journal of Educational Management*. https://doi.org/10.1108/IJEM-07-2017-0181

Yeigh, T., Lynch, D., Turner, D., Fradale, P., Willis, R., et al. (2020). Using blended learning to support whole-of-school improvement: The need for contextualisation. *Education and Information Technologies*. https://doi.org/10.1007/s10639-020-10114-6

Yudt, K., & Columba, L. (2017). The effects of blended learning in pre-service elementary mathematics teachers' performance and attitude. *National Teacher Education Journal, 10*(1), 17–25. http://www.ntejournal.com/

7 A vision for the future of schooling

Positioning Blended Learning in relation to school improvement

Relevant Australian Professional Standards for Teachers: 1.2; 1.5; 2.6; 3.4; 3.6; 4.5; 5.1; 5.4; 6.2; 6.3; 6.4; 7.4

Chapter synopsis

As indicated in previous chapters, the dynamics of disruptive innovation in education were on full display under the unprecedented COVID-19 pandemic conditions. In the years to come, mountains of detailed research and myriad case scenarios will no doubt showcase the diverse strategies that schooling systems around the world implemented in order to adapt to COVID-19 conditions, with most of them plunging (or being pushed) headlong into some form of online learning as a major focus for teaching and learning (Newcomb, 2020). Most likely, studies will unpack how most schools and districts found themselves coping – rather than strategising – transitioning to remote teaching with no time, limited resources and little training. However, the most interesting research in the years to come will have little to do with how well schools coped under COVID-19 conditions. Rather, it will explore how they used the experience to inform their next chapter of school improvement.

The question is whether school communities will leverage the 'teachable moment' that was manifest in pandemic conditions. Many won't. Many schools and practitioners will simply return to their comfort zone because they lack the imagination, the will or the resources to do otherwise. As noted by Lynch (2012), the enculturating effect of a long-held tradition that is schooling is hard to break. Some schools and practitioners will take the opportunity to deliberately reflect upon the lessons they learned and redefine 'normal' teaching and learning in a way that aligns more suitably with the world of technological disruption that has been so clearly outlined in previous chapters (Wei et al., 2017).

This chapter provides a practical framework for those schools who wish to reflect upon what they have learned and leverage it in order to fulfil their vision for future improvement as a blended school. Because every school has its own unique school improvement objectives, this chapter is scaffolded around a series of 'big questions' that are designed to stimulate reflection and empower schools to adopt Blended Learning in a way that is relevant to their own particular school improvement agenda.

This chapter begins by focusing on the particular skill sets required to integrate Blended Learning within a whole-of-school improvement initiative, as informed broadly by the school improvement and Blended Learning research. Furthermore, it will provide specific contextualising models designed to convey how to go about positioning Blended Learning within a distinct school context. It will then delineate the important relationships between Blended Learning and school improvement, as well as the purpose and function of technology as part of an overall school improvement initiative. Finally, it will propose how a school's Blended Learning journey can be monitored and managed by three crucial and interconnected components: a supportive coaching, mentoring and feedback (CMF) structure, a holistic **progressive evaluation** structure and evidence-driven decision making within a teacher-as-researcher (TaR) framework.

Requisite skill sets for integrated Blended Learning

We begin this chapter by asking what fundamental skill sets are required to integrate Blended Learning within a whole-of-school improvement initiative? This is a crucial question because, as discussed in previous chapters, integrated Blended Learning is disruptive by its very nature. Thus, in order for it to be a positive disruption, some essential agreements and skill sets are required.

One prerequisite for success is a commitment to some fundamental change management principles from both leadership and community members. If a Blended Learning strategy is truly 'integrated' and 'whole school', then it is likely that the full spectrum of community members will be pushed out of their comfort zones by the initiative (Waite, 2019). Board members, school leaders, teachers, support staff, parents and students (current and future) will likely be discomfited in some way by the notion of integrated Blended Learning. Many will confront principles and practices that they may have never considered, while others will be expected to embrace conditions that they never agreed to or believed in. As we have noted in prior chapters, the recognition of this fact, and the need for a collaborative change management culture with shared principles and practices, is fundamental for success.

While much has been written about change management, the McKinsey Group's 'Four Building Blocks for Change' provide a solid framework for schools making the transition to integrated Blended Learning. Like Blended Learning itself, McKinsey's basic tenets focus upon empowering the 'learner' in the change scenario (Basford & Schaninger, 2016). In this case, presented in Table 7.1, school community members are being called upon to transition to new and potentially confronting teaching and learning conditions.

The first building block in the McKinsey model is to foster understanding and conviction. In the case of a school undertaking Blended Learning integration, all community members will first need to fully understand the rationale behind the initiative and how it

Table 7.1 Overview of McKinsey's Integrated Transition Framework

Objective	Requirement	Leadership skill/ strategy
	I understand what is being asked of me and it makes sense.	Fostering understanding and conviction
'I will change my mindset and behaviour if …'	I see that our structures, processes, and systems support the changes I am being asked to make.	Reinforcing with formal mechanisms
	I have the skills and opportunities to behave in the new way.	Developing talent and skills
	I see my leaders and colleagues behaving differently.	Role modelling

(Adapted by the authors)

will benefit them in concrete ways. This is an essential step in order for them to dedicate themselves to the initiative in an authentic way. School leaders must develop a change story that helps all stakeholders understand where the school is headed, why it is changing, and why this change is important. Furthermore, it is important to recognise and address misunderstandings about the initiative, so the provision of a feedback loop to gauge how the story is being received is highly recommended.

The second building block is to reinforce change in formal ways. The business world has long leveraged KPIs and bonus conditions to incentivise change. Formally embedding Blended Learning objectives in job descriptions and employment conditions can make the change 'real' for staff. However, it should be remembered that rewards and incentives aren't always about money. Intangible reinforcement is effective as well, especially in the field of education – a field that has sadly never been known for material reward. Frequently shared success stories that feature team and individual achievements can make the change real for those who may have been on the fence, and thus these sorts of incentives can have genuine impact. Furthermore, concrete examples of change can be easily imitated to generate momentum.

Success stories are not enough to reinforce change, however. It is equally important to publicise how and when objective progress milestones are being attained. Formal reports that feature the attainment of evidence-based success metrics can make the change visible and can ensure further authentic integration rather than superficial gestures of commitment to the initiative. On that note, it's important to remember that teachers – especially the most experienced practitioners who may have endured years of pedagogical trends and professional development buzzwords – need to see evidence that integrated Blended Learning is not just another fad that will go away if they wait long enough. In order to get on board with the change, they need to recognise that it is now an integral part of their job, that progress is being made by those around them, and that it's not going away.

Perhaps the most obvious building block for change is to develop talent and skills, as we discussed in detail as part of Chapter 5, but it is also all-too-often the one that attracts the least attention in regard to allocated time and money. Effective training strategies need to be in place to efficiently identify training needs and to provide the right support. This requires self-assessment conditions that allow community members to honestly express where they are in their understanding of blended principles and practices, as well as their competency in associated technical skill sets. These conditions must also consider those who may be too confident about their abilities and who are unaware of what they need to learn. Furthermore, the training must be relevant. Training is obviously not a 'one-size-fits-all' endeavour in a K-12 school community that is implementing a broad scope and sequence of technological integration conditions and Blended Learning practices. Finally, authentic integration requires that role-appropriate training is in place for all community members, including school leaders, teachers, students and parents. It is not enough to assume everyone will be able to adapt to integrated Blended Learning conditions, and school leadership in particular must ensure that everyone is able to embrace the school's vision. That means accurately estimating and budgeting sufficient time and money to meet the needs of current and future teachers, students and parents. Marketing, recruitment and training strategies for these target audiences must ensure that transformative Blended Learning conditions are inclusive and attract new community members, rather than act as an exclusive barrier to entry.

McKinsey's final building block is to role model the desired change. This is a potent element in Blended Learning integration. Role modelling of positive change is essential, and it needn't be limited to people in formal positions of authority – or even to individuals. In fact, group change modelling can be easy and effective when a school starts with demonstrated blended administrative practices. For example, when school leaders leverage technology in ways that empower teachers to control the pace, place and pathways for the fulfilment of their own administrative responsibilities, everyone in the community can experience and model the benefits of blended administrative conditions, empowering teachers and other staff to be more confident in transitioning to blended classroom practices.

While McKinsey's change management building blocks provide solid foundations for the transition to Blended Learning, a certain **dispositional balance** is also required of all community members in the face of such change. Dispositional balance refers to the community's capacity to recognise and respect various stakeholder perspectives throughout the period of change. In this context, successful change requires balanced thinking, planning, communication, collaboration:

- **Balanced thinking:** In periods of major change, school community members must all embrace their roles as open-minded inquirers who are ready to explore, experiment, fail, learn and improve. They also need to recognise and accept that lessons can come from any direction in the community – from any stakeholder in teaching and learning. Furthermore, the community of inquirers needs to be able to balance both 'macro' and 'micro' priorities. The big picture which is often a top down vision targeting abstract strategic goals and organisational objectives needs to balance with the practical realities and priorities of teachers, students and parents on the ground. The latter are often manifested by pragmatic anxieties about what will happen 'in my classroom' or 'for my child'. Leadership needn't micro-manage and obsess over the detailed concerns of every teacher, student or parent – but they shouldn't dismiss them either. Micro worries may be indicative of unforeseen macro challenges; they should be considered and unpacked to determine whether they might represent larger obstacles or opportunities. When community members give voice to comments like 'yeah, but what about … ?' or 'have you ever considered that … ?', leadership can perceive them as 'blockers' who are resistant to change. Leaders will gain much by listening to worriers; they represent focus groups whose input can contribute to the success of the initiative – especially if they are empowered to recommend constructive solutions to the problems that they perceive. In this respect the goal to achieve a macro/micro thinking balance echoes the alignment component of the ACE model we have discussed in prior chapters. In both cases the aim is to align thinking and attitudes in support of an improvement agenda (Figure 7.1).
- **Balanced planning:** Integration of a Blended Learning strategy must feature both systemic and organic planning. Strategies must be proactive and structured with documented implementation priorities and 'SMART' milestones: specific, measurable, achievable, relevant and timely. However, planning must also be reactive and flexible in ways that respect teachers' professional creativity and invites them to explore and experiment in their own ways. An approach that systematically reviews progress towards targeted objectives and welcomes independent exploration and unexpected discoveries can provide a balance that ensures school communities achieve their destination, while allowing them to learn and adapt to unforeseen challenges and opportunities encountered during their development journey. Most importantly, a balanced implementation strategy should take 'baby steps' at the start of the journey. Balanced planning should not over-invest in untested assumptions about what will work or facile assumptions about what won't work. It should include the same responsible, 'minimum viable product' mindset that features

Macro Thinkers

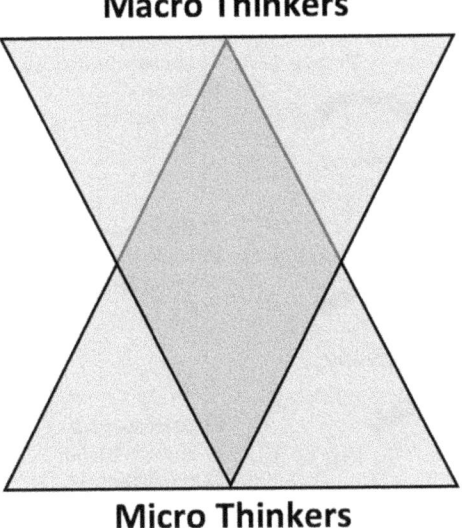

Micro Thinkers

Figure 7.1 Balanced macro-micro thinking (created by the authors).

in the design thinking of entrepreneurial start-ups.[1] Such an approach allows schools to invest on a small scale to test what is 'good' before spending more time and money to achieve something 'great' (Figure 7.2).

- **Balanced communication:** Successful transition to Blended Learning requires inclusive, comprehensive communications with all stakeholders in mind. Communication must be timely, accessible and multi-directional. For example, the initial 'vision' for integrated Blended Learning must be shared well in advance of any concrete assigned actions. It is human nature to resist change, and all organisations (especially schools) are vulnerable to 'change fatigue'. Therefore, it is important to inform community members of the 'blended vision' well in advance, and to let them know what specific role they can play in making this vision a reality. The change will seem less threatening to them if they are given sufficient time to understand the rational and details of the initiative, the potential impact it will have upon their specific roles and how they can play a part in managing the transition. Furthermore, messages should be accessible and free of educational and technical jargon. The vision must be expressed in terms that everyone can understand, including students and second language speakers. Finally, communication must be multi-directional. School leadership must invite, listen to and demonstrate that they hear the perspectives from all community members – especially those who fear change. The macro and micro inquirers mentioned above must openly communicate with due consideration and respect for one another's priorities and concerns. This represents an essential approach involving coordinated communication and collaboration, and without these essential agreements for communication, stakeholders will feel anxious, marginalised and disenfranchised – hardly firm foundations for successful innovation. One simple practice for effective communication and collaboration is to use Blended Learning conditions and practices to communicate,

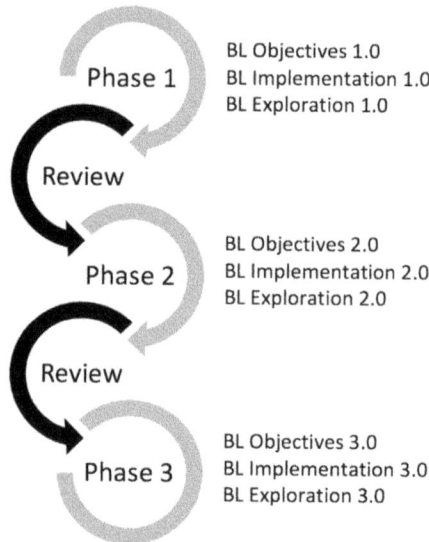

Figure 7.2 Balanced proactive/reactive planning (created by the authors).

implement and collaboratively manage every stage of your plan. Under these conditions, the 'blended' medium becomes the message: blended project management conditions will not only increase the likelihood of balanced inquiry, planning, communication and collaboration – it will allow them to actually experience the benefits of 'going blended'.

- **Balanced collaboration:** Community members must be authentic co-constructors of the integrated Blended Learning initiative, for a number of reasons. First of all, no single individual in a school community knows it all. No one has the whole picture. Successful change occurs when community members have mutual respect for one another's unique role and associated skill sets. This is especially important when it comes to integrated Blended Learning. In his book, *Class Clowns: How the Smartest Investors Lost Billions in Education,* Jonathon Knee (Knee, 2016) presents a series of depressing case studies of failed EdTech Business ventures. Significantly, a major common failing for these companies was the fact that they featured insufficient mutual respect for those three distinct professional skill sets that must work in harmony for success: education, technology and business (Startups.com, 2017). In this regard the transition to integrated Blended Learning requires input from and respect for multiple perspectives: board members, parents, students, school leaders, primary teachers, secondary teachers, financial managers, pedagogical specialists, pastoral care specialists, information technology specialists, facility managers, admissions and marketing specialists, etc. When all points of view are taken into consideration a school community can not only envision what is possible, they can create a plan that is feasible and gradually build an embedded Blended Learning community in stages that are viable and enduring (Figure 7.3).

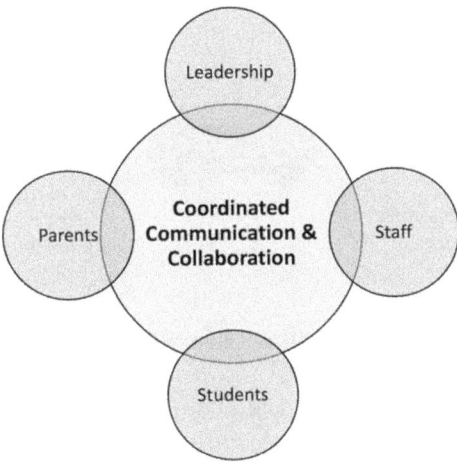

Figure 7.3 Balanced communication and collaboration (created by the authors).

Contextualising models

While prerequisite skills and dispositions are fundamental for successful implementation of integrated Blended Learning, it's equally important to ask how important school context is for the implementation of Blended Learning models for whole-of-school improvement. Blended Learning is not a one-size-fits-all endeavour. In fact, Blended Learning is not merely student-centred; it can also be community-centred, with capacity to suit a school or school group's unique needs and context. Previous research by the authors has explored the capacity of Blended Learning to support whole-of-school improvement when it is introduced with suitable contextualisation to meet the specific needs and culture of local schools (Yeigh et al., 2020).

The application of Blended Learning must be positioned within a continuum framework delimited by the characteristic imperatives of the Knowledge Economy at one end, and by the capabilities and needs of the local school at the other end, particularly the school's ability to use ICT to promote learner agency. Under these contextual conditions, integrated Blended Learning becomes something more. It becomes 'embedded Blended Learning' (eBL) signifying that it is entrenched and endures in relevant ways, with capacity to meet Knowledge Economy imperatives within the specific contextual capabilities and needs of an individual school or school group.

Contextualising the eBL project in this way naturally incorporates any school improvement agenda that may be taking place in response to Knowledge Economy imperatives. Such an approach 'embeds' Blended Learning within the immediate context of the local school environment, ensuring that the approach is relevant and appropriate to the authentic capabilities and needs of the school (Arnett, 2019). This overall contextualising process empowers schools to integrate Blended Learning in ways that address global issues associated with the Knowledge Economy while also addressing the pertinent issues of the local school and has thus been a major concern of the eBL project reported in Chapter 8 of this book. Yeigh et al. (2020) refer to this as the **Knowledge Economy-Local School (KELS) continuum**, a framework that can help schools to determine where they

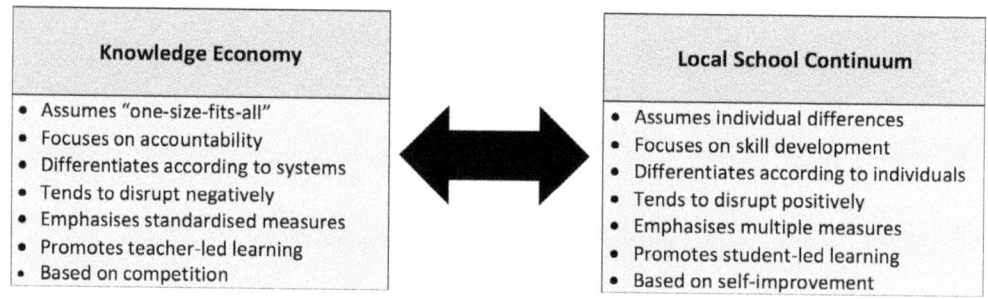

Figure 7.4 Overview of the KELS continuum (created by the authors).

are currently operating and how they could progress in their use of Blended Learning as an integrated pedagogy (Figure 7.4).

A full audit of the local context can provide schools with a useful reality check in defining their vision for Blended Learning improvement. Before determining where they are going, schools should first take stock of where they are. With a few preliminary questions, school communities can survey their Blended Learning terrain, locate an achievable destination and plot a journey that suits their particular context. For example:

- What external compliance obligations must the school meet, and do they feature potential constraints/opportunities for Blended Learning integration? For example, what regulatory bodies is the school aligned with and what requirements should be taken into consideration for integrated Blended Learning (e.g., local/national government authorities, HR contractual standards, accrediting agencies, authorising bodies, examination boards and conditions, teachers' unions conditions, health and safety standards, data security standards, etc.)?
- What does the physical/digital infrastructure of the school community look like, and does it feature potential constraints/opportunities for Blended Learning integration? How could the physical spaces and resources at school and home influence the Blended Learning vision (e.g., single/multiple campus conditions, home access conditions, student–teacher ratios, classroom space and furnishings, staffroom and office conditions, library and resource centre conditions, network, hardware, software resources, SIS, technical support systems, data integration conditions, etc.)
- What are the stakeholder dispositions of the school community towards technology in education, and do they feature potential constraints/opportunities for Blended Learning integration? To what degree are your community members' attitudes toward Knowledge Economy priorities and technological disruption blockers or springboards for the transition to integrated Blended Learning?
- What do the stakeholder competencies look like, and do they feature potential constraints/opportunities for Blended Learning integration? To what degree are their technical and pedagogical skill sets fit for purpose for the transition to integrated Blended Learning?
- What does the budget of the school community look like, and does it feature potential constraints/opportunities for Blended Learning integration? How much time and money is the school able to allocate to the vision – in the short and long term?
- What are the stakeholder priorities, and do they feature potential constraints/opportunities for Blended Learning integration? To what degree can your digital transformation strategy

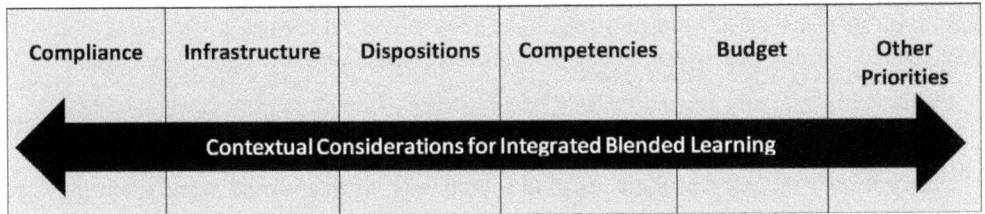

Compliance	Infrastructure	Dispositions	Competencies	Budget	Other Priorities

Contextual Considerations for Integrated Blended Learning

Figure 7.5 Auditing areas to consider as part of the contextualising process for Blended Learning (created by the authors).

target what your community cares about most? How can Blended Learning address what leadership, teachers, students and parents may want to reduce, increase, maintain and improve – in regard to both pedagogical and operational priorities? (See Figure 7.5.)

This final question brings us to perhaps the most important contextual consideration for Blended Learning integration: What is the relationship between Blended Learning and school improvement?

Relationship between Blended Learning and school improvement

When we come to the relationship between Blended Learning and school improvement, we confront the question of how Blended Learning models can be implemented to target school improvement. No one likes change for the sake of change, and thus it is important that Blended learning be integrated with a clear and relevant relationship to specific objectives for school improvement. With respect to this, much has been written about technology's potential to improve education. The power of technology to meet global education challenges has been the subject of reports by NGOs such as the World Bank and OECD (Schleicher, 2012), UNESCO (2016) and the Bill & Melinda Gates Foundation (2010). Comprehensive reports on the subject have also been compiled by multiple government and independent agencies such as the US Department of Education (2020), the UK Department for Education (2014) and The Indian Ministry of Human Resource Development (2016). Education thought leaders such as Fullan (2012), Robinson (2015), Prensky (2012), and Horn and Staker (2017) have published and presented extensively on the topic. While such global perspectives can open minds regarding the potential for strategies such as integrated Blended Learning to address global challenges, real change happens in the local context of a school community, and relevant change must therefore target specific areas of school improvement.

Once a school community has assessed their improvement priorities, then integrated Blended Learning can be judiciously applied in the right places and the right degrees. As indicated above, an essential first step is a comprehensive assessment of improvement priorities; it is essential that schools get feedback from leadership, teachers, students and parents regarding what they want to reduce, increase, maintain and improve in their teaching and learning experience. Furthermore, it is important that both pedagogical and operational priorities are considered. As Fullan (2012) and others have observed, the power of Blended Learning to address operational challenges cannot be underestimated.

The power of integrated Blended Learning for pedagogical improvement has been referenced in previous chapters. Organisations such as the Christensen Institute (2019), International

Society for Technology in Education (2007) and the Aurora Institute (2011; cf. https://www.aurora.edu.au/) have clearly illustrated the capacity of Blended Learning to provide a more student-centred learning experience, giving students increased control over three key areas:

- control over the path of their learning – empowering them to choose what to study and when;
- control over the pace of their learning – empowering them to advance when they are ready and review when necessary; and
- control over the time and place of their learning – empowering them to learn when and where they choose, face-to-face and online, on-campus and off-campus.

Most schools would embrace the primary pedagogical objective of Blended Learning: giving learners greater control over their learning. However, many would debate whether their students are ready and able to take control of their learning. We argue, however, that learner capacity could be a potential priority for school improvement, that is, investigating to what degree students in the school community are ready to assume responsibility for a more personalised learning experience, and what can be done to develop their capacity to take control? Working from this perspective, Figure 7.6 suggests an **eBL design framework** for designing strategies that feature a scope and sequence for integrated Blended Learning, assisting schools to develop students' independent learning capacity in three key areas:

- capacity as learning agents – empowering students to responsibly manage the way they learn;
- capacity as active inquirers – empowering students to build knowledge through active investigation, exploration and problem-solving;
- capacity as effective collaborators – empowering students to work effectively in partnership with others to achieve a common purpose or outcome.

		BL Objectives for Learner Capacity		
		Agency managing how they learn	**Inquiry** building knowledge via investigation, exploration and problem-solving	**Collaboration** working in partnership for a common outcome
BL Objectives for Learner Control	**Pace**			
	Place			
	Pathway			

Figure 7.6 Overview of Blended Learning objectives for learner control in relation to learner capacity (created by the authors).

We posit this framework as a design tool for embedded Blended Learning. When schools connect learner control objectives with the targeted development of learner capacity objectives, they can develop a potent and purposeful framework for school improvement. Of course, as indicated above, curriculum leaders must be invited to identify their own priorities when identifying pedagogical objectives for school improvement.

While Blended Learning's potential to improve learner capacity is clear, schools should not overlook its potential to improve organisational capacity as well. Governments, NGOs and thought leaders have long recognised the power of technology (and by association Blended Learning) to confront the fundamental challenges that underpin the global education crisis: the burden of increasing enrolments and expectations upon public schools; the increasing number of teachers leaving the profession and decreasing number of new teachers; insufficient budgets and resourcing for schools. In short, it is clear that the traditional model of education simply cannot keep pace with current and future education demands. While reports by groups like the OECD and World Bank illustrate how technological integration can help developing nations to build organisational capacity and education access, the same can be said of any school anywhere – in developed or developing nations. This means that Blended Learning conditions can empower schools, school groups or other educational organisations to maximise operations and leverage limited resources. Under traditional conditions, school assets are 'siloed' on individual campuses, and schools often compete with one another to hire qualified staff. However, under Blended Learning conditions a connected network of campuses can share the cost of human resources, as well as digital resources and licence fees, maximising organisational capacity. For example, a highly experienced (and expensive) mathematics teacher can support learning as a blended head of department across multiple campuses. Furthermore, a school that lacks a critical mass of enrolments to hire a teacher in a 'speciality subject' such as psychology or economics can invite their students to join the course virtually, led by a teacher at a sister campus. Figure 7.7 shows how, under collective Blended Learning conditions such as these, schools can potentially extend their course offerings, open educational access, increase enrolment, manage costs and provide students with a broader, more flexible range of educational opportunities under both face-to-face and online conditions.

		BL Objectives for Organisational Capacity		
		Resources sharing staff, services and digital resources	**Access** extending the range of learning opportunities	**Collaboration** working in partnership for common outcomes
BL Objectives for Organisational Control	**Pace**			
	Place			
	Pathway			

Figure 7.7 Overview of Blended Learning objectives for organisational control in relation to organisational capacity (created by the authors).

This also provides us with important insights into the functional role of technology within a Blended Learning environment.

Purpose and function of technology

So, what is the point of EdTech integration? Earlier chapters have established that there are three essential understandings regarding the role of technology in Blended Learning. The first is that the use of technology itself does not define what Blended Learning is. The technology is not an end in and of itself; it is simply a means by which certain aspects of Blended Learning – in particular the online aspects – are delivered. The second essential understanding is that the critical function of technology resides in its capacity to optimise teaching and learning conditions in ways that enhance the role of the teacher – not replace it. The third understanding is that technology integration should transform – not simply enhance – teaching and learning.

The specific technology that schools use to support personalisation of learning is not the critical issue. A wide range of technical options can be used in myriad ways to increase student control over pace, place and pathways for learning. An individual teacher may choose to use a few rudimentary Google files that feature hyperlinked YouTube clips. A school may decide to take a coordinated approach that leverages the full functionality of Google Classrooms and associated Google tools across subjects. A district may develop an integrated strategy that relies upon a sophisticated learning management system for end-to-end synchronous and asynchronous teaching, learning and data management. Whatever technology a school chooses to integrate, it should suit the local context and optimise the scale of teaching and learning with a focus upon and respect for user experience and the preparation of learners to experience success in the knowledge and gig economies.

Quality user experience has long been an obsession for successful e-commerce companies. Sadly, the same cannot be said for e-learning. The fact is, while teachers are highly experienced as instructional designers in their use of classroom time and space, they are relatively inexperienced as instructional designers of effective user experiences in digital time and space. In short, the quality of user experience depends upon how intuitive the use of technology is in support of a seamless 'user journey'. For Blended Learning conditions, technology should be integrated in ways that make the student journey clear, efficient and consistent. Obviously, technical conditions for a quality user experience will depend upon the user context: 'user friendly' criteria for a 16-year-old will differ greatly from those for a 7-year-old. No matter what the context, each student should enjoy a suitable level of clarity, efficiency and consistency in their technical experience. Ideally, this requires the school community to agree upon the range of digital components and resources that constitute the school's learning platform from K-12. This reinforces the need to have teachers and other staff members work collaboratively in both the design and implementation of Blended Learning, as doing so provides increased nuance to the process of contextualisation and can be used to develop an initial model or schema for the implementation phase.

Furthermore, the school should agree upon a scope and sequence of digital literacies and competencies to be developed on their shared platform. This shared technical landscape will make life easier for both students and teachers in their Blended Learning journey. Students will be more confident in Blended Learning conditions that feature a degree of continuity in the use of technology by different teachers, and when they feature an increasing degree of sophistication in the use of technology in ascending year levels. Furthermore, such frameworks can build confidence in teachers who are new to digital instructional design as well. They can learn and grow with their colleagues under shared platform conditions. In this respect a common set of technical tools and recommended conventions for basic instructional functions such as content transmission, communication and collaboration can make the prospect of designing a Blended Learning journey less daunting to teachers. If the school has not yet documented K-12 standards regarding which technical tools and practices are recommended for the sake of a consistent user experience, it is worth doing so in order to create a solid technological foundation for integrated Blended Learning. Likewise, it is worth developing processes whereby teachers and students can be encouraged to explore and experiment with new, alternative technology so that they can be evaluated and potentially incorporated where relevant.

Mapping the degree and nature of Blended Learning from K to 12 is an important part of the purpose and function of technology integration. However, before setting out on the transition to Blended Learning, schools really need to agree upon how 'blended' the student experience will be from K-12, and what the associated volume of technical integration will look like. The Aurora Institute's **Dimensions of Blended Learning matrix** (Figure 7.8) provides some good cues for reflection and decision making about the big questions that need to be addressed for whole-school Blended Learning. For instance, schools must determine what the level of Blended Learning practices will be in each year group with respect to the volume of online instructional materials, resources, assessment and communications. Furthermore, they need to confirm the degree of student-centred instruction in terms of attendance requirements, student roles and responsibilities and degrees of individualised instruction in each year level. Finally, schools need to consider logistical issues such as instructional support models, instruction schedules and locations, and technological infrastructure.

The Aurora Institute's matrix offers a sound framework that can stimulate reflection upon the purpose and function of technology in a school's Blended Learning model.

Whatever the purpose, technology integration should not only suit the practical context for K-12 users, it should also valorise the role of the teacher and enhance the impact of they can have in the learning process. Wherever possible, technology should be used in ways that liberate teachers from mundane, lower-order instructional tasks, and elevate their role in transformative teaching and learning. Arthur C. Clarke's (1980) frequently referenced quote that 'Any teacher that can be replaced by a machine should be!' simultaneously embraces the inevitable influence that technology will have on education while recognising the sacrosanct role that teachers will always have in education. It reminds us that education is a social contract – a complex, human dynamic between teacher and learner. In this day and age, few would argue that a teacher's critical role is to take attendance and transmit information. As illustrated by Hattie and Zierer (2018), the critical difference a teacher can make to learning outcomes resides in the range of productive and dynamic connections they build and maintain with their students – a personal understanding of when and how to intervene in order to support and/or challenge learners. When schools leverage technology purposefully, they can automate lower order activities in ways that enhance rather than replace the role of the teacher. When technology releases teachers from mundane instructional activities, they have more time to concentrate on the higher order teaching and learning activities that Hattie identifies as having the most substantial influence upon student achievement.

Level of Blended Learning

Less Online ———— More Online ———— Mostly Online

Learning Object ——— Lesson ——— Unit Module ——— Single Course ——— Full Curriculum

Dimension	Less Online	More Online	Mostly Online
Characteristics of Instructional Models			
Instructional Material	Course minimally uses digital content, resources, and tools to supplement instruction		Use of digital resources and tools are integral to content, curriculum and instruction
Instructional Resources		Digital content, resources, and tools expand and enhance the curriculum and content	
Assessment	Whole-class assessments, used primarily in the classroom, during the school day as the primary means of feedback	A combination of traditional and online assessments are used inside and outside the classroom	Greater amount of digital, real-time data and feedback allow for individualized instruction
Communication (Student-Teacher & Student-Student)	Occurs primarily synchronously and in the physical classroom	Is a mixture of synchronous and asynchronous, and may be in the physical classroom or online	Occurs primarily asynchronously and online or from a distance
Student-Centered Instruction			
Attendance	Students are required to attend a physical classroom 5 days a week	Students attend a physical classroom less than 5 days a week and work online at other times	Students have flexible physical classroom and/or location attendance requirements
Student Role	Student is primarily the recipient of teacher provided instruction. Teacher sets day-to-day pace	Student takes active role in learning with reliance on digital content, resources and tools. Student has more control of own pace	
Individualisation of Instruction	All students expected to complete same instructional pathway	Students engage with digital content to customize their instructional pathway	Students engage with digital content and have multiple pathways; competency-based and not tied to a fixed school calendar.
School Considerations			
Instructional Support Models	"Direct student learning" through traditional teacher roles and staffing models	"Facilitate student learning" through a team approach with a significant reliance on technologybased tools and content	"Coordinate student learning" through the expanded use of technology-based tools and content, as well as the effective use of outside experts and/or community resources
Instruction Schedule and Location	Fixed daily schedule, with instruction primarily in physical classroom	Mixed schedule, with online and physical instruction	Highly flexible schedule, with instruction possible 24x7. Learning centers support instruction.
Access to Support	Support is school-based, and provided primarily by the teacher during the class period.	Support structures in place 24x7, in addition to teacher support (e.g. online tutoring, home mentors, and technical support services)	
Technological Infrastructure	School or classroom based with students using shared classroom computer resources. Access to infrastructure ends with class period.	Available across school campus with students checking out computers from a lab or bringing their own. Access to infrastructure is during school hours.	Available on and off campus with students using their own device. Access to infrastructure is 24x7.

Blended Learning Characteristics Driving the Changing Roles of Educators

Figure 7.8 Aurora Institute Dimensions of Blended Learning matrix (adapted by the authors).

While increasing teacher efficacy and impact is an important function of technology integration, enhancement is not the ultimate goal as Puentedura's (2020) SAMR model illustrates (Figure 7.9). Ultimately, technology should be implemented in ways that transform teaching and learning. Under optimal conditions, the valorised teacher aspires to use technology to completely redesign past learning tasks and create new personalised learning activities under blended conditions that were previously inconceivable.

Of course, developing transformative uses of technology doesn't happen overnight. As previously discussed, school improvement through Blended Learning is a journey that requires a balanced plan and measured steps. It takes time in a process that invites practitioners to collaboratively experiment and develop in their use of technology, to monitor evidence of the effects on learning outcomes and to reflect upon appropriate improvements and adjustments. Three interconnected components can play a crucial role in monitoring and managing the progress of a school's Blended Learning journey: (1) a supportive coaching, mentoring and feedback (CMF) structure, (2) a holistic progressive evaluation structure and (3) evidence-driven decision making within a teacher-as-researcher framework.

Role of coaching, mentoring and feedback (CMF)

When designing Blended Learning to support a school improvement initiative, school leadership must consider the function of coaching, mentoring and feedback in implementing Blended Learning to this purpose. Ongoing collaborative application, experimentation and development are essential to any school's Blended Learning journey, and a structured approach to professional coaching, mentoring and feedback (CMF) can be an invaluable asset in helping a school to arrive at its destination. When faced with major innovations and initiatives, schools sometimes take an 'organic' approach, relying upon their natural teamwork culture for progressive experimentation, observation, feedback and reflection. Frankly, the comprehensive investment in time and money for Blended Learning transformation is too high to entrust it to something as amorphous as 'school culture'. Formal structures are required – structures capable of connecting CMF with the other two fundamental resources for gradual school improvement: progressive evaluation and evidence-based decision making. CMF is one of those areas that require a balance between systemic and organic planning, as recommended earlier in this chapter. A balanced CMF framework should be proactive and structured with documented

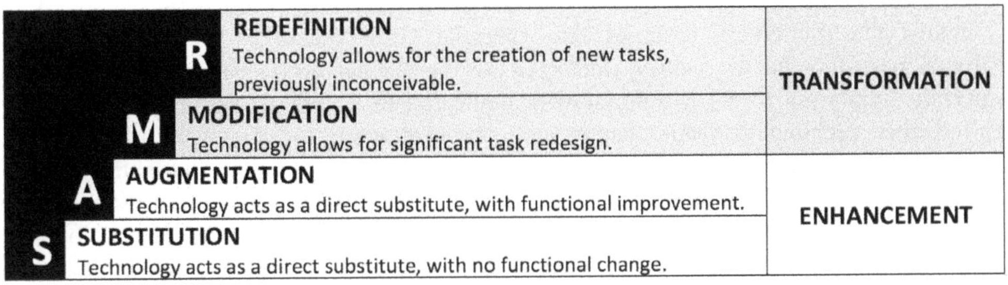

R **REDEFINITION** Technology allows for the creation of new tasks, previously inconceivable.	**TRANSFORMATION**
M **MODIFICATION** Technology allows for significant task redesign.	
A **AUGMENTATION** Technology acts as a direct substitute, with functional improvement.	**ENHANCEMENT**
S **SUBSTITUTION** Technology acts as a direct substitute, with no functional change.	

Figure 7.9 Representation of Puentedura's SAMR model of transformational technology (created by the authors).

implementation priorities and SMART milestones, but it must also be responsive and flexible in ways that respects teachers' professional feedback, creativity and needs.

Lynch and Smith (2014) offer some sound points of reference for a structured CMF approach, which can be adapted to meet the contextual needs of any school community. Mentoring is a structured, sustained process for supporting professional learners through significant career transitions. Normally, 'mentoring' refers to a one-to-one relationship in an organisation, where a senior experienced person or specialist offers guidance, help, support and advice to facilitate the learning or development of a junior or less experienced member of staff. Specialist coaching is a structured, sustained process for enabling the development of a specific aspect of a professional learner's practice. It features the explicit and implicit intention of helping individuals to improve their performance in various domains, and to enhance their personal effectiveness, personal development, and personal growth. Collaborative coaching is a structured, sustained process between two or more professional learners to enable them to embed new knowledge and skills from specialist sources in day-to-day practice. The repetitive use of the phrase 'structured and sustained' in these definitions is hardly accidental: unstructured collaboration can often be sporadic due to typically overloaded academic calendars and inconsistent due to the diverse nature of teaching groups and departments.

The structure for effective coaching, mentoring and feedback does not need to be complex – nor rigid. In fact, a few basic activities – when implemented in a sustained manner – can drive a CMF cycle that is capable of adapting to the organic and evolving needs of both teachers and the school year on year. For instance, a CMF cycle for any initiative should commence with a teacher-centred reflection survey that captures teacher feedback on two basic questions: 'What can the school do to support you in achieving our specific initiative objectives?' and 'What can you do to support your colleagues in this regard?' The first question is obviously designed to target specific teacher objectives for the year, while the second invites teachers to nominate themselves as collaborative coaches in their own right, sharing and observing practices which they believe to be their areas of strength. Furthermore, a CMF cycle should always feature safe, constructive dialogue between the classroom teacher and their mentor(s), and between the teacher and their coach(es). These sorts of dialogues are necessary in order to identify needs and set SMART objectives for improvement. Once objectives are agreed upon, scheduled classroom observations by mentors and coaches should be accompanied by constructive feedback targeting only the agreed-upon objectives. Finally, teachers must have scheduled opportunities to respond in writing to observer feedback – and put it in relevant context for future progress. Of course, any CMF framework is built upon the premise of trust. Teachers must know that they are in a 'safe place' in order to honestly appraise themselves and one another, without negative consequences.

Finally, the framework assumes that essential CMF outcomes are documented in a digital portfolio that is securely managed by the teacher and their supervisor. This is especially important to a CMF framework dedicated to Blended Learning development. As indicated previously in this chapter, one simple practice for effective CMF is to use Blended Learning conditions and practices for communicating and collaboratively managing this process. In effect, Blended Learning conditions can offer teachers the same learner-centred control over pace, place and pathway in their professional development that it provides students in their academic development. Furthermore, data housed in a digital portfolio can be anonymised and play a powerful role in progressive evaluation and evidence-based decision making for the whole school, improvement initiative or even school district.

Need for progressive evaluation

A key question in all this involves determining what the function of progressive evaluation is in implementing Blended Learning for school improvement. CMF structures are most effective in promoting sustained and purposeful school improvement when they are integrated with comprehensive and progressive evaluation structures. Systematic data collection, analysis and reporting are essential features of a whole-of-school improvement culture. In the Blended Learning journey, it is literally the 'dashboard' that helps a school to reach its destination. Like some dashboards, school evaluation structures can often be overly complex and confusing. Technology integration for Blended Learning conditions can provide a potential tsunami of digital information. Schools need to take great care in delineating exactly what success looks like, as well as what the relevant success metrics and associated data sets are. Furthermore, they need to determine how and when data is captured, analysed and reported upon to inform decision making.

Before we examine the 'what, how and when' of progressive evaluation, it is important to first address potential anxieties about 'big brother'. Under well-managed, technical-integration conditions, there are no secrets; data capture and analytics can provide powerful data regarding all kinds of user behaviour. Good learning management systems, educational software and digital tools feature comprehensive data analytics and reporting functionality can make the dynamics of teaching and learning more transparent than ever before. For some, this is a slippery slope toward 'big brother' evaluation conditions. Under bad school leadership they would be right. However, under good school leadership, stakeholders would have confidence in a shared understanding of the difference between facts and judgements. Good progress evaluation operates on the common principle that a single piece of measurable user behaviour data captured by a single digital component represents only a single piece of the teaching and learning process; that single piece of data must never be considered in isolation from the range of other available qualitative and quantitative data sets – or out of context from the particular Blended Learning conditions and objectives with which they are associated. Fortunately, well-managed CMF practices that privilege instructional context and professional dialogue over hard data can mitigate the risk of facile and reductive 'big brother' judgements.

With that essential agreement in mind, the first step in progress evaluation is to define the success metrics and progress indicators associated with the school's initial improvement objectives. What is the school's original rationale for Blended Learning implementation? Is it to address pedagogical priorities such as increasing student control over their own learning or developing learner capacity for inquiry, agency and collaboration? Is it to address organisational priorities such as optimising school resources, increasing student access and enrolment, developing professional collaboration or stakeholder engagement in a more 'connected' school community? Whatever the objectives are, school leadership must identify what success looks like and identify the associated success metrics – that is, the quantitative and qualitative evidence of progress as related to each objective.

As indicated above, Blended Learning conditions can provide powerful new forms of quantitative and qualitative feedback regarding user behaviours and user perceptions. Digital quantitative data such as user login frequency and duration, page views, click rates, discussion posts and responses, and automated assessments can paint a detailed picture of user behaviour as well as identify the resources with which they engage in a digital environment. Furthermore, integrated technology can provide teachers and students with rapid real time opportunities for 360 degree qualitative feedback under a range of contexts such as teacher-to-student feedback regarding students' use of class time, student-to-teacher observations regarding the value of specific learning activities or resources, student-to-student feedback regarding collaboration in group activities, and teacher-to-teacher feedback during and after classroom observations. The extensive range of data available under blended conditions can generate a comprehensive profile of the teaching and learning dynamic. That being said, we are all too familiar with the fact that profiling can be a very dangerous activity. That is why the subject of observer feedback – be it a teacher, student or administrator – must be regularly invited to reflect upon the composite picture that the data points and place it in context of their personal learning conditions and purposes. This is a specific example where progressive evaluation can and should be fairly integrated into the CMF framework described above.

Of course, schools may choose to extend their progressive evaluation parameters beyond their original objectives to explore potential unforeseen benefits or side-effects of Blended Learning. As discussed above in regard to balanced planning, the process must embrace exploration and review unforeseen discoveries. For example, while a school's progress evaluation should focus upon their original Blended Learning objectives such as increased learner control and capacity, they should also remain available to unforeseen discoveries and make choices regarding possible correlations between Blended Learning conditions and such things as student performance in internal and external assessments, trends in levels of stake-holder satisfaction, trends in student and teacher retention, and even long-term trends in their graduates' university admissions and alumni destinations. Such short- and long-term data sets can provide timely evidence affirming whether the school is moving in the right direction toward their Blended Learning objectives, whether adjustments are required to get them on track, or whether new additional objectives should be considered. In business start-up terms, this is known as the capacity to 'pivot' – the ability to reassess, adapt and adjust one's original objectives as a result of evaluation feedback or unforeseen market challenges and opportunities. After all, the Frisbee 'flying saucer' began with a simple pie tin manufacturer, the Frisbie Pie Company in 1871, until it was discovered that they were more popular when thrown through the air than when placed in the oven. This point brings us to the issue of how and when progressive evaluation structures and CMF feedback can be used to inform timely decisions for both the organisation and its community members.

Role of evidence-based decision making

The purpose of gathering evidence from CMF feedback and progress evaluation is to inform the decision making around Blended Learning for school improvement. The stakes are high in Blended Learning implementation, and we emphasise again that in this respect school leadership is responsible for ensuring that all community members get a suitable return on investment. With judicious and timely use of evidence generated by CMF and progressive evaluation systems, school leadership can make responsible proactive and just-in-time decisions that allow them to fulfil their duties and achieve the improvement objectives. Evidence-based decision making is thus essential to the implementation of purposeful and successful Blended Learning in support of school improvement.

A connected approach can ensure that CMF and progressive evaluation activities are coordinated and scheduled to inform decisions for both school and teacher progress. Areas for team and individual improvement that are agreed upon, developed and monitored in the CMF process can be cross-referenced with agreed upon data sets in the progressive evaluation process. Likewise, hard data generated in the progressive evaluation system can be contextualised, unpacked and addressed in the CMF system. In a Venn diagram approach, these two circles not only provide an important system of checks and balances – they also overlap with and inform a third circle of school improvement activity, wherein evidence from both systems combine to inform the collaborative decisions that teachers and leadership make about the priorities to be addressed and planned actions to be taken in their shared and respective improvement journeys. In this context, an agreed upon action research model with a clear sequence for professional planning, action, observation and reflection can meet both organisational and individual needs in a way that uses progressive evaluation data in informative ways. Under such a model, a teacher-as-researcher framework empowers both leadership and teachers to identify areas for professional development within the above-mentioned CMF structures, and invites them to draft the next iteration of improvement and progressive evaluation.

The timing for this three-way dynamic between CMF, progressive evaluation and evidence-based decision making needs to be carefully considered. For instance, CMF structures can feature scheduled formative reviews of teacher and school progress at strategic points throughout the year, inviting community members to make adjustments that can support or extend achievement of improvement objectives as necessary. This three-way process can leverage the principles of Blended Learning itself in achieving their objectives – empowering teachers and leadership to collaborate in negotiating and controlling their improvement pace, place and pathways. While scheduled formative activities permit timely short-term adjustments, the importance of scheduled summative activities must not be overlooked – especially in regard to planning and budgeting for the next stage of improvement in the coming academic year. In this regard an annual progress evaluation process should conclude with a carefully scheduled, comprehensive, summative report. This report is not just a critical review of how far the school has come in fulfilling its improvement objectives; it is the foundation for the next stage of the school's improvement journey and the rationale for the next budget. A summative annual report formally represents the evidence-based decision making of school leadership. It identifies key issues to be addressed, it recommends associated strategies and it calculates the projected costs of requirements such as training time, training resources, technical resources and personnel.

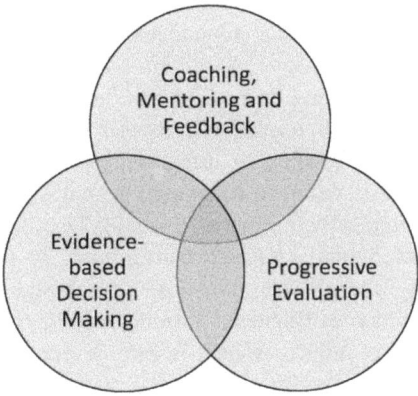

Figure 7.10 Integrated CMF, evaluation and decision making (created by the authors).

In this way, evidence-based decision making has a dual function – it serves as the capstone of one stage in the annual process for implementing Blended Learning for school improvement and it provides the cornerstone for the next stage (Figure 7.10).

Chapter summary

In this chapter we have attempted to articulate a clear design approach for Blended Learning in support of school improvement. This approach emphasises many of the key concepts and principles introduced in earlier chapters of the book, including the importance of effective school leadership, the purpose of Blended Learning in relation to the Knowledge Economy and the need to contextualise this purpose, the importance of evidence and the role of collaboration (CMF) to effective Blended Learning integration. Getting these things right is important when setting-up for the relevant skills sets and instilling appropriate levels of dispositional balance. Beyond that, however, it is also important to use SMART principles to ensure that coordinated communication and collaboration takes place within a blended approach to school improvement, and that an appropriate audit be undertaken initially, in order to include all stakeholders in both the design and ownership of the improvement agenda. Importantly, a key focus for this chapter has been on the relationship between Blended Learning and school improvement. In the next chapter (Chapter 8), we provide an example of how this relationship has played out in an authentic circumstance, seeking to illustrate how the concepts and principles highlighted in Chapter 7, and indeed across this entire book, can be implemented in a real-world context.

Glossary

Dimensions of Blended Learning matrix   A procedural design matrix by Aurora Institute, adapted here by the authors, to provide key questions and scaffolding for the considerations that need to be addressed for whole-school Blended Learning, including the level of Blended Learning practices for each year group, the degree of student-centred instruction to take place, and logistical issues such as instructional support models, instruction schedules and locations, and technological infrastructure.

Dispositional balance   Refers to a school community's capacity to recognise and respect various stakeholder perspectives in relation to transitional change. In this respect, the dispositions requiring balance are how we think about the various perspectives, plan to include these perspectives, pursue balanced communication between stakeholders, and seek balanced collaboration.

eBL design framework   A framework proposed by the authors to assist embedding the learning objectives for learner control in relation to learner capacity, and the learning objectives for organisational control in relation to organisational capacity, both within a Blended Learning environment that is designed to support school improvement. These framework functions are depicted graphically in Figures 7.6 and 7.7.

Knowledge Economy-Local School (KELS) continuum   A two-dimensional continuum designed to help identify where a school or other educational institution is operating with respect to the implementation of Blended Learning, as this implementation is appraised in relation to the imperatives of the Knowledge Economy versus the capabilities and needs of the local school.

McKinsey's Integrated Transition Framework   A model for organisational transformation, based on identifying the effectiveness of organisational performance across seven inter-dynamic dimensions. This model is important for successful change management in relation to implementing Blended Learning in that it provides a clear procedural approach to this implementation, based on the McKinsey Group's 'Four Building Blocks for Change': foster understanding and conviction for change; reinforce for change; publicise the achievement of change milestones and develop talent and skills for change.

Progressive evaluation   Refers to the systematic collection, analysis and reporting of data as essential to the development of a whole-school improvement culture within an embedded Blended Learning environment. As noted in this chapter, CMF structures are most effective in promoting sustained and purposeful school improvement when they are integrated with comprehensive and progressive evaluation structures.

Note

1 Ries, E. *The Lean Startup Methodology.* Retrieved June 1, 2020, from http://theleanstartup.com/principles.

References

Arnett, T. (2019). *One major barrier to high-quality Blended Learning.* Retrieved September 11, 2019, from www.christenseninstitute.org/blog/one-major-barrier-to-high-quality-blended-learning/?_sft_

Aurora Institute. (2011). *iNACOL National Standards for Quality Online Courses (v2)*, 6. Retrieved June 3, 2020, from https://aurora-institute.org/resource/inacol-national-standards-for-quality-online-courses-v2/

Basford, T., & Schaninger, B. (2016). The four building blocks of change. *McKinsey Quarterly.* Retrieved May 25, 2020, from www.mckinsey.com/business-functions/organization/our-insights/the-four-building-blocks–of-change

Bill & Melinda Gates Foundation. (2010). *Next generation learning – The intelligent use of technology to develop innovative learning models and personalized educational pathways.* Retrieved March 12, 2016, from www.bespacific.com/bill-melinda-gates-foundation-next-generation-learning/

Christensen Institute. (2019). Disruptive innovation. Retrieved November 10, 2019, from www.christenseninstitute.org/disruptive-innovations/

Clarke, A. C. (1980). Electronic tutors. *Omni Magazine, 2*(9), 77.

Fullan, M. (2012). *Stratosphere: Integrating technology, pedagogy, and change knowledge.* Pearson Canada.

Hattie, J., & Zierer, K. (2018). *10 Mindframes for visible learning: Teaching for success.* Routledge/Taylor & Francis.

Horn, M. B., & Staker, H. (2017). *The blended workbook: Learning to design the schools of our future.* Wiley & Sons.

International Society for Technology in Education. (2007). *National educational technology standards for students* (2nd ed.), (NETS-S). Author. http://cnets.iste.org/inhouse/nets/cnets/students/pdf/NETS_for_Students_2007.pdf

Knee, J. S. (2016). *Class clowns: How the smartest investors lost billions in education.* Columbia Business School Publishing.

Lynch, D., & Smith, R. (2014). Improving teaching through coaching, mentoring and feedback: A review of the literature. *MIER Journal of Educational Studies, Trends & Practices, 4*(2), 136–166.

Lynch, D. E. (2012). *Preparing teachers in times of change: Teaching school, standards, new content and evidence.* Primrose Hall Publishing Group.

Newcomb, T. (2020). Why do I want digital experiences for my kids if it looks like this? Experts fear parent backlash against online learning. The 74. Retrieved April 22, 2020, from www.the74million.

org/article/why-do-i-want-digital-experiences-for-my-kids-if-it-looks-like-this-experts-fear-parent-backlash-against-online-learning/?utm_source=Ed%20Digest&utm_medium=email&utm_campaign=4%2F10%2F20

Prensky, M. (2012). *Technology and the quest for digital wisdom.* St. Martin's Press.

Puentedura, R. R. (2020) *An intro to the SAMR method: The two-pass ladder.* Retrieved June 12, 2020, from http://hippasus.com/blog/archives/501

Robinson, K. (2015). *Creative schools: Revolutionizing education from the ground up.* Allen Lane.

Schleicher, A. (2012). *Preparing teachers and developing school leaders for the 21st century; lessons from around the world.* OECD Publishing. Retrieved March 10, 2017, from https://unesdoc.unesco.org/ark:/48223/pf0000246124

Startups.com. (2017) *Everyone pivots: The truth about a startup pivot.* Retrieved June 17, 2020, from www.startups.com/library/expert-advice/startup-business-pivot

The Indian Ministry of Human Resource Development (MHRD). (2016). *Themes and questions for policy consultation on school education.* Retrieved November 12, 2016, from https://mhrd.gov.in/nep

UK Department for Education. (2014). *Education Technology Action Group (ETAG) reflections and recommendations.* www.naec.org.uk/artefacts/reports/educational-technology-action-group-our-reflections

UNESCO Institute for Statistics. (2016). *The world needs almost 69 million new teachers to reach the 2030 education goals.* Retrieved March 8, 2017, from https://unesdoc.unesco.org/ark:/48223/pf0000246124

US Department of Education. (2020). *National Education Technology Plan.* Retrieved June 13, 2018, from https://tech.ed.gov/netp/

Waite, C. (2019). *6 insights about school innovation from 173 schools you may never have heard of.* Retrieved November 1, 2019, from www.christenseninstitute.org/blog/6-insights-about-school-innovation-from-173-schools-you-may-never-have-heard-of/?_sft_topics=personalized-blended-learning,teacher-of-the-future,higher-education

Wei, Y., Shi, Y., Yang, H., & Liu, J. (2017). Blended learning versus traditional learning: A study of students' learning achievements and academic press. *International Symposium on Educational Technology, 2019*, 223. https://doi.org/10.1109/iset.2017.57

White, J. (2019). *5 blended-learning trends to watch.* Retrieved November 12, 2019, from www.christenseninstitute.org/blog/5-blended-learning-trends-to-watch/?_sf_s=teacher+design+of+blended+learning

Yeigh, T., Lynch, D., Turner, D., Fradale, P., Willis, R., Sell, K., & Lawless, E. (2020). Using Blended Learning to support whole-of-school improvement: The need for contextualisation. *Education and Information Technologies.* https://doi.org/10.1007/s10639-020-10114-6

8 Using embedded Blended Learning to create the outstanding school

Relevant Australian Professional Standards for Teachers: 1.2; 1.5; 2.6; 3.4; 3.6; 4.5; 5.1; 5.4; 6.2; 6.3; 6.4; 7.4

Chapter synopsis

Summing up what we have said in the prior chapters of this book, technological innovation exerts a fundamental impact on the structure of society in terms of the way people live, socialise, work and learn, a societal circumstance known collectively as the **Knowledge Economy**. This has resulted in calls for schools and other education providers to develop new teaching strategies that incorporate technology designed to improve student outcomes and support a shift to more student-centred learning. This represents what is essentially a new learning paradigm for education, and from this perspective the research literature positions Blended Learning as a pedagogical approach designed to harness the positive power of technological disruption in ways that are intended to increase student-centred, student-led learning via the assistance of technology.

In addition, the impact of the COVID-19 pandemic on education, especially how this has driven schools to undertake large-scale online teaching and learning, also positions Blended Learning as an important pedagogical approach for today and moving into the future. It is highly unlikely that education will ever return precisely to what it used to be, partly because the impact of this pandemic seems far from over but also due to the increased use of technology that this situation has forced upon schools and teachers in general. We therefore need to consider how schools can continue to use technology to address the issues this pandemic has created. In this respect Collie and Martin (2020) emphasise the need this has created for 'teacher adaptability', that is, teachers being adaptable in relation to how they teach and how they achieve professional capacity within the context of online teaching and learning, and Lieberman (2020) identifies the development of what he terms the 'digital savvy' teacher as a key imperative for education moving into the future. These suggestions reinforce the need to upskill teachers in the use of ICT as a primary point of reference for ongoing teacher adaptability.

We also noted that Blended Learning is still developing as a distinct pedagogical format, and because of this does not have a single, universally agreed definition in terms of specific structure or process. However, there is general agreement that Blended Learning involves some combination of face-to-face (F2F) and online learning elements, and that the main focus for learning needs to be situated within a school setting (Horn & Staker, 2015). Connecting student learning to actual school settings is important because this ensures that the learner's online experience is informing what's happening in the classroom and vice versa, suggesting one reason why Blended Learning works best when embedded within a holistic, whole-of-school improvement initiative. This also suggests that effective use of Blended Learning necessitates a considered design approach that is sensitive to multiple factors and perspectives, in order to provide clarity of purpose for the use of Blended Learning as it may be situated within a particular context.

In order to address these concerns, it is necessary to define and position Blended Learning within the immediate context of the local school environment, to ensure that the specific Blended Learning approach is relevant and appropriate to the authentic capabilities and needs of the school. Clark and Barbour (2015) refer to this as 'intentional design', and it is the purpose of this chapter to demonstrate how an actual intentional design process was used to implement Blended Learning in a way that addresses global issues associated with the Knowledge Economy, while at the same time also able to address the issues and needs of the local school, that is, in-line with the KELS continuum as proposed in this book.

In this respect the current chapter will examine a case study in which the concepts and principles described in various chapters, and particularly in Chapter 7, were used to contextualise a Blended Learning pedagogical approach to whole-of-school improvement in two schools in Japan. Following an extensive review of the Blended Learning literature to identify key conceptual elements and their associated understandings (Willis et al., 2018a), the purpose of this study was to position and design an embedded Blended Learning (**eBL**) project across three associated phases:

1. Establishing the degree to which the schools were ready for improvement, including:

    a. teachers' attitudes toward and competencies in the use of technology;
    b. teachers' understanding of Blended Learning,
    c. teachers' readiness to engage with the change agenda associated with school improvement;
    d. school leadership readiness to manage the change agenda associated with school improvement;
    e. teachers' ability to research their teaching as the basis for professional development in relation to student achievement; and
    f. students' achievement under a blended learning pedagogy.

2. Designing and implementing an embedded Blended Learning (eBL) improvement agenda, including:

    a. constructing a whole-of-school improvement schema for incorporating Blended Learning into the improvement agenda;
    b. developing a model to explain and frame what the project was to implement (the Collaborative Blended Learning Model);
    c. developing a series of professional development (PD) units to use as the basis for teacher knowledge and understandings about Blended Learning; and
    d. establishing a digital learning management system to provide standards and record progress in relation to improvement.

3. Designing a systematic data collection schedule for monitoring and evaluating agenda progress, including:

    a. establishing clear baseline and ongoing data collection strategies, comprised of attitudinal and behavioural data (Readiness Survey, Leadership Survey, Teacher BL Survey), as well as standardised student achievement data (school ISA data, PAT-R and PAT-M data);

b. constructing a systematic data collection timeline for the purpose of ongoing monitoring and evaluation to support and guide the project; and

c. determining a data analysis and project reporting timeline for monitoring and evaluating the eBL project in a valid and authentic manner.

Data collection was targeted as an essential skill set for the eBL Project because it is essential to the provision of evidence-based decision making for school improvement, and in this respect represented a core focus for the overall project design and implementation. The logic of this approach is presented in Figure 8.1, which provides an overview of the relationships between school improvement, project implementation and student learning in terms of the data collection process.

eBL methodology

We note that the eBL Project adopted pragmatism as its theoretical framework for research purposes, largely because pragmatism uses an inductive approach toward data collection and analysis to determine what, and how, things work in real-world settings. Within this framework, the eBL Project employed a methodology based on **explanatory research design** to identify the important concepts, principles, behaviours and attitudes that appeared to effect the project. The importance of this design is that it allowed us to inductively analyse project information, forming a good basis for authentic, evidence-driven decision making. The relationship between project implementation and theoretical framework may seem less relevant to the contextualising process at 'first blush', but be aware that having a clear theoretical framework is important because this framework is what provides a bridge between project implementation and meaningful project evaluation. It's always good to know what sort of theoretical framework is most relevant to a school project you may be involved with, in order to ensure you are able to perform a meaningful evaluation of the project as it proceeds.

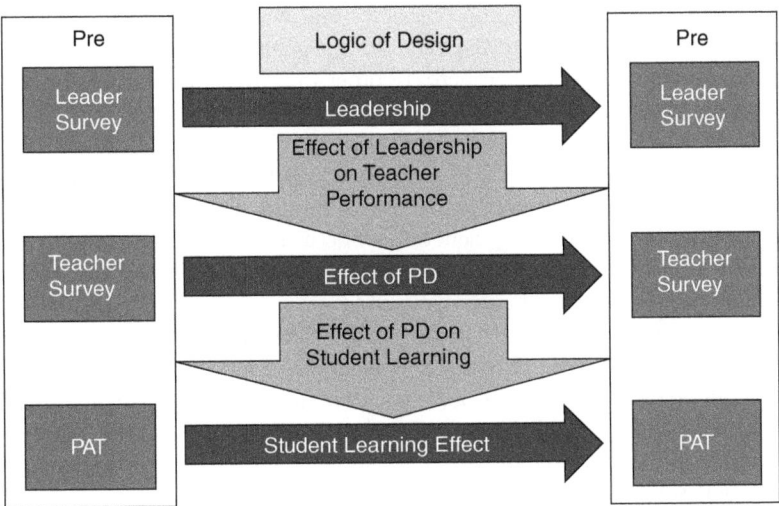

Figure 8.1 Overview of relationships between data collection and school leadership, teacher professional development and student learning.

Within the explanatory research design methodology, a mixed methods approach was used to collect data for the project, with quantitative data captured using Likert-type scales and qualitative data obtained using semi-structured interviews conducted by trained interviewers. The quantitative data consisted of standardised student achievement data, teacher surveys and school 'readiness' data. The qualitative data consisted of teacher and leadership interviews, led by trained interviewers during various periods at the participating schools, aimed at determining teacher and leadership attitudes, beliefs and ideas about the eBL Project. An overview of teacher confidence ratings in relation to their professional learning was also included in the data collection process, as this provides some insights regarding changes in teacher confidence across the project. This professional learning occurred via a series of professional development (PD) units that were developed for the project, specifically for the purpose of developing teacher knowledge and skills in areas deemed important to successful Blended Learning and school improvement. These units introduced teachers to Blended Learning, ICT use, curriculum design, data-driven decision making and strategies for collegial collaboration. The main focus for these units was on theoretical and applied knowledge about Blended Learning, the teacher-as-researcher (TaR) and team collaboration.

Data collection measures

A primary focus for the eBL Project was student achievement, as mediated by teacher professional learning in the PD units. In line with this focus, the following measures were designed to capture student achievement (PAT-R & M and ISA) in relation to teacher attitudes and behaviour concerning the project (BL Teacher Survey), within the whole-of-school improvement initiative (Readiness Survey and staff interviews) which took place at the participating schools.

The standardised tests (PAT-R & M and ISA) were used to show the level of student learning outcomes in the core areas of literacy and numeracy over a 3-year period. While not comprehensive in terms of the overall school curriculum, these tests do provide significant insight into important student learning outcomes and were thus able to act as proxies for outcome effectiveness in relation to the eBL Project goals and outcomes. A brief overview of each quantitative measure is given here, in order to provide an example of how this part of a project design can occur.

PAT-R & M – These *Progressive Achievement Tests* (PAT) were used to provide a standardised measure (specifically formatted for purposes of comparison) of student achievement over time. This allowed us to assess progressive change in student academic achievement within the participating schools, while at the same time compare results with normative data from other schools. The use of PAT tests thus allowed for both intra- and inter-school comparisons of student achievement.

ISA – The *International Schools Assessment* (ISA) program is designed specifically for grades 3–10 in international schools. It is based on the OECD's *Programme for International Student Assessment* (PISA), and assesses student learning in the areas of reading, writing and mathematical literacy (grades 3–10), and scientific literacy (grades 7–10). ISA data is standardised in order to allow comparisons between approximately 400 international schools globally (around 90,000 students). ISA data is thus useful for making inter-school comparisons based on scores that have been amalgamated across the designated areas. It does not provide area-specific analyses, however, and although aligned with PISA areas it is important to note that the ISA program is not endorsed by the OECD. For these reasons we also included the PAT measures to indicate student achievement in more specific areas.

BL Teacher Survey – The *BL Teacher Survey* was a project-specific measure created to function as an exploratory tool for building theory and to aid in providing a measure of teacher change over the course of the project. Included in the survey are items intended to measure teacher attitudes and behaviours regarding important aspects of the eBL project, such as the use of ICT (in the classroom as well as general skills), face-to-face classroom interactions, student-centred learning, the inquiry context, and teachers' use of student data. The BL Teacher Survey is conceptually linked to a **BL Schema**, which underpinned the overall improvement agenda. This schema was co-designed by all stakeholders, including teachers, school leaders and academic mentors. In addition, input by students via their teachers, and from parents via school leaders and teachers, also contributed to the construction of the schema for this project.

Readiness Survey – The Readiness Survey is used to measure alignment, capabilities, and engagement within the school from the perspective of the teachers and school leaders (using separate versions of the survey). In this respect, alignment relates to how clear and congruent school goals, strategies and priorities are to staff. Capabilities assess whether there is sufficient information, resources and skills within the schools to do the work and meet the project goals as required. Engagement refers to the motivational energy or commitment of staff, and thus incorporates a willingness to exert effort and act as an advocate for successful project outcomes. Research suggests that maximising these three things will increase a school's ability to make effective improvements when instituting a significant change program, such as involved in a school improvement initiative or implementing a Blended Learning pedagogy (Yeigh & Lynch, 2017; Yeigh et al., 2018). The Readiness Survey was used to provide information about how functional and effective the relationship between school leadership and teacher behaviours was in terms of ensuring that the participating schools were ready for implementing successful project change.

Contextualising the eBL Project

There were two main teacher skill sets considered important for positioning and contextualising the eBL Project: The school's pre-project relationship with technology as an instructional tool, and the teachers' pre-project understanding of the connections between 'evidence' and their own teaching. A teacher-as-researcher (TaR) inquiry approach was used to determine the degree to which these skill sets were present within the project schools, targeting the teachers' use of and attitudes toward technology, their understanding of evidence-driven decision making as a basis for professional learning and making pedagogical change, and defining what they thought a contextualised, high-quality model of Blended Learning might look like for their school. At the heart of this inquiry lay a focus on developing the foundations for a fully blended instructional approach at the participating schools, requiring teacher understanding of how to use technology to drive student-centred learning and how to develop evidence to inform their teaching practices.

Building skill sets: the TaR inquiry

As noted in Chapter 7, the purpose of the teacher-as-researcher (TaR) inquiry is to provide a framework for school improvement programs by investigating the key issues that impact students, teachers and schools. The objectives for the inquiry used to assist contextualising the eBL Project were to:

- develop a collaborative understanding of Blended Learning;
- provide a relevant background for the eBL project;
- determine the teachers' use of and attitudes toward technology;
- instil a clear understanding of evidence-driven decision making as a basis for professional learning and pedagogical change;
- begin defining what a contextualised, high-quality model of Blended Learning might look like for the case study schools, based on an inquiry-based learning approach.

The TaR inquiry approach was considered important for helping to contextualise the eBL Project because one of the key features of Blended Learning as an emerging pedagogy is that it focuses on the relationship between practice and research. This relationship is crucial to the ongoing development of Blended Learning as a distinctive pedagogy because it allows us to evaluate the effectiveness of the pedagogical decisions we make in relation to the practice of Blended Learning in schools and classrooms. In this respect, how we design Blended Learning requires us to make certain decisions regarding how we will implement it as part of our practice, and then be able to evaluate and make judgements about those decisions from an informed point of view. There thus exists a clear need to collect data in relation to these teaching decisions, with data collection and analysis normally viewed as a function of research. A depiction of this relationship is shown in Figure 8.2, indicating how the different elements of the TaR inquiry cycle interacted with Blended Learning data collection in relation to the case study eBL Project.

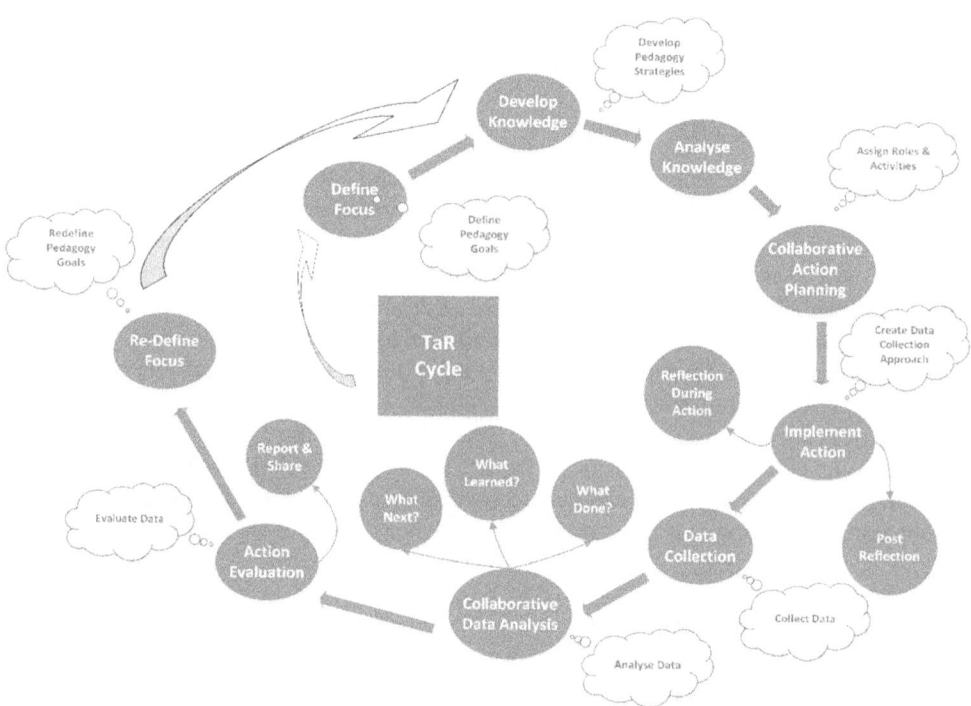

Figure 8.2 Overview of the relationship between Blended Learning and the TaR cycle.

A meaningful 'take-away' from this part of the chapter is that the use of research to inform our understanding of Blended Learning is an important contextualising principle. In this respect, integrating research into applied Blended Learning is highly appropriate whenever we want to assess, compare or evaluate the decisions we have made about how to implement Blended Learning as an applied pedagogy or teaching practice. We can therefore make use of research to identify the type of relationship that exists between different aspects (often called 'factors' or 'variables') of a particular situation, in order to determine (say) which teaching strategy works best within a given situation, how one management program might compare against another, which variable (amongst several) exerts the most influence on learning, which model of Blended Learning might work better for teaching a particular type of lesson, what type of technology might work best for younger learners, etc. The point is that a natural correspondence exists between research and Blended Learning, and there thus exists an intuitive logic to the use of a TaR inquiry to help develop the foundational skill sets needed by teachers, in preparation for the implementation of a whole-school improvement program that is based on Blended Learning. This is particularly important for laying an appropriate foundation for evidence-driven decision making on the part of teachers, as well as in terms of helping to contextualise Blended Learning to the specific characteristics of an individual school or group of schools.

Positioning skill sets: the BLSschema

The BL Schema represents a collaborative conceptualisation of how to contextualise the eBL Project in relation to the improvement agenda of the case study schools, as presaged in Chapter 7. For the eBL Project this schema provided an underlying framework for the Collaborative Blended Learning Model used by these schools (Figure 8.4), designed to support this model within a change agenda impacting teachers. In this respect the BL Schema operated as a mechanism to articulate, scope, direct and guide each school, its leaders and teachers, to understand the overall relationship between Blended Learning and school improvement in relation to what needed to change and what these changes would 'look like' in terms of classroom application at the local school level (Lynch et al., 2014). Figure 8.3 provides a visual representation of how this schema was conceived in relation to the case study eBL Project, highlighting how the schema centred on student learning via a Blended Learning pedagogy that was used to filter the various components of the school improvement agenda.

As an initial part of the contextualising process, this schema was collaboratively construed as a series of pedagogical elements and outcomes via discussions and meetings involving the school leaders, teachers and research team, with prior discussions with students and parents having been undertaken by the teachers and school leaders. The pedagogical elements included clear descriptions of the goals for student learning, specific blended teaching strategies, what types of face-to-face (F2F) interactions were to be involved, how to use digital technologies to support teacher and student inquiry, what constituted student-centred learning and how to construct an inquiry context. For each of these elements, relevant evidence was also described in the BL Schema, using a hierarchical descriptive system to show progressive development for each element. This is an excellent way to 'custom-fit' an integrated improvement initiative, such as the eBL project, into a specific context (Ingvarson et al., 2014; TEMAG, 2014), and although this entire schema is far too large to show here, Table 8.1 provides an example of how the BL Schema was originally conceived in this manner.

We note that the BL Schema was further developed for specific application to teacher curriculum planning, via successive iterations across the eBL project. Discussion of this

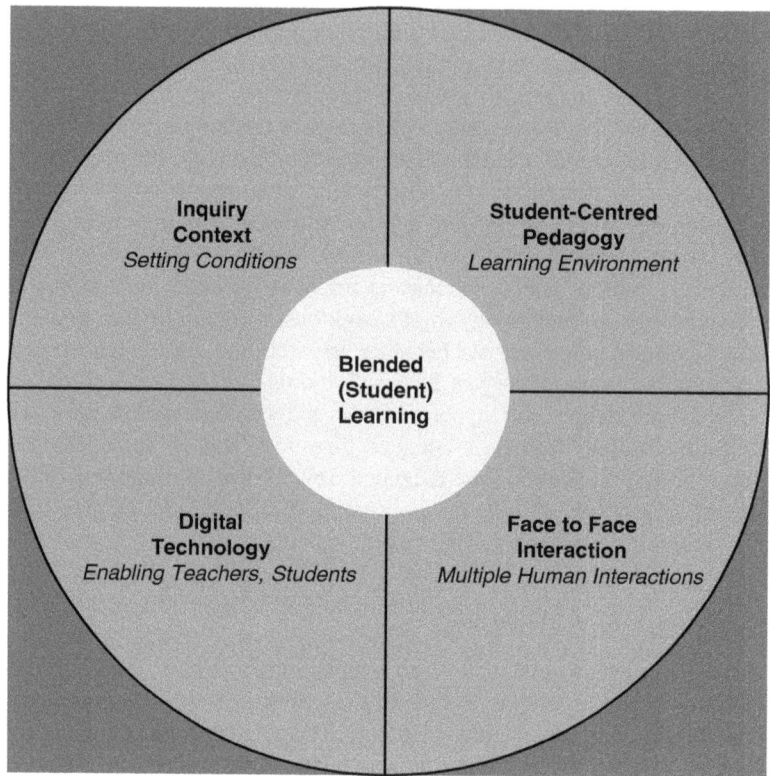

Figure 8.3 Visual representation of the underlying BL schema.

further application has been published elsewhere (Yeigh et al., 2020), but here we simply want to detail how this schema was originally developed as a strategy to support the process of contextualising, in order to provide an example of how to begin the process of contextualisation in general terms.

Integrating skill sets: the CBLM

The application of these elements to the eBL Project was encapsulated in a Collaborative Blended Learning Model (CBLM), which seeks to capture how the important relationships of the underlying BL schema are meant to operate in the service of overall school improvement. Figure 8.4 provides a simplified overview of the CBLM, showing how its basic dimensions (student and teacher) interact to support specific project outcomes that underpin the teacher skill sets considered important for positioning and contextualising the eBL Project for these particular schools.

The assumptions of this model are crucial to the intent of Blended Learning as a contextualised pedagogy, and are what characterise Blended Learning as a distinct pedagogical approach for an embedded Blended Learning project, as opposed to the role of technology per se, which some might expect to be more the case (cf. Willis et al., 2018b). When understood from this perspective, the CBLM can be seen as a modern pedagogical model in

Table 8.1 Example elements from the BL schema

Goals for student learning	Specific Blended Teaching strategy	F2F interactions	Digital technologies	Student-centred learning	Inquiry context
1.1 Teacher is able to articulate: – The vision for the school – His/her role in delivering on the school's vision – The component pieces that he/she personally has to engage with for success	2.1 Curriculum implementation is aligned with vision and values	3.1 Teacher in student interactions: – Uses open ended questions – Checks for understanding	4.1 Teachers deliberately use 'off the shelf' digital technology product/s	5.1 Students can: – Articulate the goal for learning – Explain what they are learning	6.1 Statements of inquiry drive process, along with Big Question foci and the use of provocations to find out and test things; focus on deep conceptual learning
1.4 Teacher references individual student and collaborative learning profiles in plans and can provide explicit insight into each student's current performance level based on a hierarchy of thinking orders	2.4 Collaboration with teaching team members becomes central for teaching and learning effects Efficiencies and increased capacities for dealing with individual students is created	3.4 Teacher incorporates feedback from students to inform next teaching steps	4.4 Teachers develop their own digital technology product to enhance learning (e.g. design an app)	5.4 Students decide pace of their learning (e.g. students negotiate submission dates)	6.4 Students engage with problems that are significant to them and their immediate world, propose a solution and test for fit and effectiveness and report on findings using various ICTs
1.5 Teacher develops a plan for each student: – based on data in the form of an individual student learning profile (i.e., identified learning need) and managed through technology	2.5 Teacher incorporates path, place and pace options into learning engagements	3.5 Learning environment customised to meet student learning goals: collaborative configurations, resource and study centres, ICT devices, furniture configurations, appropriate digital technology and the technical resources used	4.5 Teachers use adaptive technology as part of the learning management system	5.5.Students decide path for their learning (e.g. students negotiate use of external academic programs)	6.5 Students set and engage with problems that are significant to them and their immediate world, propose a solution and test for fit and effectiveness, and report on findings using various ICTs

(Created by the authors)

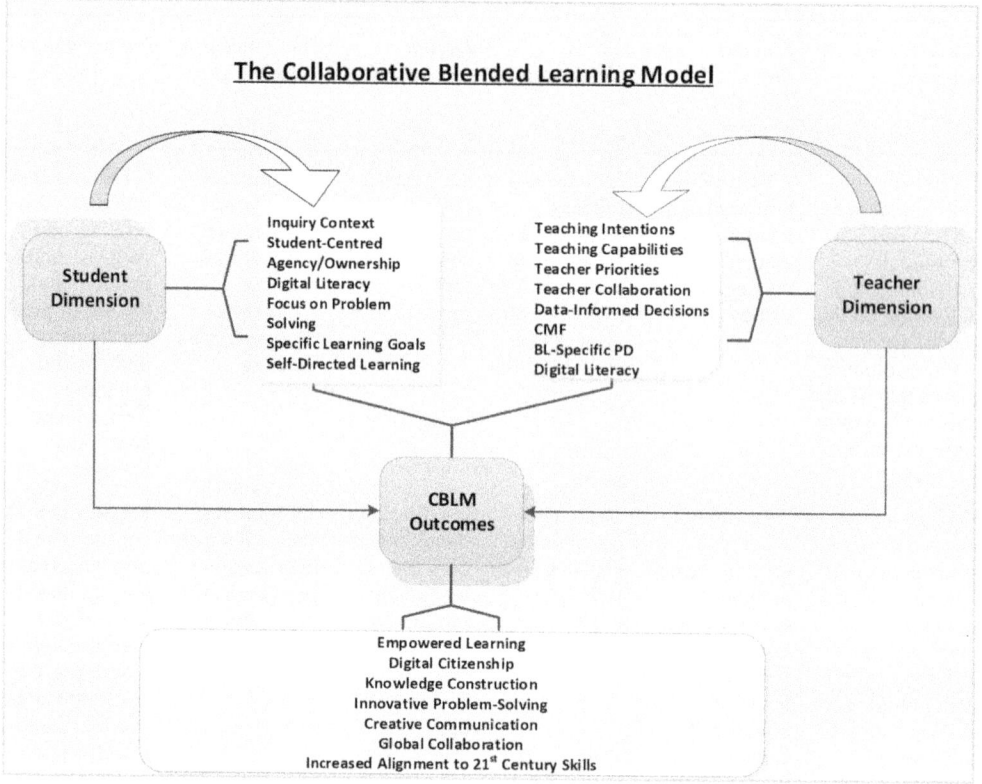

Figure 8.4 Overview of the CBLM as contextualised for the eBL Project.

which the classroom and online learning elements inform and direct one another in a reciprocal manner. Importantly, the goal of this reciprocity is to change the fundamental role of the teacher and the student in a manner designed to better differentiate and personalise student learning, that is, to increase student control over the learning that takes place in schools and classrooms. This is critical in that it lays the foundation for student ownership of the learning, a necessary pre-condition for genuine learner agency. Learner agency is crucial to successful Blended Learning (Arnett, 2019), and will become even more so in the wake of the COVID-19 pandemic situation that schools currently find themselves in (Gerwertz, 2020; Guttentag, 2020). Because of this, understanding how to develop a collaborative approach to teaching and learning that includes both teachers and students will be imperative for teachers and school leaders as education moves forward in pursuit of learner outcomes that reflect twenty-first-century skills. The CBLM is provided here as one example of how to plan and design for this level of collaboration.

Case study findings

To this point in the chapter we have learned why it is important to contextualise Blended Learning in order to address the imperatives of the Knowledge Economy in a way that also meets the authentic needs and goals of an individual school or school system. We also looked at key strategies for contextualising Blended Learning within an overall school improvement initiative, in order to ensure that the relevant teacher skill sets and support systems are embedded within the initiative, and in a way that supports teacher and student agency as crucial elements of education for the twenty-first century. This represents what might be termed a 'macro' understanding concerning the essential need to contextualise Blended Learning and exampling ways of designing for this at a large-scale or general level of planning. We now turn to an examination of how this more generalised understanding can be instantiated within a specific context, in order to delineate these concepts and principles in more detail. In this respect we will now report on the data and outcomes associated with the participating eBL Project schools, for the purpose of providing a case study example of how Blended Learning was actually contextualised in alignment with the design principles that have been presented throughout this book. From this perspective, the intention of the eBL Project was to build relevant skills sets, position these skills sets authentically, and integrate the skill sets in accordance with the mission and goals of the participating schools. This allowed the eBL Project to address the concerns of the Knowledge Economy within the confines of the schools' immediate classroom situations. We also learned, in earlier portions of this book, that a key teacher skill set is the ability to collect and analyse data for the purpose of monitoring and evaluating what they are doing, how they are doing it, and what effect this was having on student learning over time. This forms the basis for evidence-based decisions about teaching, student learning and school leadership with respect to the overall school improvement program. Details of how these aspects of the eBL Project were operationalised for the participating schools will now form key elements of examination. We will also examine some of the major findings that came out of the eBL case study schools, to get an idea of how much impact these skill sets had on teaching and learning at the local school level. An important caveat for these findings is that they are provided as example impact indicators only, that is, they are not intended as categorical representations of success or effectiveness. Rather, they are used here to promote one way of developing a whole-school improvement initiative that is framed within a Blended Learning pedagogy.

Readiness Survey

We will begin by discussing the Readiness Survey outcomes, as this data is foundational for the contextualising process. It provides insights into how functional and effective the relationship between school leadership and teacher behaviours is, in terms of ensuring that the school is ready for improvement and ongoing change.

We summarised the responses to this survey in terms of whether they represent a contribution to readiness for change or an inhibitor to change. Specific contributors and impediments to **school readiness** at the time of data collection are shown below, based on the initial Readiness Survey administered to these schools. At this time, staff indicated the top 5 contributors and impediments to readiness as follows, and we note that the impediments here appear to echo other areas of data collection for this project, which also indicated a desire for additional time, more specific guidance and increased (or more consistent) leadership feedback. We also note the potential for further development that seems inherent to the contributors here, as this reminds us of the relatively strong support for the overall project that was found in the BL Survey ratings and teacher confidence ratings, as examined subsequently.

Contributors	Impediments
• Staff are ready to be responsible for improving student achievement. • Teamwork and cooperation within work units/departments or teams is sufficient. • The school's values have been clearly articulated to me. • Staff are happy with this school as a place to work. • Staff are generally treated with respect and dignity in this school.	• The school is not one of the best schools to work for this part of the country. • The school staff do not have all the information about students that they need to raise academic performance in this school. • The resources required to teach students are not readily available. • Staff in the school do not get focused training so they can meet the school's expectations. • The school's professional learning programs have not made teachers and administrators more effective in their work.

A breakdown of the specific readiness elements is shown in Figure 8.5, categorised by the survey components (alignment, capabilities and engagement). Note there are no 'needs work' elements in the alignment section of these responses, but a majority of these do exist in the capabilities section. Thus, there appears to be clear understanding and support for the school's mission and goals on the part of teachers (alignment), but this is coupled to less satisfaction or clarity around issues of support and feedback (capability). Of interest, the 'needs work' elements relating to capabilities seem to again highlight the teachers' desire for increased feedback (availability of key information and evaluations on performance) and more specific guidance (levels of professional learning and availability of resources).

The engagement section of the survey responses shows moderate satisfaction with the work environment and a strong sense of collegial support. Receptivity to feedback and perceptions concerning organisational support are both viewed as needing further work however. This may reflect a desire to provide more 'bottom-up' feedback to school leaders by the teachers, as they also reported in their qualitative feedback for this project (teacher interviews), as well as a perception that more specific guidance and feedback is needed, in particular ICT skills and collaborative team performance according to other report data.

Overall the readiness report data reveals strong support for the goals and mission of the school, and moderate satisfaction with how these goals are being pursued, yet low satisfaction with the organisation and guidance provided by leadership. This data thus provides highly relevant information about how the school leadership team is impacting on the teachers' project engagement, and suggests clear direction for modifying the leadership approach to providing feedback to teachers about their project engagement moving forward.

BL Survey

We began analysis of the BL Survey data by performing Exploratory Factor Analysis (Principal Component Analysis) to identify the underlying structure of the survey. This analysis revealed a number of survey sub-factors (distinct categories that the different survey items could be classified by), as follows:

• ICT skills, attitude and behaviour change due to the BL Project (ICT).
• Impact of professional development on student-centred learning, inquiry approach, collaboration, and core team inquiry (PD).

Key Readiness Elements

Report
developed by

Southern Cross
University

Alignment

• Committed to being responsible for improving student achievement	○
• Levels of teamwork and cooperation	○
• Focus on making teaching more effective	○
• Clarity on school Values	○
• Clarity on the Strategic Plan	●
• Clarity on what good teaching is	○
• Clarity on goals to focus upon	○

Capabilities

• Availability of key information	○
• Levels of professional learning	●
• Leadership competency	○
• Availability of resources	●
• Levels of Skills to achieve goals	●
• Extent of evaluations on performance	○
• Level of capable staff to achieve goals	○

Engagement

• Satisfaction with workplace	○
• Receptivity to feedback	○
• Levels of organisation	○
• Levels of support	○

Reading the Report

Student Academic Performance: This graph represents your overall school performance in NAPLAN literacy elements over three years in comparison to similar schools and all schools.

Staff Readiness Indicator: The readiness score and its positioning on the 'readiness scale' represents the level of staff alignment, capability and engagement in the school. It is an indicator of the readiness level of staff to engage in a whole-of-school teaching improvement strategy.

Top 5 Contributors and Impediments to Readiness: Based on the readiness survey that staff completed, this section provides an outline of key indicative elements that will contribute or impede readiness of the school to undertake whole of school teaching improvement (or a change strategy). ● ○ ○

Key Readiness Elements: Coloured circles represent: Red = Needs Work; Amber = Getting There; and Green = On Track. These are relative scores within the school.

Readiness for Teaching Improvement - Detailed Report

For more information on the detailed report where a comprehensive breakdown of all associated elements in this report are revealed, please contact:

Name: .... Position: .... Email: .... Phone: ....

Schiemann, W.A. (2012), The ACE advantage: how smart companies unleash talent for optimal performance, Society for Human Resource Management, Alexandria, VA.

Figure 8.5 Key readiness elements.

- Core Team Work importance in the BL Project and impact on teaching (CTW).
- Leadership oversight and feedback.

The ICT, PD and CTW subscales were all found to have a single underlying factor, each of which explained over 70 per cent of the variance for each item (this supports item integrity). The Leadership subscale, however, was found to have two underlying factors: *Leadership Feedback* and *Leadership Oversight*. Together, these two factors accounted for 92 per cent of the variance within the Leadership items.

As can be seen in Table 8.2, internal reliability for these subscales is high. This provides evidence that each subscale item is measuring the same subscale construct (the same variable or factor) as the other items in that subscale, thus affording confidence that the subscale items are consistent in the way they are measuring each construct.

EFA interpretation

These findings are interesting because they suggest that two different aspects of leadership are being represented in the Leadership item responses, one focusing on oversight and the other on feedback. In this respect it is important to note that whereas the mean (average) rating for Leadership Oversight (4.52) was the second-highest rating for these subscales overall, the mean rating for Leadership Feedback (3.45) was the lowest, and that the standard deviation (SD) for Leadership Feedback (1.48) was the highest SD for these ratings overall (i.e., the responses for this subscale had the least amount of agreement/most amount of disagreement). This may seem like a lot of mathematical 'jargon' at this point, but these findings are important because they accord with the Readiness Survey data also analysed for this project, in that both data sets identified strong leadership guidance (especially at the beginning of the project) coupled to inconsistent ongoing feedback as a relevant issue for the project. Thus we were able to use corresponding data from the Readiness Survey and the BL Survey to reinforce a particular 'message' important to the ongoing direction of this project, in this case noting that a certain disconnect seemed to be occurring between leadership feedback and leadership oversight that required attention on the part of the school leadership team.

To dig a bit deeper into this information, we also performed cluster analysis to assess whether there were different teacher profiles (different groups of teachers) that could be distinguished based on responses to the BL Survey subscales. In this respect the same two cluster solutions were found when analysing the survey items separately and as subscales, in both cases identifying one group of teachers who scored higher on all 5 subscales, and another group of teachers who scored lower on all 5 subscales. Importantly, the relative predictors for this grouping structure were (from most important to least

Table 8.2 Cronbach's alpha and descriptive statistics of subscales

	Cronbach's alpha	N of items	Mean	Std. deviation
ICT	.875	4	4.45	0.99
PD	.868	4	4.51	1.13
CTW	.883	4	4.89	1.11
Leadership Feedback	.972	4	3.45	1.48
Leadership Oversight	.959	4	4.52	1.37

(Created by the authors)

important) CTW, Leadership Oversight, ICT, PD, and Leadership Feedback. That is, CTW most differentiated between the clusters (or teacher groups), while Leadership Feedback least differentiated between the clusters. This was also important information for the project, because it highlighted differences in the way teachers think about and respond to their experiences with the eBL Project, thus providing direction in terms of the particular strengths and limitations we had to focus on to move project engagement forward for the teachers.

Student achievement data

As noted prior, we also included standardised measures of student achievement to help evaluate the impact of the project on student learning, as well as to act as a proxy for teaching effectiveness. Two types of standardised data were used for these purposes, data from the *Progressive Achievement Tests* (PAT) and from the *International Schools Assessment* (ISA) program.

ISA data

The *International Schools Assessment* (ISA) data is useful for making inter-school comparisons based on scores that have been amalgamated across designated areas (literacy and numeracy, for grades 3–5 and 6–10). Figure 8.6 shows the percentages of ISA scores as the project progressed that are above and below the year-1 project scores. As we can see, grades 3–5 have almost equal year-2 scores above and below their year-1 scores, thus presenting a fairly static picture in terms of improvement. Grades 6–10, however, have a greater proportion of scores at project end that are higher than their year-1 scores, as well as a larger proportion of scores significantly higher, and with no scores being significantly lower. Because of this, overall ISA change for the schools

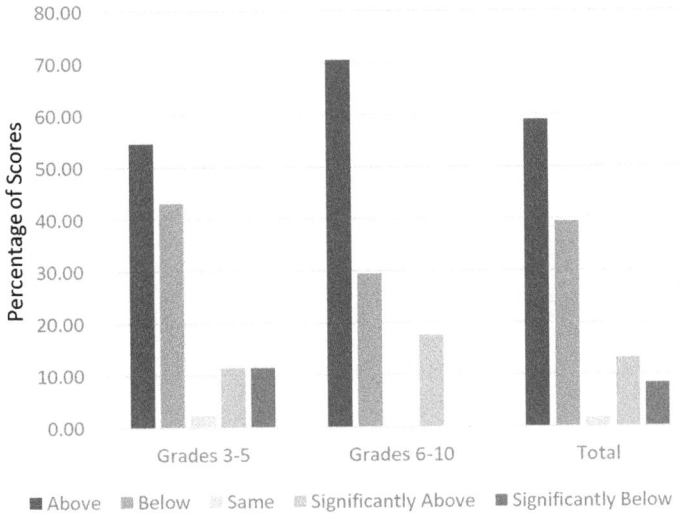

Figure 8.6 Percentage of year-2 ISA scores above and below year-1 ISA scores.

during this period shows positive improvement, but it will also be important for change management moving forward to closely examine differences between the ways that grades 3–5 and 6–10 are prepared for literacy and numeracy, in order to determine why these test differences occurred.

School PAT data

Progressive Achievement Test (PAT) assessments are informed by a growth mindset, which means they are intended to assist teachers in differentiating their teaching for the purpose of addressing individual differences and learning needs in relation to student-centred learning. In this respect we analysed two types of PAT data for the eBL Project, the PAT-R (Reading) and the PAT-M (Mathematics). Figure 8.7 (Reading) and Figure 8.8 (Mathematics) provide example snapshots of the PAT data for this project, and it is important to note that in both

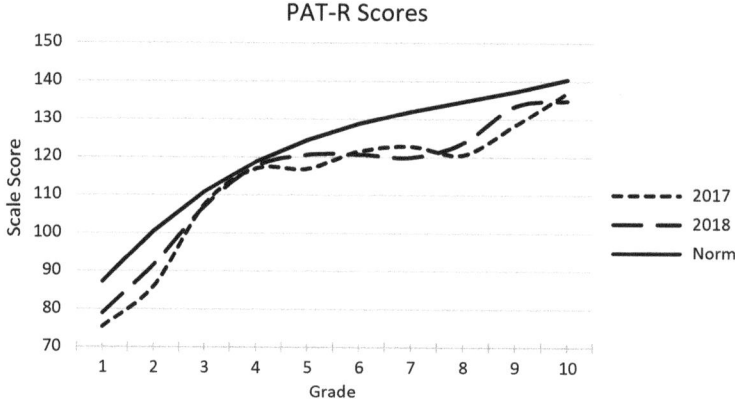

Figure 8.7 Overview of PAT-R comparisons, year-1 (2017)–year-2 (2018).

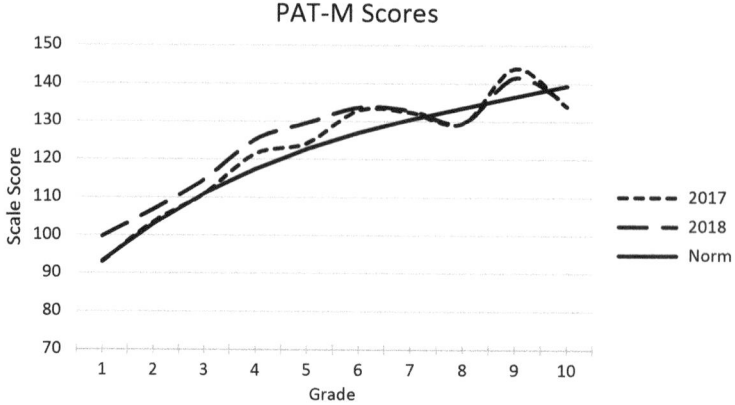

Figure 8.8 Overview of PAT-M comparisons, year-1 (2017)–year-2 (2018).

reading and maths there has been general improvement across this initial period for the participating schools. However, it is also important to note that for reading this improvement has been minimal and remains below the reading norm, whereas for mathematics the improvement has been largely above the norm. We suspect this may have to do with 'English-as-a-second-language' as a general issue for international schools (which the eBL Project schools are), but for whatever reasons an important outcome of these findings is that additional investigation is required concerning reading, in order for these schools to improve their reading outcomes moving forward.

Closer analysis of this data also reveals that the grades at which the 2018 reading scores have fallen below their 2017 counterparts are grades 6 and 7, and then again at grade 10. Similarly, although the year-2 maths scores show substantial improvement in general, and are mostly above the norm for mathematics, there is a notable dip in improvement for grades 8 and 10 across these assessment years. This may be a cohort function (particularly for grade 10), but obvious questions would also be whether the same teacher(s) was delivering mathematics for grades 8 and 10, and, importantly, whether a different instructional approach was being used for these grades. Information of this sort is crucial for focusing the ongoing project in terms of its instructional approach and student achievement goals, and thus forms an important source of evidence-driven decision making for the project.

Teacher confidence data in relation to the PD units

Another area of interest is the teachers' self-ratings concerning how confident they were with various aspects of their project involvement, as a consequence of their engagement with the professional development (PD) units that were created to support specific skill set learning in the case study schools. Table 8.3 shows correlations between reported confidence levels before PD unit 1, after PD unit 1 and after PD unit 2, in relation to reported levels of confidence with technology (this was reported pre-project by the teachers as part of a technology self-audit).

As shown in Table 8.3, there is no relationship between these variables before taking part in the PD units. That is, teachers' confidence with, for example, applying technology within the school's BL framework and effectively incorporating ICT skills into curriculum planning had no relationship with their confidence with technology in general. Upon completion of the PD units, however, there were positive relationships between these things, suggesting the teachers became progressively more confident about their use of technology in relation to classroom teaching and learning as a function of their involvement with the PD units.

We can also note an increase in confidence for other items of importance for the eBL Project from this data, including being able to incorporate ICT skills into curriculum planning and being able to experience positive change in relation to the PD units. Data collection, which overlaps to a large extent with the teacher-as-researcher (TaR) process being used to underpin teacher self-evaluation for the project, seems more inconsistent in these ratings however, and probably reflects the teachers' desire for more specific mentoring in this particular area (as also reported in the teacher interviews).

Of particular interest are the teachers' responses concerning the degree to which their PD learning will help them to meet the needs of students, and the degree to which their professional learning will result in improved student outcomes. In this respect note that initial confidence for both these items was negative, yet confidence in their BL Project

Table 8.3 Pearson's Correlations between confidence with technology and the PD units

	Confidence with technology		
	Pre-unit1	Post-unit1	Post-unit2
I am confident with using computers and other technology.	.262	.499t**	.433*
I am confident that I understand what the Blended Learning (BL) project is about.	.191	.312	.181
I am confident that I can use and apply technology within the school's BL framework.	.142	.435*	.419*
I am confident that I can incorporate ICT skills into my curriculum planning effectively.	.122	.493**	.506**
I am confident that my BL project will meet the needs of my students.	-.207	.112	.289
I am confident that my professional learning will result in improved student outcomes.	-.246	.173	.542**
I am confident that I understand how to collect student data for my BL project.	.070	.355*	.296
I am confident that I understand how to collect data on my teaching for the BL project.	-.068	.510**	.202
I am confident in my ability to experience positive change in relation to Professional Development (PD) as part of the school's BL project.	-.141	.369*	.543**
I am confident that I understand how to implement Teacher as Researcher (TaR) practice in relation to the school's BL project.	.097	.240	.388*

Note. * $p < .05$ (2-tailed); ** $p < 0.01$ (2-tailed); $N = 33$.
(Created by the authors)

meeting the needs of students grew more positive across PD units 1 and 2; and confidence that their professional learning would result in improved student outcomes became highly significant by the end of PD unit 2.

These correlations are of interest because they show how important it is that teachers have the necessary ICT skills to use in their classrooms (cf. Willis et al., 2018b). They also demonstrate that it is not necessary for teachers to know about all aspects of ICT, but rather that they need to have quality experiences with ICT related to what they might do in the classroom. Similar findings were also evident in the qualitative interviews, where one group reported having been introduced to appropriate technology by a member of the leadership team, and the subsequent benefit from this process. Overall, these correlations are of interest because they testify to the positive impact of the PD units on skill development within a whole-of-school improvement program, even suggesting the development of some risk-taking by teachers. They also attest to an emerging digital literacy on the part of the teachers, which is important for the promotion of student success within a Blended Learning environment.

We include these findings here because they testify to the importance of school-specific PD as part of the contextualising process. These units were created to meet the specific needs of teachers at the local level of the participating eBL Project schools, yet they also included universal elements of Blended Learning as core features, which allowed the teachers to understand the larger picture of Blended Learning as an instructional approach designed to address concerns of the Knowledge Economy.

Triangulation of the *eBL Project data*

We have examined these various data sources for the eBL Project in order to gain ideas about how to monitor and evaluate what might be called 'contextualising effectiveness'. It is crucial to position Blended Learning in relation to any 'given' school context we might be working with when implementing a blended pedagogy, and using targeted data collection from various sources such as these can assist in many of the early and ongoing decisions that have to be made about how to integrate Blended Learning into a particular school or learning situation. It is also important to be able to monitor and evaluate the effectiveness of these decisions from an evidence-driven perspective, especially decisions that might relate to the underlying goals and purpose of the improvement initiative that Blended Learning is meant to support. From this perspective we hope you are able to appreciate the need to contextualise Blended Learning, as well as the added value that occurs when Blended Learning is integrated into a holistic (whole-of-school) improvement initiative that operates on the basis of a clearly defined mission and specific improvement goals (as represented in the BL Schema used to underpin the eBL Project).

In this respect we have used the eBL Project as a case study in this penultimate chapter, to show the importance of the contextualising process, as well as to demonstrate possible strategies for incorporating research into an applied Blended Learning approach, as follows:

- From the Readiness Survey data we have been able to see that in terms of readiness for improvement the project schools have good alignment to the mission and goals of the improvement agenda, yet elements of capability and engagement require further attention, providing ongoing direction for the school improvement agenda.
- The nature of this attention was then highlighted by additional data from the BL Survey which showed that divided perceptions about leadership existed amongst the teachers, with leadership oversight seen in quite positive terms but leadership feedback being perceived as insufficient. This data thus suggested an area of leadership that required adjustment in order to improve teacher engagement with the eBL Project moving forward.
- Cluster analysis further revealed that this division was somewhat polarised amongst the teachers themselves, having received quite different survey responses from two different teacher groups: a more 'positive' group of older, more experienced teachers, and a more 'negative' group of younger, less experienced teachers. This information clarified which teachers to work with in relation to improving project understanding and satisfaction amongst the teachers.
- Analysis of teacher confidence in relation to the professional development units – which were created specifically to build relevant teacher skill sets for the project – showed increasing confidence in relation to several individual skill sets, especially in relation to how to use ICT to support student learning. This data provided support for the use of PD as a dedicated strategy for skill development when implementing a whole-school approach to Blended Learning.
- Student achievement data revealed that learning improvement had taken place for the participating schools under the Blended Learning regime, with greater learning improvement having taken place at the middle and upper school levels, and mainly in the area of mathematics. This suggested that a close examination of possible teacher or cohort effects was required in order to better understand why this same learning effect was not also occurring at lower levels and in relation to English literacy.

Chapter summary

The particular importance of this chapter is that it can be used to illustrate the relationship between Blended Learning and research quite clearly. It also demonstrates how Blended Learning can be used in support of a whole-school improvement initiative, and from an inclusive and collaborative perspective that includes all stakeholders in the design and implementation processes. In this respect Chapter 8 has provided an overview of key concepts and strategies for contextualising Blended Learning in an authentic and broadly effective manner and has offered a case study analysis of one way to approach this sort of implementation successfully. To this end, we have highlighted that the need for technological innovation in modern education suggests a natural relationship between Blended Learning and whole-of-school improvement initiatives. We revisited the notion that education systems are currently operating in a Knowledge Economy that requires the incorporation of technological innovation to support student learning, and noted that Blended Learning provides a flexible yet robust approach to applying technological innovation in positive ways that are able to address the concerns of the Knowledge Economy.

We then analysed particular concepts, principles and strategies for contextualising Blended Learning in this manner, and reviewed how they had been used in the eBL Project to demonstrate the contextualising process within an authentic setting. We demonstrated how to apply these concepts, principles and strategies on the basis of this project by examining various data sources from the project schools, and looking in particular at how these contextualising elements (the concepts, principles and strategies) had been used to inform and direct change management during the eBL Project. We also interpreted the findings from this project to gain insights concerning how to make data-driven decisions for modifying and re-focusing the project moving forward.

In this respect our case study analysis of the eBL Project has shown how to operationalise the KELS continuum, that is, how to contextualise Blended Learning in order to build specific and relevant skill sets, position these skill sets authentically and in a relevant manner for the particular educational situation at-hand, and integrate the skill sets in accordance with the mission and goals of an intended school improvement program. Using this continuum, the eBL Project was able to address the concerns of the Knowledge Economy within the confines of immediate classroom situations, as well as provide important strategies and insights for building teacher capacity and social capital as part of the school improvement program.

We hope you have found this chapter helpful in terms of understanding how to design for and implement Blended Learning in ways that are authentic and genuine to the intentions of its applied purpose, that is, in ways that are relevant and effective to the mission, goals, needs and capacities of the immediate school and situation it is intended to support, as suggested by the KELS continuum we discussed in prior chapters of this book. In our final chapter (Chapter 9), we will offer a summary of what might be called our Blended Learning journey, as well as offer some ideas for ongoing research in the area of Blended Learning that could be used to further crucial concepts and principles of the book.

Glossary

eBL   embedded Blended Learning. The term used in this chapter to refer to the whole-of-school Blended Learning Project that underpinned school improvement relating to the research this chapter reports on. Positioning Blended Learning within a whole-of-school improvement initiative is important because it allows evaluation of *school readiness* (see below) at a holistic pedagogical level for the participating schools (cf. Yeigh & Lynch, 2017).

BL Schema **(BLS)**   An underlying framework for the Collaborative Blended Learning Model, designed to support this model within a change agenda impacting teachers. The BLS operates as a mechanism that articulates, scopes, directs, and guides the school, its leaders, and teachers to understand what needs to change and what such changes will 'look like' in classrooms.

Collaborative Blended Learning Model   The specific, contextualised model of Blended Learning that was developed to help position this pedagogy within the local school context. A visual conceptualism for this model is provided in Figure 8.4.

Explanatory research design   The case study being reported on in this chapter adopted pragmatism as its theoretical framework, because pragmatism uses an inductive approach toward data collection and analysis to determine what, and how, things work in real-world settings. Within this framework, this case study employed a methodology based on *explanatory research design* to identify the important concepts, principles, behaviours and attitudes that appeared to effect the eBL Project. The importance of this research design is that it allowed us to inductively analyse project information, forming a good basis for authentic, evidence-driven decision making.

Knowledge Economy   Refers to the way technological advancements have changed the way people live, socialise, work and learn in modern societies, wherein most societies have moved from an economy based on industrialised outputs to an economy based on information outputs.

School Readiness   An important underlying concept for the eBL: that effective school improvement (involving school leaders, teachers and students) depends on a school being appropriately 'ready' to enact improvement measures, across three corresponding areas of knowledge, skill-sets and behaviour: *alignment* (agreement between teachers and school leaders concerning improvement goals and vision); *capabilities* (degree to which the improvement initiative is properly resourced in terms of knowledge, skill development, time, etc.); and *engagement* (the level to which a positive school-wide attitude/belief that the initiative and effort required are meaningful and worthwhile is taking place). The concept of school readiness is based on the *Theory of Planned Behaviour* (TPB), which suggests that an explicit relationship exists between attitudes, intentions and behavioural engagement (cf. Ajzen, 1991; Armitage & Conner, 2001; Lamorte, 2018).

References

Ajzen, I. (1991). The theory of planned behavior. *Organizational Behavior and Human Decision Processes, 50*, 179–211.

Arnett, T. (2019). One major barrier to high-quality blended learning. Retrieved September 11, 2019, from www.christenseninstitute.org/blog/one-major-barrier-to-high-quality-blended-learning/?_sft_topics=k-12-education

Armitage, C. J., & Conner, M. (2001). Efficacy of the theory of planned behaviour: A meta-analytic review. *British Journal of Social Psychology, 40*, 471–499.

Clark, T., & Barbour, M. K. (Eds.). (2015). *Online, blended and distance education in schools: Building successful programs*. Stylus Publishing.

Collie, R., & Martin, A. (2020). Teacher wellbeing during COVID-19. *Teacher* (Australian Council for Educational Research). www.teachermagazine.com.au/articles/teacher-wellbeing-during-covid-19?utm_source=CM&utm_medium=Trending&utm_content=TeacherWellbeing

Gerwertz, C. (2020). How technology, Coronavirus will change teaching by 2025. *Education Week.* www.edweek.org/ew/articles/2020/06/03/how-technology-coronavirus-will-change-teaching-by.html

Guttentag, S. (2020). *Looking ahead—Planning for post COVID-19 learning.* https://fs24.formsite.com/edweek/gp3qco3el3/fill?id32=EDWEEKBOX

Horn, M. B., & Staker, H. (2015). *Blended: Using disruptive innovation to improve schools.* Jossey-Bass.

Ingvarson, L., Reid, K., Buckley, S., Kleinhenz, E., Masters, G., & Rowley, G. (2014). *Best practice teacher education programs and Australia's own programs.* Department of Education.

Lamorte, W. W. (2018). *Behavioral change models: The theory of planned behaviour.* Retrieved November 7, 2018, from http://sphweb.bumc.bu.edu/otlt/MPH-Modules/SB/BehavioralChangeTheories/BehavioralChangeTheories3.html

Lieberman, M. (2020). Like it or not, K-12 schools are doing a digital leapfrog during COVID-19. *Education Week.* www.edweek.org/ew/articles/2020/06/03/like-it-or-not-k-12-schools-are.html?cmp=eml-enl-tl-news1&M=59599510&U=1790648&UUID=5a0962b1730 c8128b2846c213757611a

Lynch, D., Madden, J., & Knight, B. A. (2014). Harnessing professional dialogue, collaboration and content in context: An exploration of a new model for teacher professional learning. *International Journal of Innovation, Creativity and Change, 1*(3). www.ijicc.net

Teacher Education Ministerial Advisory Group (TEMAG). (2014). *Action now: Classroom ready teachers.* Available online: The report may be accessed via the Department of Education website at: www.studentsfirst.gov.au/teacher-education-ministerial-advisory-group

Willis, R., Yeigh, T., Lynch, D., Smith, R., Provost, S., Turner, D. & Sell, K. (2018a) *Towards a strategic blend in education: A review of the blended learning literature.* Oxford Global Press.

Willis, R. L., Lynch, D., Fradale, P., & Yeigh, T. (2018b). Influences on purposeful implementation of ICT into the classroom: An exploratory study of K-12 teachers. *Education and Information Technologies.* https://doi.org/10.1007/s10639-018-9760-0

Yeigh, T., & Lynch, D. (2017). Reforming initial teacher education: A call for innovation. *Australian Journal of Teacher Education, 42*(12). https://doi.org/10.14221/ajte.2017v42n12.7

Yeigh, T., & Lynch, D. (2018). School leadership and school improvement: A correlational analysis of school readiness factors. *School Leadership and Management.* https://doi.org/10.1080/13632434.2018.1505718

Yeigh, T., Lynch, D., Turner, D., Fradale, P., Willis, R., Sell, K., & Lawless, E. (2020). Using blended learning to support whole-of-school improvement: The need for contextualisation. *Education and Information Technologies.* https://doi.org/10.1007/s10639-020-10114-6

Yeigh, T., Lynch, D., Turner, D., Provost, S., & Willis, R. (2018). Organisational readiness and strategic leadership for school improvement. *International Journal of Educational Management.* https://doi.org/10.1108/IJEM-07-2017-0181

9 Taking stock of Blended Learning as a school-based reform journey

Thematic overview of this book

In this book we have taken a journey. This journey has focused on how schooling, with its four walls, the prominence of teacher-centred activities and compliant students sitting at desks in age-related cohorts, has largely remained enmeshed within what was explained in Chapter 1 as the industrial revolution. This first revolution, where a predominantly rural-agrarian society was transformed through the introduction of machinery into an industrial society centred on urban centres and factories, came to represent a fundamental change in the society of the time. Schools as we understand them were invented during this time, and played an important role in this first industrial society because they set in train, through a set of powerful enculturating traditions, a process of sorting future workers into a stratified work environment. Put simply, those who could do school continued on to higher learning and high-level jobs, while the others were filtered out into unskilled, semi-skilled and skilled work. This stratification continued through a further two industrial revolutions, until another profound and fundamental change – the fourth industrial revolution – occurred in global societies circa 1990.

This fourth revolution has been widely characterised in the literature as a Knowledge Economy. Importantly, it represents a contrast to previous revolution eras, in that a premium is now placed on knowledge as the basic source of industrial value, and thus one's capacity to use knowledge in new and interconnected ways is key to successful learning, employability and general satisfaction as a member of this economic society. Specifically, this economy is driven by the advent of, and advances in, modern technology, and therefore technological innovation and disruption abound such that the only constant is change. There are few unskilled jobs in the Knowledge Economy, as these have been largely taken over by technology. Because of this a highly skilled workforce is now a key requirement of the Knowledge Economy. Within this framework, a key problem being addressed by this book is that, despite such profound changes in society affecting work, learning and home life, the logic and fabric of schools continues to operate largely unchanged. A major 'take-away' from this first chapter was therefore that a disjunction exists between the imperatives of the new Knowledge Economy and the more traditional way education continues to prepare learners for engagement in the modern world. This disjunction can be understood as an inter-play between five key factors: the growth of uncertainty; the growth of new forms of economic rationality; the transformation of time into the 'extended present'; flexible space; and increasing capacity for self-organisation. These represent points of disruptive 'flexion' that were then examined in relation to modern education across the remaining chapters of the book.

In Chapter 2, we turned first to the growth of uncertainty in the case for school reform, which reveals a reform rhetoric, now many decades old, that seeks to achieve change by doing the same things differently: an oxymoron that has manifested in employers and industry groups arguing that schools are no longer graduating young people with the required knowledge, skills and mindsets needed for a modern workforce. This rhetoric of reform seems to have occurred largely because schools have been around for so long that policy makers have become myopic and captured by their own experiences in and with schools (Yeigh & Lynch, 2017). While it is true that curriculum reforms have been undertaken, many of these have taken extended periods of time to be designed and implemented, thus arriving late into schools as exponential societal change necessitates yet further revisions. They have also tended to focus on increased intensity of learning in traditional areas (numeracy and literacy for the most part), rather than on authentic attempts to revamp these areas in relation to the changing needs of society, to better match the imperatives of the Knowledge Economy, as it were. Thus an inherent reform process, by which the duration of design and implementation continually lags behind the pace of actual change, has resulted in a highly disruptive impact on teaching and learning as an implicit outcome of the Knowledge Economy. Put simply, a schooling system built on traditions and conformity is a poor fit to a world that thrives on innovation, creativity and change.

A key point of flexion for Chapter 2 was that a change is now needed in how teachers are viewed within the system of schooling. While the evidence is clear that teachers make the fundamental difference for students, and that school leaders play an equally important role in enabling teachers to be effective (Hattie, 2012), there yet remains the need for an operating logic that enables and positions teachers to interpret, locate and implement a classroom curriculum commensurate to a Knowledge Economy. In more essential terms, teachers are no longer cogs in a wheel of a tradition, but rather represent a school's necessary talent pool. Thus, in this chapter we argued that it is through Talent Management that schools and their leaders now need to work to create environments in which teachers can integrate the world of modern work and life into the fabric of a modernised, future-orientated school. This approach comes to mean that teachers are aligned, enabled and made capable such that they are highly skilled, continually learning and motivated to create, invent and innovate, linking notions of educational improvement more directly to the imperatives of the Knowledge Economy.

Missing in this complex equation is a mechanism that enables all these disparate elements to emerge and then be consolidated into a flexible and highly Knowledge-Economy-centric school. We therefore introduced Blended Learning in Chapter 3, arguing that it represents a distinct pedagogical approach that is designed to harness the power of technology in innovative and positive ways designed to address the specific needs of schools in a flexible manner. At its heart, Blended Learning is a set of capacities – limited only by the 'Talent' of the teacher – that are intended to generate customised learning programs to meet the diversity of students present in classrooms and schools, and to position the curriculum into closer proximity to the 'real world' through an ICT-driven instructional approach that can make use of virtual reality, augmented reality and artificial interline functions. In this respect Blended Learning is able to harness and combine supportive aspects of physical classroom learning with those of online learning to create an explicit, sophisticated, deliberate 'blend' in teaching and learning. In this manner Blended Learning comes to represent an opportunity for teachers to exploit the rapid technological developments that are occurring in information communication technologies while embracing the face-to-face classroom circumstance that is synonymous with growing up and attending school.

Many books and articles have been published over many years proclaiming yet another good idea that education should embrace. We have been conscious of not falling into this trap, so in Chapter 4 we introduced an exposé of the evidence which informs the effective school. Using this exposé as our roadmap for positioning Blended Learning in relation to the traditional school, with the goal of transforming it, we then identified a series of maxims that can be used to represent the teaching and learning design considerations for an approach to effective schooling based on Blended Learning. These maxims embody the preliminary design considerations to examine when planning for effective schooling from a Blended Learning perspective, as follow:

First, there is a growing evidence base which has highlighted what works in teaching and learning, and which emphasises that teachers must reconceptualise themselves away from the notion of teacher as an 'artist' who diligently and creativity makes up a lesson on the whim, to the teacher as a 'scientist' who collects evidence, analyses and tests it for fit and purpose, and then uses this to view themself as core Talent in the success equation, thus focusing on continuous learning as a fundamental characteristic of their professional identity.

Second, and returning to Knowledge Economy logic, classroom teaching must move from teacher-centred to student-centred. This goes hand-in-hand with the Knowledge Economy imperatives concerning technological innovation, self-organisation and the need for a highly skilled workforce that is adept at a self-directed use of technology. With this in mind personalised learning becomes a necessary teaching goal when planning for effective schooling from a Blended Learning perspective.

Third, neither the teacher nor school leaders are isolated from such transitions. School leaders play an important role in positioning and enabling teachers to transform the schooling experience and work to generate the required teacher attributes by applying Talent Management principles. We examined this key role in detail in Chapter 5, and in summary our findings are that the impact of school leaders in the student learning outcome equation is second only to teachers. The effective school leader, while concerned with standards and various other constraints that make all organisations sensible and sustainable, is foremost focused on enabling and positioning their teachers for transformational change and corresponding positive effects in students. The modus operandi of an effective school leader who is operating in full cognisance of the Knowledge Economy is centrally directed at increasing the capacity and capability of their Talent. This Talent, of course, is the teacher, and the leader achieves such increases through an enabling mechanism that bridges the traditional/future divide – which we argued in Chapter 3 has created a change malaise in schools – known as Blended Learning. Put colloquially, Blended Learning comes to represent the best of 'both worlds' when it comes to planning for effective schooling in response to the imperatives of the Knowledge Economy. Our central message in Chapter 5 was thus about the key role that school leaders play in planning for and implementing an effective school via building enduring states of alignment, capability and engagement through a Transformational Leadership approach and a learning-focused mindset.

In Chapter 6 we further examined our evidence-based mandate by noting the research that informs Blended Learning. In particular, we investigated the current state of research evidence regarding Blended Learning in general, that is, how the outcomes from Blended Learning compare to other common pedagogies, and what the research literature says regarding the efficacy of various specific models of Blended Learning. In this respect a key take-away from Chapter 6 was that Blended Learning, as a pedagogy, is focused on how to use technology in ways that promote student-centred, personalised learning.

We also examined how to establish some important parameters for implementing Blended Learning, using the Blended Learning continuum to show how different models of Blended Learning can be used to control for the level of personalised learning that takes place. Following on from this, Chapter 6 reiterated the critical role that school leaders play in leading the changes that need to occur when implementing Blended Learning, noting in particular the need for principals and other school leaders to understand how to make use of social capital within online and Blended Learning environments. We concluded the chapter by identifying areas, concepts and specific strategies by which school leaders can plan for successful online and Blended Learning, as has been necessitated by the COVID-19 pandemic. Thus, another take-away from this chapter is that the need for Blended Learning is likely to remain prominent as education progresses into the future, in light of the impact of the COVID-19 pandemic.

In Chapter 7 we focused on the particular skill sets required to integrate Blended Learning within a whole-of-school improvement initiative, as informed broadly by the school improvement and Blended Learning research literature. The purpose and function of technology was a key consideration for this chapter, because it defines how the use of technology is to be appraised as part of an overall school improvement initiative, as well as how technology can be supported by a dedicated coaching, mentoring and feedback (CMF) regime. From this perspective it is crucial to understand that CMF represents a Talent Management strategy that the school leader uses to build the required states of alignment, capability and engagement in teachers to effect the overall future school vision. In a parallel manner CMF also provides scope for the required evaluations of both teachers and the overall Blended Learning project to be evaluated in an objective and formative environment. In simple terms, CMF represents a Knowledge Economy logic to professional learning in the future school.

As also noted in Chapter 7, a key consideration in all this is the logic of a Blended Learning continuum, which we have operationalised in the form of the KELS continuum. This continuum is essentially an implementation schema that works to identify and decide the mix of face-to-face and online instruction that will operate in any given situation relating to the classroom curriculum within a school improvement initiative. Understanding the need for a continuum of this sort is important because the decision on how much face-to-face versus online instruction is needed is central to the pedagogic logic that the teacher applies when wanting to achieve specific learning outcomes with their students.

Overall, Chapter 7 provided a clear design approach for Blended Learning in support of school improvement that incorporated many of the key concepts and principles introduced in earlier chapters of the book, including the importance of effective school leadership, the purpose of Blended Learning in relation to the Knowledge Economy and the need to contextualise this purpose, the importance of evidence and the role played by collaboration (CMF) in support of Blended Learning integration. A major take-away from this chapter was that getting these things right is important when setting-up for the relevant skills sets and instilling appropriate levels of dispositional balance. A key focus for this chapter was therefore on the relationship between Blended Learning and school improvement.

In Chapter 8 we returned to the evidence base logic one final time, in this instance to report on original research exampling how Blended Learning can be implemented in schools according to the concepts and principles of design and implementation presented in the earlier chapters of the book, especially those described in Chapter 7.

What was revealed in this chapter was that successful Blended Learning initiatives are enmeshed in a pedagogic framework. In simple terms how the form and function, as well as the location of such initiatives into the school curriculum, need to follow an established and evidence-based set of guidelines and principles, and what these can look like in practice.

Summary of the book's themes

What we have outlined in this book are the cornerstones of a new vision for schooling. In this respect a core proposition has been that Blended Learning has come to represent a vehicle by which schools and school leaders can transform teaching and learning within particular school contexts. In line with this logic is that a change in how the school leader views and thus positions the teacher in the school is also required. A change in which the teacher is recognised as the required Talent, and Blended Learning becomes the means through which school and curriculum transformation can occur in ways that are meaningful to the modern needs of teaching and learning. Our vision for the future school, while predicated on the use of Blended Learning, also embraces the key points that we have summarised in previous sections herein. There are a set of requisite skills that teachers must have to operate with and engage with Blended Learning. Further, their classroom curriculum planning is balanced in terms of thinking, overall planning, communication and collaboration. These considerations are further embedded in the context of the specific school, and in line with our evidence base call, use an evidence-based contextualising model to ensure a perfect fit. This contextual consideration can essentially be understood as an audit and thus provides a series of questions that the school leader asks with their teacher as they plan for the what, when, where, how and why of their transformation to Blended Learning. While simply using Blended Learning sounds seductive, this book also revealed a further set of organisational and resource considerations which come to represent the capacity and enabling elements that Blended Learning requires. The Blended Learning journey is fruitful but it comprises a set of complexities which require leader-centric orchestration as well as teacher-centric skilling and a student-centric pedagogy.

Ongoing learning about contextualised Blended Learning

As this book has revealed, Blended Learning comes to represent a strategy for transforming the traditional school effectively into a school fit for the Knowledge Economy that is further unfolding as we continue into twenty-first-century schooling. Further studies on the use of Blended Learning in relation to student achievement are needed in additional education contexts to expand these ideas further. There are many issues that affect Blended Learning from the perspective of students and teachers and their attitudes towards it, and thus it will be important to have more studies in this area designed to investigate the use of Blended Learning as a construct and as an applied pedagogy within specific contexts. In line with this, a clear overall take-away from this book is that there is no single formula that guarantees learning, and in this respect Blended Learning should be embedded within an overall school curriculum. It is certainly not useful to implement Blended Learning in isolation or without specific direction to guide it, and we urge ongoing research to investigate applied Blended Learning in relation to specific school improvement agendas in order to further this area of knowledge and understanding.

We end by emphasising that the imperative for this sort of research seems all the more urgent in light of the COVID-19 pandemic that has impacted on education worldwide, especially with respect to the possibility that schools are likely to close again, perhaps in a cyclic or sporadic manner as this pandemic continues to work its way through societies (Guttentag, 2020). Because of this, future research will also need to take a close look at what schools can do to address the issues this pandemic has created for schools forced into online-only teaching and learning. In this regard Lieberman (2020) suggests that a primary goal for education moving forward is the development of what he terms the 'digital savvy' teacher, identifying the need to upskill teachers in the use of ICT as a primary point of reference for ongoing teacher adaptability. The eBL Project has identified some ways of supporting this type of digital competence, but further research in this area is also necessary.

We trust you have enjoyed learning about Blended Learning as you worked your way through this book, and that you will seek to apply your learning to new school situations in your own right as a teacher or school leader. Building and sharing knowledge as an overall education community is the best way to develop a collaborative understanding of what Blended Learning is and how best to use it in the interests of your students. We trust you have found this book helpful in that respect, and wish you every success as you continue in your own blended journey.

References

Guttentag, S. (2020). *Looking ahead—Planning for post COVID-19 learning.* https://fs24.formsite.com/edweek/gp3qco3el3/fill?id32=EDWEEKBOX

Hattie, J. (2012). *Visible learning for teachers: Maximising impact on learning.* Routledge.

Lieberman, M. (2020). Like it or not, K-12 schools are doing a digital leapfrog during COVID-19. *Education Week.* www.edweek.org/ew/articles/2020/06/03/like-it-or-not-k-12-schools-are.html?cmp=eml-enl-tl-news1&M=59599510&U=1790648&UUID=5a0962b1730c 8128b2846c213757611a

Yeigh, T., & Lynch, D. (2017). Reforming initial teacher education: A call for innovation. *Australian Journal of Teacher Education, 42*(12). http://doi.org/10.14221/ajte.2017v42n12.7

Index

9 780367 407407